Figureheads
OF THE
ROYAL NAVY

Figureheads
OF THE
ROYAL NAVY

David Pulvertaft

FOREWORD BY
ADMIRAL THE LORD BOYCE

Seaforth
PUBLISHING

Frontispiece: Courtesy of the National Museum of the Royal Navy

First published in Great Britain in 2011 by
Seaforth Publishing
An imprint of Pen & Sword Books Ltd
47 Church Street, Barnsley
S Yorkshire S70 2AS

www.seaforthpublishing.com
Email info@seaforthpublishing.com

British Library Cataloguing in Publication Data
A CIP data record for this book is available from the British Library

ISBN 978 1 84832 101 4

Typeset and designed by Roger Daniels
Printed and bound in China

CONTENTS

ACKNOWLEDGEMENTS

I STARTED taking an active interest in the figureheads of the Royal Navy about a year before I left the service in 1992 as I realised that, once retired, I could no longer assume the easy access to the naval establishments and royal dockyards that I had enjoyed in the past and it was there that many of the carvings resided.

With the foundation of my database being the figureheads still under naval ownership, I investigated the collection of the National Maritime Museum (NMM) – the largest in the land – where the then Curator of Antiquities, Caroline Roberts, allowed me to make copious notes from their records and then to meet the figureheads themselves, most of which were in store and only available 'by appointment'. I am indebted to her for such a start.

Through my membership of the South West Maritime History Society, the Plymouth Naval Base Museum Trust and The Society for Nautical Research (SNR) I have acquired many good friends who have in their own way encouraged my research and provided all sorts of clues to where I might find new examples of these fascinating carvings. Dr Michael Duffy of the University of Exeter provided an academic slant, Lieutenant Commander Lawrie Phillips was ever forthcoming in offering snippets that came his way and figurehead historian Richard Hunter has proved to be a long-standing colleague with whom I have been able to explore the more difficult identities and who has always been most generous with items from the Richard Hunter Archives.

Help from the many contacts who work in Portsmouth has been eased by my membership of the Friends of the Royal Naval Museum and HMS *Victory* with Matthew Sheldon and Richard Noyce, now of the National Museum of the Royal Navy, deserving special thanks for their help over the years. Jenny Wraight, the Admiralty Librarian, has been a mine of information; first when the library was in Old Scotland Yard in Whitehall and more recently from her desk in the Portsmouth Naval Base as a member of the Naval Historical Branch.

In preparing for this book, my thanks go first to its publisher, Robert Gardiner, who encouraged me to dig deep into my own archives to select a suitable cross-section of subjects and images to do justice to this rather specialist subject and then suggested that I should include what were the uncharted waters, for me, of ship plans and ship models. To enter these fields of expertise was somewhat daunting and I make no attempt to be authoritative on either subject but simply to show where each provides figurehead evidence. I was warmly welcomed to the Brass Foundry at Woolwich by the NMM's Curator of Historic Photographs and Ship Plans, Jeremy Michell, and his colleague Andrew Choong and given every assistance to search their vast collections. The NMM's Curator of Ship Models, Simon Stephens, was equally forthcoming in his area of expertise, not only guiding me through the collection at a time when much of it was being prepared for its move to Chatham, but also pointing me in the direction of other collections of ship models where further figurehead evidence might be found.

In the last few months I have had to make contact with a large number of curators, librarians, owners and copyright holders to check that the figureheads that I had recorded many years ago are still where I first met them, to discover details of model collections, to seek permission to use certain images and to explore many other details. To all of these I offer my grateful thanks and in particular to the present NMM's Curator of Artefacts, Barbara Tomlinson, who has helped me update my earlier records from their collection and the Editor of *The Mariner's Mirror*, Dr Hugh Murphy, for permission to use the 1913 image of the fire-engine house at Devonport. My special thanks go to Richard Blundell who owns the Dickerson Archive in Australia and allowed me to examine the whole collection when I last visited that country a year ago. He has been enormously generous in providing the scans that illustrate this previously unpublished source and answering the many questions that have resulted.

It has been reassuring to have my manuscript read by two of the maritime historians whom I have come to know and admire over the years, Dr Michael Duffy and Robert Gardiner. Each of them gave me sound advice that I was only too happy to follow and, while I thank them for this, any remaining errors are entirely mine.

Finally, I thank my wife, Mary Rose, for encouraging my interest in figureheads for the last twenty years and for remaining totally supportive, despite my almost complete dedication to the book's creation over the last twelve months!

FOREWORD

FOR more than three centuries the bows of British warships were adorned with an elaborate decorative device, often in the form of a carved human or animal figure. These were emblematic of the ship's name, symbolized the fighting spirit of the Navy, and even reflected the political ideals and beliefs of the country. Sometimes large and always eye-catching, the artistic value of figureheads meant that many were retained when the ships themselves were sold or broken up – although, sadly, the later history of such collections was often one of neglect and dispersal.

In recent years there has been a revival of interest in these potent symbols of Britain's maritime heritage, much of it due to the painstaking work of Rear Admiral David Pulvertaft. He has identified and catalogued all surviving figureheads of the Royal Navy – which has encouraged a growing appreciation of their value – but in this book he has carried his research to a new level. For the first time he describes the process by which the Admiralty commissioned such work, analyses how the ship names were translated into sculpture, and looks at the lives and businesses of the carvers themselves. He has tracked down extant design drawings, some from as far away as Australia, and studied models and ship plans as objective records of figureheads that have themselves long since disappeared. All these sources are listed in a directory of immense reference value that will surely form both the starting point and inspiration for further research.

I have no hesitation in welcoming a work of real scholarship that throws much new light on this poorly understood aspect of naval history.

Admiral the Lord Boyce KG GCB OBE DL
May 2011

INTRODUCTION

FIGUREHEADS have been mounted on the bows of ships from the earliest times, giving guidance and comfort to superstitious mariners and taking on something of the 'soul' of the ship. When on the bows of warships they provided an image of the fighting spirit of the crew and thus their nation, whether their role was warfare, exploration or the protection of trade.

This book looks only at the figureheads of British warships, charting their evolution from the days before there was an established navy until the period when ship design made the figurehead redundant. For three and a half centuries ships were given names that were appropriate to their function and the ships' carvers created works of art that illustrated the names. During much of this period, the carvers also created the stern and quarter decorations that were sometimes several times more expensive than the figurehead, but this book does not stray into that field as these were demonstrations of the nation's wealth and prestige rather than the character of the ship.

While it has been deemed important to identify the figureheads with the size and role of the ship on which it served, the exploits of the ships themselves have not in general been described as this is the figureheads' story and not that of the men who manned the fleet.

There are today about 200 figureheads of the Royal Navy that have survived from their sea-service; mostly now in museum collections and naval establishments in the United Kingdom but with a handful overseas. With a few exceptions, these have not been used to illustrate this book as an interested reader can find them for himself or herself, providing they know where to look. Thus, in the 'Figurehead Directory' at the back of the book each of the survivors will be found with its present location – highlighted in **bold** type. Many of them have been repaired and restored over the years but it is not the intention here to assess how much original material remains and how much is new.

The exception to this policy is where a replica has been created in modern materials for display outside so that the original can be kept safe in controlled conditions. For those examples, both the original and the replica are listed in the Directory.

To capture the character and variety of the Royal Navy's figureheads over the years, the book has been illustrated with photographs of figureheads now lost and design drawings submitted by the figurehead carvers for approval, most of which are to be found amongst the Admiralty papers at The National Archives. As many of these have been folded within their letters of approval for well over a hundred years, image-wise their condition is far from perfect but, despite this, it is believed that photographs of the original documents show the carver's intention to best effect. For those periods when designs are not available, the figureheads shown on the plans from which the ships were built and those carved on contemporary models fill many of the gaps. Where these add to the overall knowledge of the subject, they have been included in the Figurehead Directory.

Ships that were not deemed suitable for a figurehead were given a 'scroll' – curling forward from the stem-post – or a 'fiddlehead' – curling backwards like the end of a violin. As these do not make any artistic contribution to the history of the Royal Navy, nor do they represent the name of the ship, they are not listed in the Directory. There then came a period towards the end of the nineteenth century when, due to ship design, figureheads were no longer appropriate to the bows of the Royal Navy's ships and yet some form of decoration seemed necessary. Bow decorations became the fashion, usually in the form of the royal arms within a cartouche surrounded by carved scrolls down the ship's side. Occasionally the decoration was particular to the ship and, as these were following the long-established practice of figurehead design, these too are included in the Directory.

CHAPTER 1

—◇—

SHIP NAMES[1]
AND THE FIGUREHEAD
CARVERS' TASK

[1] Captain T D Manning and Commander C F Walker, *British Warship Names* (Putnam, 1959) – with a comprehensive alphabetical Dictionary that lists for each ship name, its meaning, the dates of ships that bore the name and the battle honours won.

[2] C S Knighton and D M Loades, *The Anthony Roll of Henry VIII's Navy* (Navy Records Society, 2000).

THE first English fighting ships to be given figureheads relating to their names appeared during the reign of King Henry VIII and it is from this period, therefore, that our examination starts. 'The Anthony Roll'[2] of 1546 has some fifty-eight ship-portraits with, on the whole, uncomplicated names of people such as the *Mary* and the *Matthew* or animals such as the *Dragon* and the *Salamander*. Some of these are included in Chapter 4.

During the reign of Elizabeth I, ships were given names with warlike connotations such as *Victory*, *Triumph*, *Repulse*, *Revenge* and *Defiance* and compound names such as *Dreadnought*, *Swiftsure* and *Warspite*, all of which have continued to be used in the modern Royal Navy. During the relative peace of the first half of the seventeenth century few heavyweight ships were added to the fleet, notable exceptions being the *Prince Royal* and the *Sovereign of the Seas*.

Ships built under the Commonwealth reflected Cromwell's victories such as *Naseby* and *Marston Moor* while others that were already in commission with royalist associations were changed, such as the *Prince Royal* becoming the *Resolution*. With the restoration of the monarchy in 1660, ships were renamed; *Naseby* becoming *Royal Charles* while others were given names alluding to the King such as *Royal Oak* and *Happy Return*.

The early part of the eighteenth century again saw few warships being built but the majority that were added to the fleet, whatever their rate, had lions as their figureheads, some uncrowned [1.1] and some crowned. An example of a stylised crowned lion will be found in Chapter 5. Other animals began to appear in a form that was similar to the full-length lion such as the *Licorne*, the anglicised version of the French ship *La Licorne* [1.2], captured in 1778 and still with her French figurehead. Less comfortable, perhaps, were the *Centaur* and *Sphinx*, to be found in Chapter 5.

From about 1740, while lions continued to be carved for some ships, increasing numbers of others were given either a standing figure or a full-length figure that

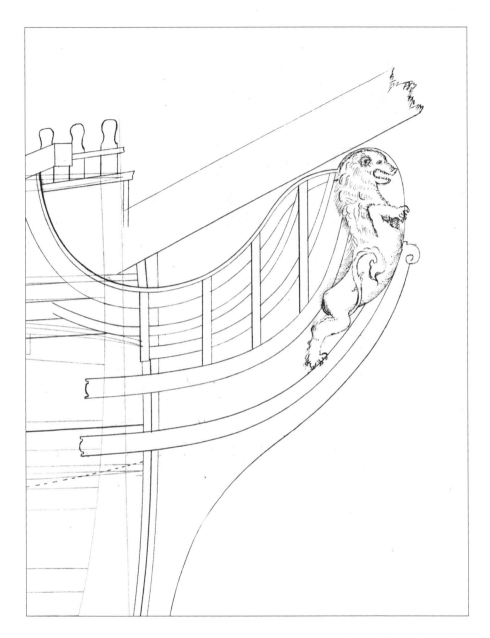

1.1
Belleisle **1761 –**
Ship plan detail.

straddled the stem-post and had its legs carved down the trailboards so that some appeared to be in a near-kneeling position. In most cases these single figures were made to represent the name of the ship, thus starting an art-form that lasted for over 150 years.

A selection of these single figures is included in Part III of Chapter 5, but the difference in style can be seen by comparing the designs of two unidentified ships. Both were drawn by the Dickersons of Plymouth, each ship clearly having a name with some warlike association. The first [1.3] is a full-length warrior dressed in classical clothing, wearing a plumed hat and holding both a shield

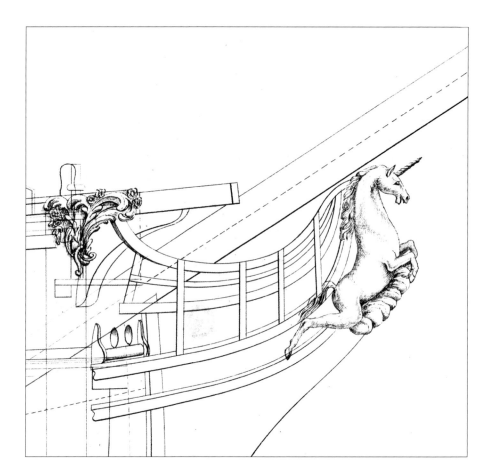

1.2
Licorne 1778 –
Ship plan detail.

1.3
Unidentified ship –
Dickerson design.

1.4
**Unidentified ship –
Dickerson design.**
DICKERSON ARCHIVE

and a scimitar while a putto blows a trumpet of victory in the trailboards. The second [1.4] is a beautiful example of a standing figure with a plumed helmet and an elaborate costume with two putti in the trailboards, each with fishes' tails suggesting they are children of a merman. One holds the sword and scales of justice while the other has a badge that probably symbolises the City of London. This design is drawn on paper with a watermark of a fleur-de-lis in a shield above the initials 'GR' dating it between 1714 and 1820.

By the nineteenth century the lion had virtually disappeared, the full-length figures no longer had their legs curving down the trailboards and demi-heads and busts had taken their place. The alternatives that were offered when

HMS *Frederick William* (110) was building in 1860 were a demi-head for £60 [1.5] or a bust – with less work involved – for £54 [1.6]. Not surprisingly, the Surveyor of the Navy selected the latter.

The expansion of the British Empire and the transition from sail to steam resulted in many more ships in the fleet with a much wider range of names than before. In addition to those factors, the Navy Board required every figurehead design to be approved in the office of the Surveyor of the Navy and the letters seeking and granting approval between about 1810 and 1860 are now preserved amongst the ADM series of documents at The National Archives at Kew. This material forms the basis of the several chapters devoted to the nineteenth century.

The approval process was simple, if a little bureaucratic. If a ship was being built in a royal dockyard that had a resident figurehead carver, he would create a design appropriate to the ship's name and would quote an estimate of its cost,

1.5
Demi-head design for HMS *Frederick William.*
THE NATIONAL ARCHIVES

1.6
Bust design for HMS *Frederick William.*
THE NATIONAL ARCHIVES

sometimes offering the alternative of a full-length figure or a bust with a cost estimate for each. The Admiral Superintendent of the dockyard would forward the designs and estimates to the Navy Board where the Surveyor of the Navy would approve or amend the design and would agree, or sometimes reduce, the allowed price. The letter would then be returned for the information of the dockyard officers and, once noted, it would be returned once more to London for filing. The whole process was monitored in huge registers, many of which are also preserved in The National Archives.

If, however, the ship was being built in a royal dockyard where there was no resident figurehead carver, such as Pembroke Dockyard in South Wales, the Superintendent there would forward a scale drawing of the bow and stern of the ship requesting that 'carve work' be provided. This gave the Surveyor rather more flexibility as he would then send the paperwork to whichever carver he wished, based partly on which of them was providing the best value for money and partly on geography, as he had to take into account the ease of shipping the

1.7
HMS *Despatch* –
Hellyer design 1847.
THE NATIONAL ARCHIVES

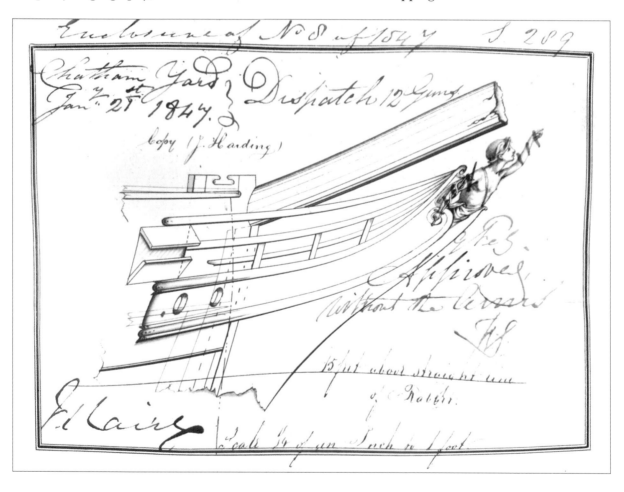

final product to the building yard. On occasions the Surveyor invited more than one carver to submit designs and estimates to create an element of competition.

The whole process is neatly illustrated in the approval of the figurehead for HMS *Despatch* (12) building in 1847 in Chatham Dockyard [1.7]. The draughtsmen at Chatham created a small drawing – only 6ins x 4ins – showing the head rails of the ship, giving it the title 'Chatham Yard Jan'y 21st 1847 – Dispatch [*sic*] 12 Guns' and quoting the scale and where the structure sat in relation to the keel. It was signed in the bottom left-hand corner by Francis J Laire, Master Shipwright at Chatham. On its receipt at the Surveyor's Office, the letter was registered in his 'Register of In-Letters Relating to Ships' and given the line number 'S289'.[3] The register records that it was referred to the Superintendent at Portsmouth on 23 January and was received back on 2 February. During that time Hellyer & Son, the resident carvers with workshops at Cosham, drew the demi-head of Hermes, the messenger of Zeus, the supreme ruler of the Greek gods, identified by the wings on his helmet and the caduceus (the herald's staff) that he carried – an appropriate figurehead for HMS *Despatch*. The estimate forwarded from Portsmouth was for £7.0.0 but the Surveyor, Sir William Symonds, decided that a bust-head would be sufficient and so deleted the arms of the figurehead in red ink and made the notation '9 Feb – Approved without the arms' and added his initials. He noted on the estimate that only £6.10.0 was allowed and the package was returned to Portsmouth for the officers to note. Eventually, the papers were filed amongst the Surveyor's In-Letters where they may be found today.[4]

[3] TNA ADM 88/7 S289 (1847).

[4] TNA ADM 87/17 S289 (1847).

CHAPTER 2

—◦—

FIGUREHEAD CARVERS

THE men – and occasionally the women – who designed and carved the figureheads of Their Majesties' ships also carved the decorations on their stern and quarter galleries. While there were periods when the stern carvings were very extensive and included details that alluded to the ship's name, it was generally on the quality of his figureheads that a carver's ability was judged and has resulted in the shorthand of referring to them as 'figurehead carvers'.

In his book *British Figurehead and Ship Carvers* the late Phil Thomas published his research into the carvers who worked on both merchant ships and naval ones, the larger half of the book being devoted to the merchant ship carvers.[1] Much of his evidence on carvers for the Royal Navy was gathered from the ledgers of the Accountant General[2] and the Yard Pay Books.[3] While this

[1] P N Thomas, *British Figurehead and Ship Carvers* (Waine Research Publications, 1995).

[2] TNA ADM 20 (1661-1795).

[3] TNA ADM 42 (1797-1815).

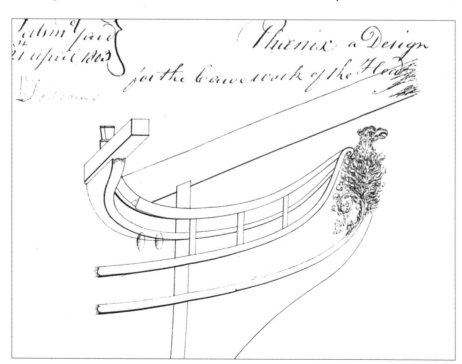

2.1
HMS *Phoenix* –
Hellyer design 1803.
THE NATIONAL ARCHIVES

information provides a detailed picture of which carvers were working in and around the dockyards and on which ships they were working, its main focus was not on the actual figureheads that they were creating. The book does, however, include a number of details not found elsewhere; for example that Cuthbert Mattingly of Plymouth carved the lion figurehead for the *Jersey* in 1736 and was allowed £17.10.0, while Cornelius Luck of London was allowed £22.18.0 in 1861 for the figurehead of the armoured frigate HMS *Resistance*. It is thanks to Phil Thomas's work that such details appear in the Figurehead Directory.

The carvers who lived in Kent tended to serve both Chatham and Sheerness Dockyards with Thomas, Matthew and John Fletcher carving for the second half of the seventeenth century and including such prestigious ships as *Sovereign*

2.2
HMS *Madras* –
Hellyer design 1844.
THE NATIONAL ARCHIVES

of the Seas and the *Royal Charles*. Several members of the Crichley family carved there during the middle half of the eighteenth century – including Abigail and Elizabeth – with replacement lion figureheads for the *Chester* and *Nassau* in 1719 and the magnificent figure of Bellerophon riding on the winged horse, Pegasus, for the 1786 *Bellerophon*. It is generally accepted that when the 1765 *Victory* was building in Chatham Dockyard, her figurehead was carved by William Savage but Phil Thomas claims that William Savage was brought in to assist Richard and Elizabeth Crichley and, as his claim is based on the payment of fees, the work probably was shared between them.[4] The final Chatham-based carver worthy of a mention is George Williams who was appointed the 'contract carver' there in 1797 and so carved the replacement figurehead for HMS *Victory* in 1802 during her rebuild, for which he was paid £50.

4   Thomas, *British Figurehead and Ship Carvers*, p 98.

2.3
HMS *Orlando* –
Dickerson design 1856.
DICKERSON ARCHIVE

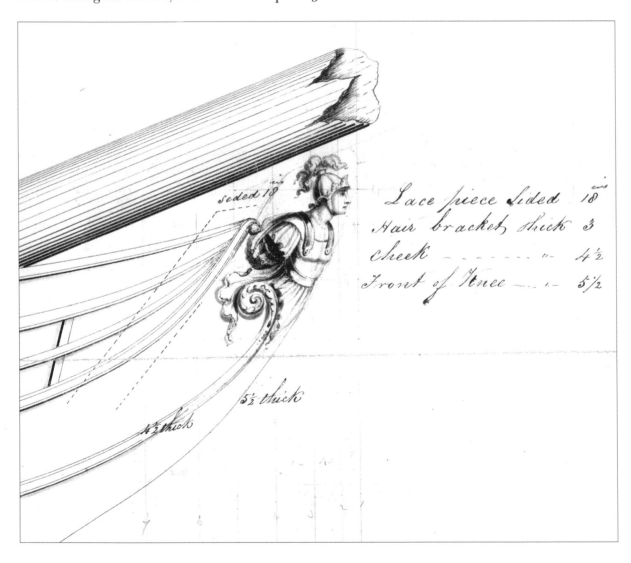

Moving up the Thames to Deptford and Woolwich Dockyards, their proximity to each other allowed a number of carvers to serve them both. Joseph Wade was made Master Carver for both dockyards in about 1720 and was paid handsomely for the refurbishment of six royal yachts between 1724 and 1742 as well as the carved work for a number of new-build warships. Several members of the Burrough family carved there; Thomas made a great deal of money from the elaborately carved and gilded 1749 *Royal Caroline* and in 1756 was paid £424 for the carved work on the *Royal George* – see Chapter 5.[5] When William Montague Burrough took over in 1790, he too created the carved work for many ships building at Woolwich, including that for the *Boyne* whose figurehead is also to be seen in Chapter 5.[6]

The two royal dockyards that are still supporting the Royal Navy today – Portsmouth and Devonport – each had a succession of resident carvers, although the dockyard at Plymouth did not acquire the name 'Devonport' until August 1843. At Portsmouth, Lewis Allen carved for a succession of ships between 1670 and 1704 but the payments to him are not sufficiently detailed to see what particular figureheads cost. William Smith carved there from 1724 to 1753, one of his first big contracts being the carved work for the 1737 *Victory* with its group figurehead, the ship model of which will be found in Chapter 5. For all her carved work he was allowed £142.12.0. In 1740 when the *St George* was rebuilt at Portsmouth with its mounted figure of St George as the figurehead, he renewed her carved work for £147.8.0. Cuthbert Mattingly carved originally in Plymouth from 1737 but moved to Portsmouth in 1760, bringing his son, William, into the business in 1778. It was William who eventually started working with Edward Hellyer, thus leading to the most successful family of figurehead carvers of the nineteenth century.

The Hellyers worked in the dockyard itself and in their own workshops at Cosham, just north of the city. The first figurehead designs by Edward Hellyer were forwarded by the Admiral Superintendent at Portsmouth in 1800 but the earliest drawing to have survived with its covering letter at The National Archives shows an 1803 replacement for the figurehead of the 1783 *Phoenix*, whose figurehead was reported to be entirely decayed [2.1].[7] This early Hellyer style of pen and ink without any shading can also be seen in the design that he submitted for the 1806 *Bulwark* – Chapter 9 – and, while they lack the sophistication of his later work, they were each successful in having the work approved. Between these early examples and 1860, when the records at Kew

[5] Thomas, *British Figurehead and Ship Carvers*, p 76.

[6] TNA ADM 106/1788 (1790).

[7] TNA ADM 106/1883 (1803).

2.4
Unnamed ship -
Dickerson design *c*1794.
DICKERSON ARCHIVE

cease, the Hellyers submitted more than 250 designs for approval, many of which will be found illustrating Chapters 6 to 15. The vast majority of their designs were submitted as pen and ink drawings with grey wash to give texture but occasionally they used colour to enhance an otherwise unimpressive design as in the design for an 1810 replacement for the 1757 HMS *Southampton* [Colour Plate 1].

While it was the Hellyers' prerogative to carve the figureheads for those ships building at Portsmouth, they were also occasionally summoned to work at Chatham and it was probably for that reason that they set up a workshop on the Thames in east London, first at Princess Stairs, Rotherhithe, and later in Brunswick Street, Blackwall. Between the 1830s and the 1850s they carved at least thirty figureheads there for ships building at Deptford, Woolwich, Chatham and Sheerness as well as a couple that were later shipped to Pembroke Yard in South Wales. In 1844 the Hellyers wrote to the Surveyor of the Navy to say that, as work was slack, they would appreciate a contract to provide the carved work for the ships building at Bombay. They were instructed to submit designs that were 'characteristic of the country' for HM Ships *Madras* (84) [2.2], *Malacca* (26), *Zebra* (16) and *Goshawk* (12) and this they did with estimates ranging from £36 to £7.[8] The Surveyor required alterations to the *Zebra* design but approved all four, a decision that he may have regretted as *Madras* had already been renamed *Meeanee* in 1843, *Malacca* was eventually built in Burma, *Zebra* was renamed *Jumna* in 1846, making the bust of a black African woman inappropriate, and *Goshawk* was renamed *Nerbudda* in 1845, making the figurehead of a bird equally wrong. The Hellyer design for a replacement figurehead for HMS *Meeanee* in 1859 will be found in Chapter 13.

In Plymouth, early ship carvers included Anthony Allen, who carved between 1691 and 1701, and Cuthbert Mattingly between 1737 and 1760 when he moved to Portsmouth. The carvers, however, who worked in Plymouth through much of the eighteenth and nineteenth centuries were the Dickersons: Samuel, James and Frederick, competing with the Hellyers of Portsmouth. Samuel Dickerson worked between 1770 and 1790, one of his most prestigious figureheads being that of the 1786 *Royal Sovereign* (100). The figurehead's design was reproduced in *Plymouth and Devonport: in Times of War and Peace* in 1900 being a group figurehead, the dominant figure being a full-length youthful George III in a frock-coat and breeches wearing a wreath of laurel leaves on his head.[9] He has a royal coat of arms in front of him, angels and Victory behind him and semi-naked figures below him trampling on a many-headed hydra. The caption records that the original Dickerson sketch was owned by Mr Sydenham.[10]

James Dickerson carved at first with Samuel, but by 1794 was describing himself as a Master Carver and amongst the numerous figureheads that he created were two that are illustrated in Chapter 5, the 1793 HMS *Caesar* and *L'Hercule*, captured from the French in 1798. One of his more lucrative contracts was the carved work for the yacht *Plymouth*, built in Plymouth and launched there in 1796 [Colour Plate 2]. The design that is in the Dickerson Archive in Australia is not actually named but it is described in a forwarding letter from Plymouth Yard as 'Ceres holding a cornucopia in one hand and a wreath of corn in the other standing erect on the knee clothed in rich drapery' so there is little doubt that this is his design.[11] The elaborate nature of the decorations

8 TNA ADM 87/14 S1661 (1844).

9 H F Whitfield, *Plymouth and Devonport: in Times of War and Peace* (E Chapple, 1900).

10 Lewis John Sydenham (1834–1910) was married to Lavinia Goldsworthy Dickerson, daughter of Frederick Dickerson, carver at Plymouth.

11 TNA ADM 106/1935 (1797).

on these yachts can be judged from the fact that his estimated cost for all the carved work for the yacht was £96.7.6, of which £11 was for the figurehead.

Frederick Dickerson was the last member of the family to carve in the dockyard, starting in 1832, describing himself as an 'artist naval carver' in the 1851 census, a 'master carver' in the 1861 census and a 'retired master carver' in 1871. During his service he carved some of the last full-length figures to be fitted to the navy's First Rates – HMS *Royal William* in 1833 and HMS *St George* in 1840 – only to carve replacements in the form of large busts when the ships were cut down to allow them to be fitted with steam propulsion in the late 1850s. Details of each of these figureheads will be found in Chapters 15 and 10 respectively.

The records at The National Archives suggest that it was not uncommon for a carver to retain a design once it had been approved, to ensure that it was closely followed. This is evident from the fact that, when full-length and bust alternatives were offered, the one that was rejected is usually filed with the correspondence while the one that was approved is often missing. The practice was followed by each of the Dickerson family and resulted in a large collection of carvers' drawings now in private hands in Australia.

It would appear that when Frederick Dickerson retired in the late 1860s he kept the designs and in due course they passed to his daughter Lavinia who was married to Lewis John Sydenham, the 'Mr Sydenham' mentioned in the book *Plymouth and Devonport: in Times of War and Peace*. They then passed to one of Lavinia's sons, an engineer in the Royal Navy, who retired as a rear admiral to New Zealand and with him went the 'Dickerson Archive'. They finally passed to the admiral's nephew who had emigrated from Devon to Australia and it is through the generosity of his son, the present owner, that they are used as illustrations to this book.

The collection consists of about 130 sheets of cartridge paper of various sizes, eighty of them containing design drawings of figureheads of named warships, the remainder being made up of studies for further development, stern carving details and associated artwork. Some appear to predate the Dickersons so perhaps were inherited by them when they took over the work; most are created for ships building at Plymouth but a score or more are on outlines created in Pembroke Dockyard prior to their passage through the office of the Surveyor of the Navy. Some sheets bear watermarks that assist in their identification while others have the Surveyor's register number that can be identified against the appropriate volume at The National Archives. It has proved to be a substantial contribution to the overall subject and is summarised in the Figurehead Directory at the end of the book.

Three examples from the Dickerson Archive show something of the range of drawings that is included.

- The bust of HMS *Orlando* [2.3] is from a three-part scale drawing of the bow, stern and quarter of the ship drawn by Pembroke Yard on 18 October 1856. The design was added by Frederick Dickerson and was forwarded by the Superintendent at Devonport on 4 November with an estimate for £18.10.0. When this had been approved and the drawing had been retained by the carver, the light vertical and horizontal lines were added so that the drawing could be scaled up to the 'larger-than-life' figurehead.

- The three unnamed sketches [Colour Plate 3] are examples of preparatory artwork showing the figures of 'Hercules' wrestling with the many-headed hydra, 'Hope' awaiting the return of her sailor with her traditional anchor and the blindfolded 'Justice' with her sword and scales.

- The unnamed standing figure, probably representing Zeus [2.4] as he is crowned and holding a thunderbolt in his right hand. Thunder clouds and flashes of lightning are carved down the trailboards with ornate scrolling. The style is typical of the late eighteenth century and the drawing is on paper with the watermark 'J.WHATMAN – 1794'.

In an attempt to keep costs under control, the Surveyor of the Navy encouraged competition between carvers and nowhere can this be better seen than the allocation of carved work for ships building at Pembroke Yard. It might have been expected that Plymouth would be given the lion's share as the transport costs of the finished product would be smaller. However, in the period from 1840 to 1860 when the records are most complete, the Dickersons offered designs for thirty-three figureheads while the Hellyers offered forty, taking advantage of the better communications between Portsmouth, Rotherhithe and London than Plymouth and London.

CHAPTER 3

———◇———

FIGUREHEAD AND ASSOCIATED COLLECTIONS

I. Figurehead Collections

WHEN a warship had come to the end of its useful life it was either sold to a commercial ship-breaker's yard or 'taken to pieces' in one of the royal dockyards, so that any sound timbers and fittings could be re-used. In either case, there was a reluctance to destroy the figurehead as it somehow represented the 'soul' of the ship; and so the carvings accumulated in the breakers' yards and royal dockyards and the early figurehead collections were created.

Devonport appears to have created the first formal collection, gathered in what had originally been a shipwrights' work-shed, built in 1826 between two of the dry docks and named the 'Adelaide Gallery' in honour of the wife of King William IV. The gallery contained a wide range of relics of the fleet from earlier years, including at least twenty-four figureheads, but these were not catalogued until after their destruction in what became known as 'The Great Fire of 1840'.[1] The fire started in the middle of the night on Sunday 27 September 1840 in HMS *Talavera* (74) that was being refitted in the northern of the two docks. The fire spread quickly via the Adelaide Gallery to HMS *Imogene* (28) in the adjacent dock, destroying both ships and the gallery with its contents. In the dock immediately astern of HMS *Talavera* was HMS *Minden* (74) and, while the ship was saved, her figurehead was destroyed. Details of the design for her replacement figurehead will be found in Chapter 13. Of the figureheads lost in the Adelaide Gallery, those that were described in sufficient detail to identify them have been included in the Figurehead Directory.

Towards the end of the nineteenth century, the Admiralty began the process of cataloguing its holdings of relics of the past, the first edition of the Admiralty Catalogue being published in 1883.[2] No doubt the Royal Dockyards were contributing to the information as the first catalogue of the Chatham Dockyard Museum was published in the early years of the twentieth century,[3] followed

[1] *The Great Fire of 1840* by Andy Endacott, May 1998 – (Plymouth Naval Base Museum).

[2] *Catalogue of Paintings, Busts, Relics, Models, &c., belonging to the Admiralty* (London, 1883).

[3] *Catalogue of Figureheads, Models, &c. in the Museum in H.M.Dockyard, Chatham* (Undated).

3.1
The fire-engine house,
Devonport Dockyard.
L to R *Horatio, Tamar,*
Raleigh, Prince of Wales,
Blenheim, Aurora and
Leda.

4 *Catalogue of Paintings, Busts,*
   Relics, Models, &c., belonging
   to the Admiralty (London,
   1906).
5 *Catalogue of Pictures,*
   Presentation Plate,
   Figureheads, Models, Relics
   and Trophies at the Admiralty;
   on board H.M.Ships; and in
   the Naval Establishments at
   Home and Abroad (London,
   April 1911).
6 Douglas Owen, 'Figureheads',
   The Mariner's Mirror Vol III
   (1913), pp 289–94 and 321–7,
   and 'The Devonport
   Figureheads', *The Mariner's*
   Mirror Vol IV (1914), pp 145–
   7.

shortly by the Admiralty's second edition in 1906.[4] These were all small-scale booklets compared with the 1911 edition that ran to 160 pages and, amongst the many hundred items listed, included brief descriptions of over 150 figureheads.[5] It is this publication that has laid the foundation for all subsequent analysis of the surviving figureheads of the Royal Navy.

It was during the years that these catalogues were being created that The Society for Nautical Research (SNR) was formed and it was through its journal, *The Mariner's Mirror*, that another page of figurehead narrative was written. The first honorary secretary to the SNR, Douglas Owen, had toured the Royal Dockyards and made descriptive notes about the various collections. He was unaware of the Admiralty catalogue (The Relics Book) until he was writing an account of what he had found, but was then able to include the Relics Book numbers in his articles.[6] Owen selected the figureheads that he considered were the most worthy from an artistic or historical perspective and, as his accounts contained much more detail than the Admiralty Catalogue, they are particularly useful. At Devonport he described no less than forty-four figureheads, giving their size, a brief description and the Relics Book number and he records that there were three distinct groups; the largest being in the fire-engine house [3.1], with others in the rigging-house and the police parade shed.

The Devonport collection remained pretty stable until 1936 when The National Maritime Museum (NMM) was created at Greenwich. The Admiralty had indicated in 1931 that, as and when the NMM was established, their Lordships would transfer a number of figureheads from the Chatham Dockyard Museum.[7] As it happened, only eight carvings were transferred from Chatham while twenty were moved from Devonport and between them formed a significant part of that new museum's collection. It so happened that this was a fortunate move as in 1941 Devonport suffered severe bombing and, amongst the devastation that resulted, six of the figureheads were lost, two of them being

7 K Littlewood and B Butler, *Of Ships and Seas: Maritime heritage and the founding of the National Maritime Museum, Greenwich* (London, 1998), p 57.

3.2
HMS *Kent* 1798–1881 – Third Rate 74 – lost 1941.
CROWN COPYRIGHT

3.3
HMS *St George* 1840–83 – First Rate – lost 1941.
CROWN COPYRIGHT

3.4
The Museum, Chatham Dockyard *c*1902.

RICHARD HUNTER ARCHIVES

8 *A Record of the Figureheads in H M Naval Establishments under Plymouth Command* – undated – but created in response to an Admiralty instruction of about 1936 (Admiralty Library Ref Dh 20).

huge, full-length figures, too large to be housed indoors – the 1789 HMS *Kent* (74) [3.2] and the 1840 HMS *St George* (120) [3.3].

These photographs had been included in a pre-war photographic archive of the figureheads in the Plymouth Command that forms the first illustrated record of the Devonport collection and therefore provides another useful stepping-stone from the 1911 Admiralty Catalogue.[8]

Of the figureheads shown in the fire-engine house, the only ones that remain at Devonport today are those from HM Ships *Tamar* and *Aurora*. Those from *Blenheim*, *Leda* and *Horatio* were amongst those transferred to the NMM, while that from *Raleigh* is now at the shore establishment HMS *Raleigh* in Torpoint, and that from *Prince of Wales* is now at the Scottish Maritime Museum at Irvine.

The Devonport collection today is housed in the fire-engine house of the Naval Base's South Yard but awaits decisions on its future. Until recently under the care of the Plymouth Naval Base Museum Trust, there are sixteen figureheads ranging from the 13ft standing figure from the 1833 HMS *Royal William* (120) to the 4ft 6in demi-figure from the 1860 wood screw sloop HMS *Rinaldo*, some of which feature in the later chapters of this book and all of which are listed in the Figurehead Directory.

The 1911 Admiralty Catalogue did not, of course, restrict itself to figureheads

**3.5
The Admiral's Walk,
Chatham.**
RICHARD HUNTER ARCHIVES

at Devonport and, in addition to the sixty-eight that have already been mentioned there, it described fifty-five at Chatham, twenty-four at Portsmouth, fourteen at Sheerness, four at Pembroke, six in naval shore establishments and four in bases overseas. The figureheads that were not included were those still attached to their ships in the many supporting roles of the period.

As already mentioned, a Dockyard Museum at Chatham was created in the first few years of the twentieth century and it is fortunate that contemporary photographs published in 1902 in *The Navy and Army Illustrated* allow each of them to be identified [3.4].[9] It was not, however, until 1938 that the first illustrated record of the Chatham collection was created.[10] Containing over fifty photographic portraits of the individual figureheads, each was given a brief description, mostly identical to that quoted in the 1911 Relics Book. The process was repeated in 1948 with a set of new photographs and showed that, despite the Second World War, the collection was little changed except that a handful of carvings had been transferred to HMS *Ganges* in Suffolk.[11]

In the 1950s, and with a desire to give visibility to this part of the Dockyard's history, eight of the figureheads were moved outside to line the 'Admiral's Walk'. Although some came and went over the years, the original line-up was *Wanderer* wood screw gunvessel, *Diana* (46), *Britomart* (8), *Conflict* wood screw sloop,

9 *The Navy and Army Illustrated* (19 April 1902).
10 *Figureheads in Dockyard, Royal Naval Barracks and Royal Naval Hospital, Chatham.* Stamped 1938. An album on linen pages containing fifty-two figurehead photographs with descriptions (Admiralty Library Ref Dh 23).
11 *Figureheads at Chatham – 31.12.48.* An album on linen pages containing forty-seven figurehead photographs with descriptions (Chatham MCD No 13234).

3.6
Inside the Portsmouth
Dockyard Museum *c*1911.

Columbine wood screw sloop, with *Amazon* (46), *Terpsichore* (18) and *Rodney* battleship in the shadows [3.5].

It was at this time that fibreglass was first used to protect figureheads in the expectation that this material would protect the wood and allow them to be displayed out of doors without fear of their deterioration. The process was not successful in the long term as the fibreglass eventually cracked and the ingress of water allowed the wood to decay without any hint of the damage being done.

The preparations to close Chatham Dockyard in 1984 resulted in much correspondence on how the figureheads should be reallocated. About a dozen went to naval shore establishments, about half a dozen were absorbed into the Greenwich and Portsmouth collections, the same number remained in the Historic Dockyard at Chatham, but, sadly, another dozen were lost to the process of decay. It is, perhaps, surprising that none of the figureheads that were moved outside to decorate the 'Admiral's Walk' suffered terminal illness and their whereabouts today can be found in the Figurehead Directory.

By comparison with the collections in Devonport and Chatham, the Portsmouth collection was always smaller but it enjoyed a relatively stable existence. The Portsmouth Dockyard Museum had been created by the

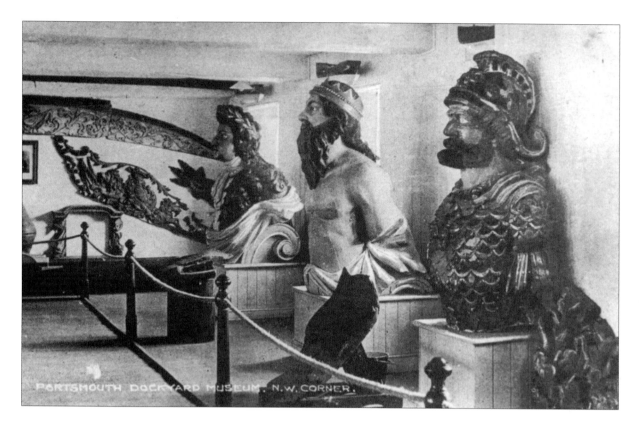

PORTSMOUTH DOCKYARD MUSEUM. N.W. CORNER.

3.7
Inside the Portsmouth
Dockyard Museum *c*1911.
RICHARD HUNTER ARCHIVES

Secretary to the Admiral Superintendent, Mr Mark Edwin Pescott Frost, between 1906 and 1911 and its first small catalogue had been printed in 1911, coinciding with the Admiralty Catalogue.[12] Douglas Owen was impressed with what he found on his visit, describing it as 'Mr Frost's delightful little museum … where all are displayed with the most loving care'.[13] He asked why the achievement in Portsmouth could not be followed in Devonport and urged that the collections should be assembled in 'a great Naval Museum'.

The illustrations show how effective the policy was of assembling the collection in a controlled environment as all the figureheads shown have survived and are today in the Royal Naval Museum at Portsmouth – *Orestes* sloop (18), *Bellerophon* (80) and *Actaeon* (28) [3.6] facing *Illustrious* (74), *Grampus* (50) and *Centurion* battleship [3.7].

Standing guard at the entrance to the museum were two very large royal bust figureheads from the Portsmouth-built ships HMS *Royal Sovereign* (121) and HMS *Royal Frederick* (110), each measuring more than 8ft in height. For some reason they were allowed to be transferred to the boys' training establishment in Gosport, HMS *St Vincent*, a move that sealed their fate as they each succumbed to rot. They are described in more detail in Chapter 15.

[12] *Catalogue of Figure-Heads, Models, Pictures, Relics, Trophies &c., H.M. Dockyard. Portsmouth* (Portsmouth, 1911).
[13] Owen, 'Figureheads', p 322.

3.8
HMS *Ganges*, Shotley, Suffolk.

As the museum evolved, its title was changed to 'The Victory Museum' in 1938 and to 'The Royal Naval Museum' in 1971. The figurehead collection has grown slowly over the years as individual items have become available from closing naval establishments and elsewhere. It was described in a booklet published in *c*1970, illustrated with neat line drawings[14] and more recently by the present author in a book that describes each of the forty-three figureheads and bow decorations in and around the museum, most of them being illustrated with watercolour portraits.[15]

The next significant dockyard collection was at Sheerness where the 1911 Admiralty Catalogue listed fourteen figureheads whose size ranged from the 9ft 9in *Goliath* (80) to the 3ft 6in *Gannet* composite screw sloop. There was no museum at Sheerness but Douglas Owen noted that the best grouping of them was to be found in the Quadrangle where they made 'a good show'. The Admiralty Board had in 1957 instructed commands to report their holdings of figureheads[16] so, by 1958 when preparations were in hand for the closure of Sheerness in 1960, the negotiations on their future were based on an up-to-date survey. Some of the collection went to Chatham, two went to museums and several – including that of the 1809 HMS *Poictiers* [Colour Plate 4] – remained in Sheerness under the care of the Sheerness Harbour Company Ltd who had taken over the management of the site.

The smallest dockyard group of figureheads in the 1911 Admiralty Catalogue was at Pembroke Dockyard where five figureheads were listed and described. While Pembroke Dockyard built some 200 ships for the Royal Navy between 1816 and 1880, it was generally not involved in taking them to pieces. The figureheads listed were, however, the exception. *Hope* (3) had become a lazarette at Pembroke and was broken up there in 1882, *Otter* (18) was a quarantine vessel at Milford, while *Saturn* (74) and *Royal Sovereign* yacht had served as the guardships there. In June 1922 a fire destroyed the mould loft and with it the dockyard's collection of ship models and figureheads.[17]

Also listed in the 1911 Admiralty Catalogue was the collection at HMS *Ganges*, the boys' training establishment at Shotley, Suffolk. In pride of place was the 9ft bust from the last HMS *Ganges* (84) that had come ashore with the training task, standing under the enormous mast that the boys would 'man' on ceremonial occasions [3.8].

The figureheads that had been gathered there by 1911 came from other boys' training ships: *Boscawen* (formerly HMS *Trafalgar* (120)), *Caledonia* (formerly

14 Captain A J Pack RN, *The Origins of the Figurehead – A description of the Figureheads in the Victory Museum and the ships to which they belonged* (Portsmouth, undated).
15 David Pulvertaft, *The Warship Figureheads of Portsmouth* (The History Press, 2009).

16 TNA ADM 1/27846.

17 *Pembrokeshire County History* Vol IV, Chapter VI, p 171.

HMS *Impregnable* (98)) and *St Vincent* (formerly HMS *St Vincent* (120)). This group was joined by others over the years and they were housed in the spacious Nelson Hall. When the establishment was closed in 1976, the figureheads were transferred, several being accepted by the Royal Naval Museum, Portsmouth.

A private figurehead collection that arose from the ship-breaking industry was that of Henry Castle & Son. The firm was established in 1838 at Baltic Wharf, Millbank, very close to the present site of the Tate Gallery. It later opened other ship-breaking yards on the Thames at Longs Wharf, Woolwich, and Anchor & Hope Wharf, Charlton. As in the Royal Dockyards, figureheads

3.9
Castles Yard, Baltic Wharf.
HMS *Orion* and
HMS *Princess Royal.*
RICHARD HUNTER ARCHIVES

3.10
Castles Yard, Baltic Wharf.
HMS *Cressy* and
HMS *Colossus.*
LONDON METROPOLITAN ARCHIVES

accumulated at all three sites but it was at Baltic Wharf that the company showed off their trophies. Over one gate stood HMS *Orion* (screw 80) and HMS *Princess Royal* (screw 91) [3.9] while over the other stood HMS *Cressy* (screw 80) and HMS *Colossus* (80) [3.10].

The headquarters and showroom on Millbank advertised that they made garden furniture and on the side wall was a painted notice saying that they also sold logs, so all the material from the wooden-walls had a use! The figureheads on display [3.11] from the roof working down the building were: HMS *Bristol* wood screw frigate, HMS *Hood* (screw 91), HMS *Collingwood* (80), HMS *Imperieuse* wood screw frigate, HMS *Cressy* (screw 80), which had been moved, and HMS *Leander* (50).

Following his 1913 articles in *The Mariner's Mirror*, Douglas Owen wrote a letter to *The Times* on how the nation's history would be better served if the figureheads from the Royal Navy's former ships were properly preserved. Philip Castle was moved to write that, if a place was found for the nation's figureheads,

3.11
Castles Millbank headquarters and showroom, *Bristol*, *Hood*, *Collingwood*, *Imperieuse*, *Cressy* and *Leander*.
RICHARD HUNTER ARCHIVES

18 *The Times* (22 October 1913).

19 *Map Record of Incidents in the City of Westminster 1940-5 –* CD 1311 – 17 April 1941.

he would offer any or all of the carvings in his care to the nation.[18] The full-length figure from HMS *Royal Albert* (screw 121) was transferred to Portsmouth as a result of this offer but, as will be seen in Chapter 15, this did not save him from the effects of the elements.

Castles created their own small museum at Millbank after the closure of Baltic Wharf in 1913 but, sadly, this and its contents were destroyed in April 1941 during the London Blitz when the site suffered a direct hit by a high-explosive bomb.[19] Fortunately, Castles had sold figureheads to interested customers and thus the field representative of the Mariner's Museum of Newport News, Virginia, was able to purchase the figureheads of HM Ships *Edinburgh* and *Formidable* and it is in that museum where they may be found today.

Another museum existed in Westminster for some years. The Royal United Service Museum in the Banqueting House, Whitehall, had four figureheads in its collection: the 1817 *Royal George* yacht, the 1845 wood paddle sloop HMS *Bulldog*, the 1854 HMS *Orion* (screw 80), and the 1876 composite screw gunvessel HMS *Condor*. The figureheads from *Orion* and *Bulldog* were displayed outside the front entrance to the museum, resulting in the loss of that from *Orion* to decay. The *Royal George* and *Bulldog* figureheads were transferred to the National Maritime Museum, Greenwich (NMM) while that from *Condor* found its way to New Zealand and is in the Te Papa Tongarewa Museum in Wellington.

The largest collection of Royal Naval figureheads today is that preserved by the NMM and, as has already been mentioned, the core collection was gifted by the Lords of the Admiralty in 1936, mostly from Devonport but also from Chatham. Others have been acquired over the years so that the total holding now is some thirty-six although, like most museums, there is insufficient space to display all the artefacts and the majority of those at the NMM are stored in their reserve collection. The numbers vary as individual examples are brought out for a particular exhibition but, on average, only about a dozen are on show at any one time.

Overseas there are small clusters of figureheads from ships of the Royal Navy; namely the museum of HMAS *Cerberus* near Melbourne, Australia, the Ballard Bunder Museum, Mumbai, India, and the Mariner's Museum, Newport News, USA. These as well as solitary items will all be found in the Figurehead Directory with examples illustrated in the appropriate chapters.

II. Ship Model Collections

Ship models of the 'sailing navy' range from the most delicate and accurate scale models constructed by specialist model-makers to sailor-made models carved in their spare time by mariners at sea, with prisoner-of-war models adding their own character and usually crafted in bone and sold by the prisoners to give them some form of income. As the last two categories were made from memory and were never intended to be an accurate representation of the ship in question, they are not included in this chapter, nor in the Figurehead Directory at the back of this book, unless they provide figurehead details not otherwise available. The scale models are often referred to as 'Navy Board' models, on the assumption that they were made for the Navy Board in the approval of a particular design. While this may have been one of the reasons why such models were made, they also served as keepsakes and presentation pieces and often include an amazing amount of detail.

Early eighteenth-century examples of these models were only partially planked so that the ship's frames could be seen, but later in the century the practice was for them to be fully planked and are then referred to as 'Georgian' models. The usual scale to which these models were made was ¼ of an inch = 1 foot (that is a scale of 1:48), although when models were made to demonstrate a particular aspect of the ship, a larger scale was sometimes used. Block models were sometimes carved from the solid with a minimum of fittings or decorations but, as some show painted representations of the figurehead, where this is the case they too have been included. As many of the warship models come from the period that is not well served by figurehead carvers' designs, they provide a most useful source of information.

By far the largest collection of models in the United Kingdom is owned by the National Maritime Museum and is described in detail in *Ship Models – their Purpose and Development from 1650 to the Present*.[20] Apart from the descriptive text, the book contains a catalogue that lists over 2,000 models, of which about 500 are from the period when figureheads were to be found on the bows of the Royal Navy's ships. Those that are only given a general title, such as, say, 'a 74-gun ship', do not help in figurehead identification but, where the ship is named and where there is a figurehead on the model that can be identified with her, they have been included in the Figurehead Directory.

The NMM collection can trace its origin to the Model Room of Somerset House in the Strand, created in the 1820s by the Surveyor of the Navy who had

[20] Brian Lavery and Simon Stephens, *Ship Models – their Purpose and Development from 1650 to the Present* (Zwemmer, 1995).

his offices there. In 1864 when the School of Naval Architecture was opened at South Kensington, the ship model collection moved there and was partly integrated with the South Kensington Museum, predecessor of the Victoria and Albert Museum and the Science Museum. In 1873 both the school and the collection moved to Greenwich, leaving behind an important nucleus that is still on display in the Science Museum. It required an Act of Parliament in 1934 to establish the National Maritime Museum but, when it was opened in 1937, the Admiralty collection of ship models was one of its important components.

A selection of the NMM's 'sailing navy' part of their collection is on display in the 'Ships of War Gallery' at Greenwich but until recently the majority of the models were in a nearby store and only accessible to researchers by appointment. However, in the autumn of 2010 about half of the models were moved to Chatham Historic Dockyard where many of them are now on view in the newly-opened 'No 1 Smithery'.

That part of the Admiralty collection that remained at South Kensington may still be found in the Science Museum, 'arranged with the object of showing the developments in structure and form which have taken place during the ages'.[21] The collection covers the whole spectrum of warships and merchantmen from the earliest times to the present day but, at its core, there are twenty or so models that display the particular figureheads of individual ships from the 1638 *Sovereign of the Seas* to the 1861 HMS *Bristol* screw frigate. A dozen ships of the eighteenth century are captured in a series of detailed perspective paintings of unrigged hull models now in the Science & Society Picture Library.[22] They were painted by Joseph Marshall between 1773 and 1775 for George III and are all shown in the Navy Board model style with their lower planks removed to display the ship's frames. To distinguish the Science Museum models from these paintings in the Figurehead Directory, the former are credited 'Science Museum' with an inventory number while the latter are credited 'Science Museum Pictorial'.

Other maritime museums in the UK such as the Merseyside Maritime Museum and the Plymouth City Museum and Art Gallery have their own model collections – including scale models – while yet more appear in unlikely locations such as Cawdor Castle near Nairn in Scotland and Arlington Court near Barnstaple, Devon. Details of the former will be found in Chapter 5 and each has been given an entry in the Directory.

Two collections overseas that have significant numbers of 'sailing navy' models

[21] G S Laird Clowes, *Sailing Ships, their History and Development as Illustrated by the Collection of Ship-Models in the Science Museum*, (Science Museum, 1932).

[22] www.scienceandsociety.co.uk

and are on public display are in North America and owe their existence to discerning and wealthy businessmen, Henry Huddleston Rogers in the United States and Kenneth Roy Thomson in Canada.

The Rogers Collection includes fifteen models originally acquired by the late-seventeenth-century Navy Board official, Charles Sergison, and bought by Rogers around 1920. One of the finest models in this part of the collection is the 1701 *St George* (96), while one of Rogers's later purchases was the model of the 1828 HMS *Royal Adelaide* (104) showing the figurehead that survived at Chatham until 1949. He bequeathed his collection to the United States Naval Academy in 1935 and it is on display in the Naval Academy Museum at Annapolis, Maryland. Its catalogue is today complemented with a website that identifies some of the previously unnamed models so that between them there are sixteen models that include British warship figureheads, adding substantially to the Figurehead Directory.[23]

The Thomson collection of ship models is part of the much wider art collection, created by the 2nd Baron Thomson of Fleet and gifted to the Art Gallery of Ontario in the year 2000. Beautifully catalogued in 2009, the collection contributes seven ship models to the Figurehead Directory, including two by the twentieth-century modelmaker, Donald McNarry – the 1716 *Carolina* yacht and the 1747 *Charlotte* yacht.[24]

The most important collection of Navy Board models in private hands is the Kriegstein Collection, owned by brothers Arnold and Henry Kriegstein in the United States of America.[25] Not only does their catalogue describe each of the models meticulously, it is beautifully illustrated and tells of the excitement they experienced during the hunt for and acquisition of many of the models. No less than ten items in the collection are included in the Directory, but the most fascinating chapter is one at the end of the catalogue describing an unfinished boxwood carving intended to be the figurehead of a ship model. Entitled 'A figurehead from the reign of Queen Anne', it is only two inches high and, although the limbs of some of the minor figures are missing, it is given a detailed description:

> The queen, seated, is shown on both starboard and port sides holding
> an orb and scepter [*sic*] in each hand with winged angels behind,
> trumpeting tritons below, and cherubs holding a crown aloft topped by a
> strutting lion.

[23] *Henry Huddleston Rogers Collection of Ship Models* (US Naval Institute, Annapolis, 1958).

[24] Simon Stephens, *Ship Models – The Thomson Collection at the Art Gallery of Ontario* (Skylet Publishing, 2009).

[25] Arnold and Henry Kriegstein, *17th and 18th Century Ship Models from the Kriegstein Collection* (Pier Books/Dupont Communications, 2007).

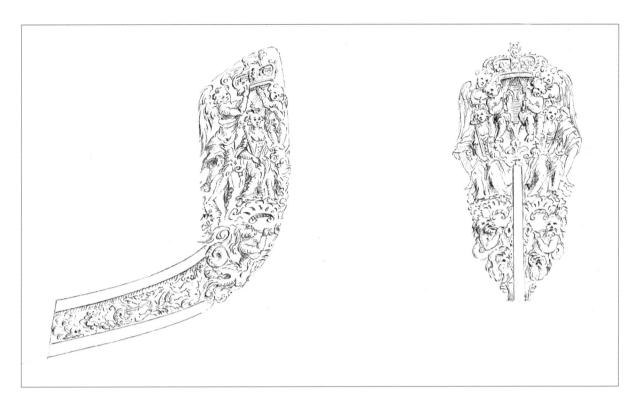

3.12
Unnamed ship –
Plymouth design, undated.
DICKERSON ARCHIVE

The Kriegsteins suggest that this would have been carved between 1702 and 1704 for the model of a First or Second Rate ship.

The fascination of this description is that it exactly matches that of an unnamed early design in the Dickerson Archive [3.12]. Each element of the group is there and the description could as well have been written for the figurehead design as the miniature carving. The implications of this are, firstly, that the Kriegstein miniature may have a Plymouth connection and secondly, if the Kriegstein assessment of date is correct, this and several similar designs in the Dickerson Archive may be earlier than previously thought.

III. Ship Plan Collections

The National Maritime Museum has the largest collection of original ship plans in the world with an estimated one million plans in its care, housed mainly in The Brass Foundry at Woolwich. Of this huge collection, the Admiralty Collection relates to about 40 per cent, with the remainder being a variety of merchant and private collections. It is, of course, only the former that are relevant to this book and, indeed, only a small proportion of the plans show figurehead details as those described as 'framing plans', 'deck plans', 'sail plans', etc., do not and it is only on some of the 'inboard profiles' that details of the figureheads are included.

Part of the Admiralty Collection has been digitised and may thus be examined on a computer screen without disturbing the originals. Commonly called the 'Sailing Navy Collection', it contains almost 8,000 plans, each of which is identified with a 'ZAZ' prefix. More than 300 of these are included in this book's Figurehead Directory and provide a significant contribution as most are of the eighteenth century and thus complement the predominantly nineteenth-century carvers' design drawings. That part of the Admiralty Collection from the introduction of steam power to the end of the figurehead era in about 1900 has not been digitised so here the original plans have to be examined. The search of these has been limited to those ships whose figurehead design drawings have not survived and this work has resulted in a further twenty additions to the Directory. They are identified with prefixes running from 'NPA' to 'NPD'.

Also stored at Woolwich is the Hilhouse Collection of ship plans created by the family that had built ships at Bristol from the early 1770s, and acquired by the NMM in 1983. The plans that contribute to the sum total of figurehead knowledge are included in the Directory with the prefix 'HIL'.

IV. Cigarette Card Collections

To quote a set of cigarette-cards as source of information about warship figureheads may at first appear frivolous but, as each provides a 'snapshot' of the available material at the time, it would have been wrong to ignore them. Two sets of twenty-five cards were issued by John Player and Son, the first in 1912 and the second in 1931. Brief details of the cards will be found under 'Bibliography and Sources'.

The artist who created the 1912 set clearly had access to the Portsmouth and Devonport Dockyard collections and to those at the Castles ship-breaking yards and this resulted in portraits that were both accurate and colourful. There were errors – such as showing a portrait of the *Royal Frederick* figurehead under the title *Royal William* – but, taken as a whole, they complement the 1911 Admiralty Catalogue which had no illustrations. The most controversial card is that for HMS *Victory* as it shows the royal arms with a uniformed marine as its supporter on the port side. The subject is addressed in more detail in Chapter 14.

Half the cards in the 1931 set showed details of the figureheads carved on contemporary ship models and, as this was several years before the collection was consolidated in the National Maritime Museum, the location of the models provides an interesting detail.

CHAPTER 4

——◦‣◦——

SIXTEENTH- AND SEVENTEENTH-CENTURY FIGUREHEADS

COMPARED with the centuries that followed, very few ships of the sixteenth and seventeenth centuries had figureheads representing the name of their particular ship.

The first few can be found in 'The Anthony Roll', a manuscript created by Anthony Anthony in 1546 that provides a complete visual record of the royal ships at the end of Henry VIII's reign and, as Anthony Anthony was an officer of the ordnance, he also included an inventory of each vessel's munitions. Although originally in three parts, the manuscript is today in two parts, one at Magdalene College, Cambridge,[1] the other in the British Library.[2] As part of their Millennium celebrations, the Navy Record Society published *The Anthony Roll of Henry VIII's Navy* that brought together for the first time in 300 years the separate parts of the original manuscript with its fifty-eight coloured ship illustrations in a style that was intended more to show the grandeur of the fleet than to attempt to be an accurate ship-portrait.[3]

Of these, two are shown with carvings on their beakheads, the *Unicorn* and the *Salamander*. The *Unicorn* had been taken from the Scots in 1544 and is shown with a standing unicorn, a supporter of the royal arms of Scotland [Colour Plate 5]. The *Salamander* is shown in an identical style, except that she has a salamander on the beakhead, that being the badge of the French kings, a beast that was said to be invulnerable to fire. She too had been captured from the Scots in 1544 but had previously been a French ship. One other illustration includes a symbol relating to the ship's name – the *Mary Rose* – notorious because she capsized off the Isle of Wight in 1545. Rather than appearing with an emblem on the beakhead, she is shown with a rose protruding from the front of her prominent forecastle. This part of the ship was not salvaged when a large proportion of her starboard side was raised in 1982, but it was discovered during the 2005 diving season and is now on display in the Mary Rose Museum. Having been built in Portsmouth in 1509, the *Mary Rose* can claim the title of being the

[1] Pepys Library no 2991.
[2] Additional MS 22047.

[3] Knighton and Loades, *The Anthony Roll of Henry VIII's Navy*.

4.1
Sovereign of the Seas –
Ship plan detail 1637.
NATIONAL MARITIME MUSEUM

first English warship to carry a figurehead symbolic of her name and certainly it must be the oldest surviving one.

During the seventeenth century a number of ships were given figureheads with equestrian themes, the earliest being the 1610 *Prince Royal* (64). The ship was included in two paintings by the Dutch painter Vroom, each showing her figurehead in some detail. The first shows the ship entering the harbour at Flushing in 1613, her long beakhead carrying a mounted St George with a dragon at the horse's side, behind which is a very large knight's helmet surmounted by a crown.[4] The second shows the ship leading the fleet into the Solent in 1623 and, while St George and the dragon are unchanged, the helmet and crown are no longer there – removed perhaps in one of her intervening refits.[5]

A similar beakhead was a feature of the 1637 *Sovereign of the Seas* (100) except

4　*The Arrival of Frederik V of The Palatine and Elizabeth Stuart in Flushing on 29 April 1613* (Frans Hals Museum).
5　*The Return of Prince Charles from Spain – 5 October 1623* (National Maritime Museum BHC0710).

4.2
Naseby –
Ship model detail 1655.
NATIONAL MARITIME MUSEUM

6 Ship plan NMM ZAZ0048.

7 Ship model NMM SLR0356
   (*c*1830).

8 Peter Norton, *Ships'*
   Figureheads (David & Charles,
   1976), p 57.

that she had King Edgar on horseback 'trampling on seven kings', an allusion to the Saxon chronicles that recorded how the other kings of Britain had acknowledged Edgar's supremacy. The ship was renamed *Sovereign* during the Commonwealth and *Royal Sovereign* on the restoration of the monarchy in 1660. Details of her carved work are shown on several ship plans in the National Maritime Museum collection, the most detailed being a nineteenth-century 'reconstruction' shown here [4.1].[6] The NMM ship model collection also includes a model of the ship made around 1830 for Sir Robert Seppings (the Surveyor of the Navy) but, although the detail is delicately carved and several of the trampled kings are shown, King Edgar's head has been lost.[7]

The Commonwealth period also produced an equestrian figurehead on the bow of the 1655 *Naseby* (80) built at Woolwich. The contemporary diarist, John Evelyn, described it as having Oliver Cromwell on horseback trampling figures from Scotland, Ireland, Holland, France, Spain and England, each identifiable from their clothing, while a 'fame' held a laurel wreath over his head.[8] A Navy

Board model in the National Maritime Museum collection shows the scene, even though the victims' identities cannot be seen [4.2].[9] Not surprisingly, the *Naseby* – whose name had commemorated the Roundheads' victory over the Royalists – was renamed *Royal Charles* at the Restoration and the figurehead was replaced.

Other mounted equestrian figureheads of the period included the 1670 *Prince* (100), built at Chatham, a model of which is in the Science Museum collection in London,[10] the 1671 *Royal James* (100), built at Portsmouth, and the 1682 *Britannia* (100), built at Chatham with carved work by Thomas Fletcher. Models of the last two are in the Kriegstein Collection in the United States.[11]

A more elaborate style of figurehead can be seen on the bow of another model in the NMM collection, that of the 1669 *St Michael* (90), built at Portsmouth [4.3].[12] A double-headed bird looking somewhat like an eagle, plucking at its breast feathers, has behind it a figure on some form of chariot with a small putto between them. The model was identified as coming from the *St Michael* from a Van de Velde drawing also in the National Maritime Museum collections that shows the bird and the reclining figure.[13] Rather than a double-headed eagle, the bird is in the contemporary heraldic style of a pelican that, when shown feeding her young, was known as 'a pelican in her piety'. The connection between Christian sacrifice and St Michael is not too difficult to imagine.

Despite the use of individually-designed figureheads on some ships, the most commonly used device in the seventeenth century was the crowned lion and about twenty examples from ship plans and ship models will be found in the Figurehead Directory. Most of the models are in the National Maritime Museum collection including that from the 1683 *Mordaunt* (48)[14] [4.4] but others will be seen to come from Annapolis – the 1693 *Sussex* (80); from Ontario – the 1699 *Nassau* (80); and from Wilton House near Salisbury – the 1678 *Hampton Court* (70).

One final example of a seventeenth-century animal figurehead was a unicorn

4.3
St Michael –
Ship model detail 1699.
NATIONAL MARITIME MUSEUM

9 Ship model NMM SLR1110.
10 Ship model Science Museum No 1895-56.
11 Arnold and Henry Kriegstein, *17th and 18th Century Ship Models from the Kriegstein Collection* (Pier Books/Dupont Communications, 2007).
12 Ship model NMM SLR0002.
13 Drawing NMM PAF6608.
14 Ship model NMM SLR0004 (1681).

[15] British Museum
1874,0808.97.

4·4
Mordaunt – **Ship model
detail 1683.**
NATIONAL MARITIME MUSEUM

on the bow of the 1660 *Mary* (8) yacht. It is illustrated in a beautifully detailed drawing by Willem Van de Velde the elder and, unlike the lions that are full-length but static in their form, the unicorn is shown leaping from the bow.[15] Trinity House used to own a contemporary model of the yacht but it was lost during the Blitz in 1940 and has been replaced by a replica made in 1952 by the modelmaker Robert Spence.

1. HMS *Southampton* –
Hellyer design 1810.
(THE NATIONAL ARCHIVES) CH. 2

2. *Plymouth* yacht – Dickerson design 1797.
(DICKERSON ARCHIVE) CH. 2

3. Hercules, Hope & Justice – Dickerson artwork.
(DICKERSON ARCHIVE) CH. 2

4. HMS *Poictiers* –
Sheerness 1992.
(AUTHOR'S COLLECTION) CH. 3

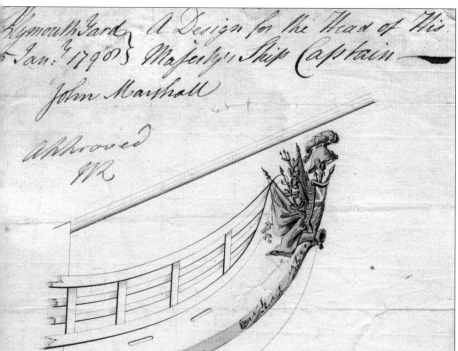

5. *Unicorn* – The Anthony Roll.
(BRITISH LIBRARY) CH. 4

6. HMS *Captain* – Dickerson design 1798.
(DICKERSON ARCHIVE) CH. 5

7. HMS *Castor* – Dickerson design 1798.
(DICKERSON ARCHIVE) CH. 5

9. TS *Conway* – HMS *Nelson* 1992.

10. HMS *Britannia* – Royal Naval College Dartmouth 1992.
(AUTHOR'S COLLECTION) CH. 9

H.M.S. HIBERNIA.

1st-Rate ship launched in 1804
at Plymouth and broken-up in 1902.
For many years she served as
a Depot ship at Malta.

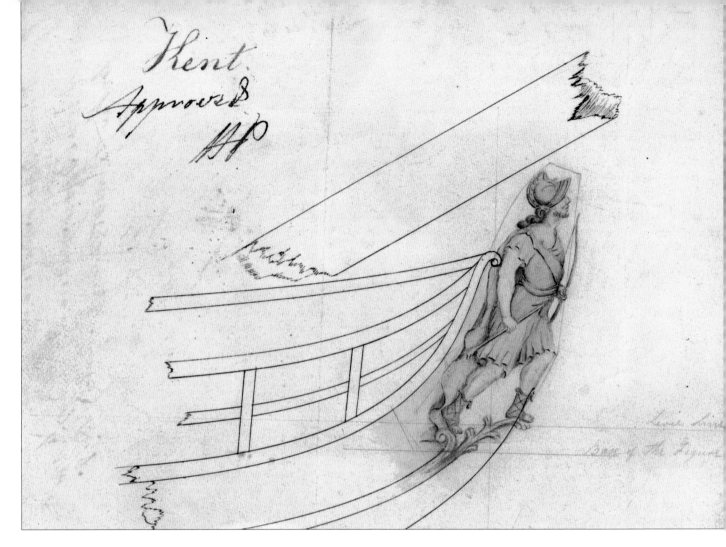

12. HMS *Kent* – **Navy Board design 1819.**

(DICKERSON ARCHIVE) CH. 9

13. HMS *Zephyr* – **Dickerson design 1809.**

(THE NATIONAL ARCHIVES) CH. 10

14. HMS *Terpsichore* – HMS *President*, London.
(AUTHOR'S COLLECTION) CH. 11

15. HMS *Sybille* – Dickerson design 1844.
(THE NATIONAL ARCHIVES) CH. 11

16. HMS *Cadmus* – Admiralty House, Plymouth 1992.
(AUTHOR'S COLLECTION) CH.11

17. HMS *Leander* – HMS *Collingwood*, Fareham 1992.
(AUTHOR'S COLLECTION) CH. 11

18. HMS *Centurion* – Topsham, Devon 1992.

19. HMS *Lacedaemonian* – Hellyer design 1812.

20. HMS *Madagascar* – Hellyer design 1812.

24. HMS *Hope* – Hellyer design 1811.
(THE NATIONAL ARCHIVES) CH. 14

25. HMS *Inflexible* – Dickerson design 1844.
(DICKERSON ARCHIVE) CH. 14

21. HMS *Seringapatam* – Greenwich 2010.
(NATIONAL MARITIME MUSEUM) CH. 13

22. HMS *Constance* – Dickerson design 1844.
(THE NATIONAL ARCHIVES) CH. 14

23. HMS *Constance* – HMS *Excellent*, Portsmouth 2009.
(RICHARD HUNTER ARCHIVES) CH. 14

26. HMS *Queen Charlotte* –
HMS *Excellent*, Portsmouth 2009.
(RICHARD HUNTER ARCHIVES) CH. 15

27. HMS *Royal William* –
HM Naval Base, Devonport.
(AUTHOR'S COLLECTION) CH. 15

OPPOSITE PAGE
28. HMS *Windsor Castle* – HMS
Cambridge, Wembury 1996.
(AUTHOR'S COLLECTION) CH. 15

VICTORIA
First Rate Battleship

1844 Laid down and designated Victoria
1858 Launched as H.M.S. Windsor Castle
1869 ~ 1907 H.M.S. Cambridge

This plaque was unveiled by
H.R.H. The Duke of Kent , K.G.
26 th March 1987

29. HMS ***Calcutta*** **– Privately owned, Norfolk 1995.**

(AUTHOR'S COLLECTION) DIRECTORY

31. HMS *Fisgard* – HMS *Raleigh*,
Torpoint 1992.
(AUTHOR'S COLLECTION) DIRECTORY

30. HMS *Eclipse* – Auckland 2011.
(ROYAL NEW ZEALAND NAVY MUSEUM) DIRECTORY

33. HMS *Penguin* –
HMAS *Penguin*, Sydney,
Australia.
(AUTHOR'S COLLECTION) DIRECTORY

34. HMS *President* –
Fishmongers' Hall, London.
(AUTHOR'S COLLECTION) DIRECTORY

32. HMS *Martin* – HMS
Nelson, Portsmouth.
(CROWN COPYRIGHT) DIRECTORY

CHAPTER 5

EIGHTEENTH-CENTURY FIGUREHEADS

DESPITE the fact that orders were issued several times during the eighteenth century limiting the amount of carving that was permitted for various classes of warships, a wide variety of styles continued to be employed throughout the period. The First and Second Rate ships were often given complex assemblies of figures referred to here as 'group figureheads'; the Admiralty favoured figureheads in the form of a lion and, for smaller ships, there was a whole range of full-length figures, either 'standing' on some form of platform or with their legs sweeping down the trailboards in what sometimes appeared to be a near-kneeling position.

Details of the group figureheads come mainly from contemporary ship models while those for the lions and full-length figures come principally from the ship plan collections in the National Maritime Museum, supplemented by carvers' designs.

I. GROUP FIGUREHEADS

A theme that was included in several of these carvings was to have a bust and the royal coat of arms on the centreline with figures on each side that together created an image of Britain and her maritime prowess. A fine example is that for the 1719 *Britannia* (100), built in Woolwich Dockyard, whose model is in the National Maritime Museum collection.[1] On the centreline is a large crown over a circular coat of arms and an upright lion stands guard on each side. Behind each lion is an angel holding up the crown with a standing figure below and a bust where the main carving merged into each trailboard.

The carvers had some difficulty in putting such designs on paper but an illustration in the Dickerson Archive of Australia can be used to decipher the components [5.1]. It is marked 'Britannia' and, although undated, contains so many characteristics that are shown in the *Britannia* model above and that of the 1737 *Victory* described below, that it is almost certainly a design for the 1719

[1] Ship model NMM SLR0223.

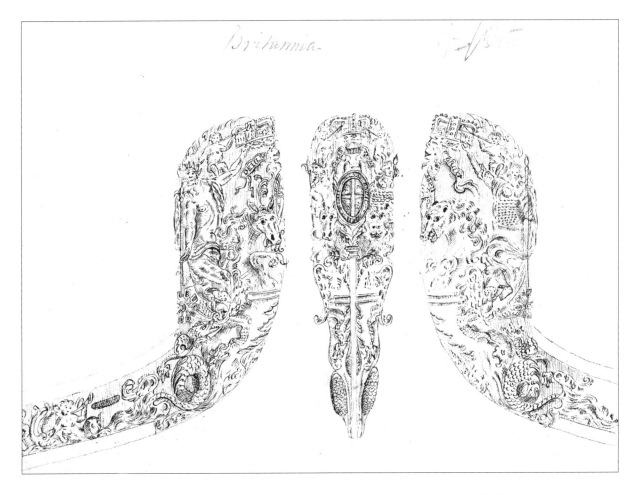

Britannia.

5.1
Britannia – **Plymouth design, undated.**
DICKERSON ARCHIVE

Britannia. The large crown surmounts the forward facing royal arms which themselves are topped with a royal helmet and a ribbon inscribed with the monarch's motto, 'Dieu et Mon Droit'. On the starboard side is a horse whose foreleg is raised but whose body is formed into a twisted serpent's tail. On this heraldic 'sea-horse' sits a crowned King Neptune, supporting the royal crown with his left hand and with a trident in his right hand. A small putto sits above Neptune's shoulder blowing a trumpet; a mermaid is by the horse's waistband while others play music in the trailboard. The port side of the figurehead is similar with a serpent-tailed lion – a heraldic 'sea-lion' – replacing the horse (his features being particularly leonine in the central drawing) while an armour-clad Britannia replaces King Neptune.

There are two contemporary models of the 1737 *Victory* (100), built in Portsmouth Dockyard, that show her figurehead in detail, one in the National Maritime Museum collection,[2] the other at Cawdor Castle, Nairn, Scotland, believed to have been acquired by John Campbell of Cawdor who was one of

2 Ship model NMM SLR0449.

the Lords of the Admiralty in 1741 [5.2]. The central crown, royal arms, helmet and inscribed ribbon can all be seen and the transition from the horse's body to the serpent's tail is more easily seen than in the *Britannia* drawing. King Neptune glowers, the putto still has his trumpet but there is an additional sea-monster appearing below Neptune's foot. On the starboard side of the model Britannia wears a laurel wreath, her lion is very fierce and another sea-monster emerges. The work of the model-maker is beautifully fine and the full-sized figurehead must have been awesome.

A double equestrian figurehead that carries similar messages appears on the bow of the model of the 1719 *Royal William* (100).[3] The mounted king is shown

3   Ship model NMM SLR0222.

5.2
Victory – **Ship model detail.**
COURTESY THE DOWAGER COUNTESS
CAWDOR

wearing the armour of a Roman warrior with a laurel-wreath on his head. A putto holds a crown above the head of the horse which is trampling on human enemies. Between the two prancing horses is an oval frame holding the royal monogram.

A very similar figurehead was carved for the *Royal George* (100), built as *Royal Anne* but renamed in 1756. The ship model is another in the National Maritime Museum collection made in 1772–3 [5.3].[4] The royal arms and crown are much less prominent but the prancing horses are vigorously carved and the king is again in the costume of a warrior with a laurel wreath on his head. The putto holds a crown over the king's head and, once more, the nation's enemies are being trampled under foot.

The specification for the original figurehead for the most famous of all the

4   Ship model NMM SLR0336.

5.3
Royal George –
Ship model detail.
NATIONAL MARITIME MUSEUM

5·4
Cambridge –
Plymouth design, undated.
DICKERSON ARCHIVE

ships of the line, the 1765 *Victory* (100), built in Chatham Dockyard, was published in *The Mariner's Mirror* in 1922.[5] The mass of carvings was topped by a bust of George III, clad in armour and adorned with laurels, over a shield that was surrounded by four cherubs' heads and wings representing the four winds and gently blowing the country's success over the four quarters of the globe. The principal figure on the starboard side was Britannia seated on a triumphal arch, supporting the king's bust with one hand while her foot was trampling down Envy, Discord and Faction represented by a fiend or hag. Behind Britannia was a flying figure representing Peace, holding a branch of palms, denoting peace, in one hand while crowning Britannia with laurels with the other. Behind the arch was the British lion trampling on rich trophies of war, while the arch was supported by figures representing Europe and America. The port side was equally complicated, the principal figure being Victory, trampling on Rebellion represented by the five-headed Hydra. Behind Victory was the flying figure of Fame holding a trumpet and behind her an escutcheon with the royal arms and an arch supported by figures representing Asia and Africa. Genii appear in the trailboards holding a cornucopia, representing the

5 'Carved Work of the "Victory", 1765', *The Mariner's Mirror* Vol VIII (1922), pp 281–3.

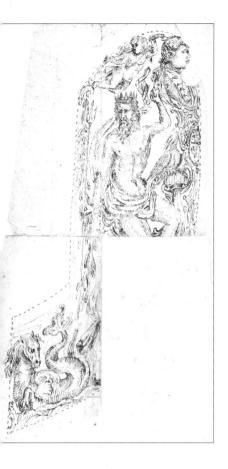

happy consequences after victory, and symbols of navigation denoting success in all parts of the globe.

With such a description to hand, the drawing for the figurehead of the 1755 *Cambridge* is more easily deciphered [5.4]. The bust of the king is crowned with a laurel wreath. The principal figure below him is King Neptune, crowned, holding his trident and half-seated on a 'sea-horse' whose lower half curls into a serpent's tail. Two putti appear behind the royal bust while there is a ferocious dolphin in the trailboards. The drawing is one of those that were retained by the Dickerson family of Devonport and is now preserved in the Dickerson Archive in Australia. It is undated but is very similar in style to the figurehead for the *Cambridge* described in the Accountant General's ledger for 1755[6] and, even though that carving was made by Thomas Burrough of Deptford, the two would appear to relate to the same ship.

A variation to this theme was given to the 1777 *Duke* (90) in which a royal bust and coat of arms had a full-length figure of King Neptune standing as a supporter [5.5]. The drawing is from the Dickerson Archive in Australia and, despite its lower quarter being missing from repeated folding, shows the detail that was provided at the time. This drawing has been identified from the NMM ship plan that is almost identical, including the bird that stands on a pot of

5.5
Duke – **Plymouth design, undated.**

6   Thomas, *British Figurehead & Ship Carvers*, p 76.

5.6
Majestic – **Ship plan detail.**

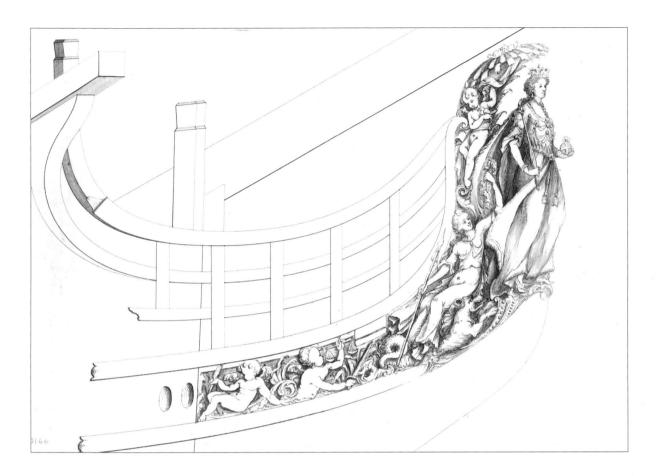

flowing water beside the royal arms.[7]

In the last quarter of the eighteenth century, ships of the line were given rather simpler figurehead designs. The 1785 *Majestic* (74), built by Adams & Barnard of Deptford, had a large figurehead of a seated George III, crowned, robed and holding the orb and sceptre [5.6]. His throne incorporated the royal arms while a lion rampant stood guard above the trailboard in which the monarch's motto 'Dieu et Mon Droit' was displayed amongst several English roses.[8] A figurehead in a similar style had been given to the 1773 *Princess Royal* (90) in which the formally dressed and seated princess held an olive branch and a classical scene unfolded below her – perhaps Artemis, goddess of hunting, as there were hunting-dogs in the trailboard of the somewhat damaged ship plan.[9]

Queen Charlotte, consort of King George III, was portrayed in the figurehead of the 1790 *Queen Charlotte* as a standing figure in formal robes, crowned and carrying the orb and sceptre. Over her head swept a canopy on which were perched two doves and at her sides were figures of Britannia and Peace with several other figures in the trailboards [5.7]. The figurehead design[10] is filed

5.7
Queen Charlotte -
Figurehead design 1790.
NATIONAL MARITIME MUSEUM

[7] Ship plan NMM ZAZ0213.

[8] Ship plan NMM ZAZ0703.

[9] Ship plan NMM ZAZ0347.

[10] Ship plan NMM ZAZ0166.

11 Ship plan NMM ZAZ0167.
12 Ship plan NMM ZAZ1243.
13 Edward Fraser, *Bellerophon,
    The Bravest of the Brave*
    (Wells Gardner, Darton & Co,
    1909), p 30.

5.8
Boyne – Ship model detail.

with the ship plans of the NMM and, unusually, has a companion showing the figurehead from the opposite side.[11] Another version of the design, this time in colour, is held by the Corporation of the Hull Trinity House, while a limewood carver's model is on display at the Chatham Historic Dockyard. The model was first owned by the then Surveyor of the Navy and was passed down through his family until it was sold at auction in 2005.

Single figures mounted on horseback also appeared at this time, two examples being the Duke of Marlborough and King William III. The Duke of Marlborough was shown on the 1785 *Ramillies* (74) commemorating his victory over the French in 1706. He is wearing a plumed hat, has his sword in his hand and his family arms are in the trailboard, as are a cannon and other trophies of war.[12] William III appeared on the 1790 HMS *Boyne* (98) that commemorated his victory over James II at the Battle of the Boyne in 1690 [5.8]. The contemporary ship model is one of those on display at the Science Museum, London.

A variation of this theme was the figurehead carved for the 1786 *Bellerophon* (74), built by Graves of Frindsbury on the River Medway. Her figurehead was described as the naked figure of the young Greek hero, Bellerophon, riding bareback on the rearing winged horse, Pegasus, wearing a golden helmet with white plumes and a short red cloak flung back from his shoulders.[13] When the ship was sold for breaking up in 1836, the Admiral Superintendent at Portsmouth was Sir Frederick Maitland who had commanded *Bellerophon* when Napoleon Bonaparte surrendered on board in 1815. The admiral bought the figurehead and some of her stern carvings and had them installed in the mould-loft of the dockyard but all that remains today is the helmeted head of Bellerophon, now in the National Museum of the Royal Navy, Portsmouth.

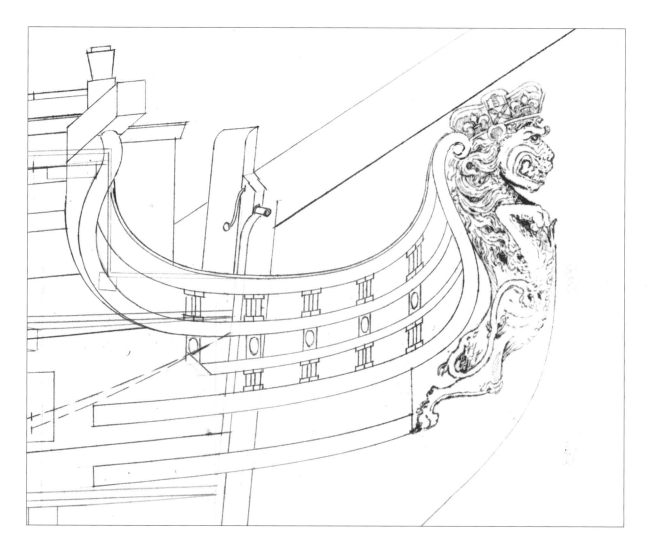

II. LIONS

An analysis of the eighteenth-century ship plans and ship models shows that, while the use of lions as figureheads was widespread in the Royal Navy, twice as many full-length or standing human figures were carved for the fleet. While each human figure was created to relate to the individual ship's name, this was not possible with lion figureheads whose only distinguishing feature was whether or not it was wearing a crown. Lions from the first half of the century tend to be in a somewhat 'compressed' style as in the example from the 1736 *Jersey* [5.9].

A fine surviving example of this type of lion is in the collection of the National Maritime Museum, Greenwich although he has travelled widely to various exhibitions over the years. Wearing a crown with alternate cross and fleur-de-lis motifs, his forelegs hold a small cartouche bearing St George's cross and his

5.9
Jersey – **Ship plan detail.**
NATIONAL MARITIME MUSEUM

mane and double tails are carved in high relief. He was originally displayed in a private museum in Uffculme near Cullompton in Devon and was sold through the auction house of Bearnes of Torquay in 1971. It is not known from which ship he came but, measuring about 7ft in height, he would have been from a Fifth or Sixth Rate ship.

It had been hoped that by analysing the many lion figureheads by ship's rate and date that some pattern of their distribution would emerge. However, except for the fact that very few First or Second Rate ships were given lion figureheads, the spread across the remaining rates and across the whole of the eighteenth century was surprisingly even.

III. FULL-LENGTH FIGURES

The picture is very different for the most widely used of all the eighteenth-century figureheads – the simple full-length figure. Analysis of more than a hundred that are included in the ship plans collection of the National Maritime

5.10
Caesar – **Dickerson design, undated.**
DICKERSON ARCHIVE

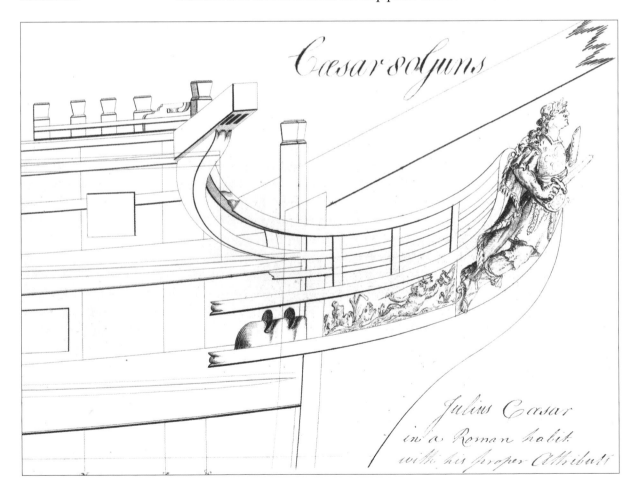

Museum shows that they did not appear until about the middle of the century but, thereafter, they were mounted on all classes of ships with the exception of First and Second Rates.

The range of ship names was not nearly as broad as it became in the nineteenth century and, in consequence, the subject-matter for the figureheads was more traditional. As might be expected, the larger the ship, the more impressive was its figurehead, a fact that is illustrated in the ship plans and contemporary models.

Of the Third Rates, two that were named after rulers of the distant past were *Caesar* and *Alfred*. On the 1793 *Caesar* (80), built in Plymouth Dockyard, the great Roman general was shown as a warrior with laurel wreath, sword and shield and, presumably to give it a nautical flavour, the figure of Neptune in the trailboard with his trident, a cornucopia and a sea-monster [5.10]. Both Samuel and James Dickerson were carving in Plymouth at this time and later correspondence between the dockyard and the Navy Board records that £44.8.0 was allowed for the work.[14] On the 1778 *Alfred* (74), built in Chatham Dockyard,

14   TNA ADM 106/1935 (1795).

5.11
Alfred – **Ship plan detail.**
NATIONAL MARITIME MUSEUM

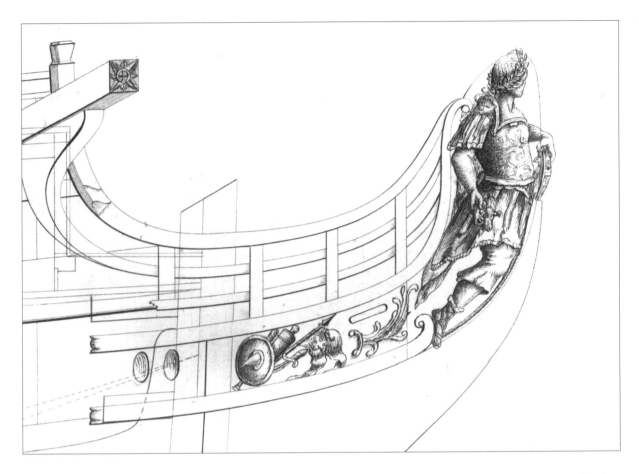

5.12
Bedford – **Ship plan detail.**
NATIONAL MARITIME MUSEUM

[15] Ship plan NMM ZAZ0563.

[16] Ship plan NMM ZAZ1304.
[17] Ship plan NMM ZAZ0985.

the king is shown on the ship plan in the National Maritime Museum collection [5.11].[15] He is wearing a crown and holds a mace of office while in the trailboards the carvers have added some cakes, that are to remind the viewer of the story of when he was chastised for burning a peasant woman's meal, and a harp that he played when he disguised himself as a wandering minstrel to gain access to the camp of the invading Danes.

Two other Third Rates with a regional association were each launched in the 1770s and have ship plans in the National Maritime Museum collection on which their figureheads are shown: *Bedford*[16] and *Cumberland*.[17] The 1755 *Bedford* (74) was named after the Duke of Bedford (created in 1694) and, although he is dressed as a Roman warrior, the association with the modern family is shown by his carrying a ducal coronet in his right hand and in all probability the family arms would have been carved on his shield [5.12]. The figurehead of the 1774 *Cumberland* (74) was in the form of King Neptune, crowned, full-bearded and brandishing his trident in a powerful manner. Creatures from the sea appear in the trailboard [5.13].

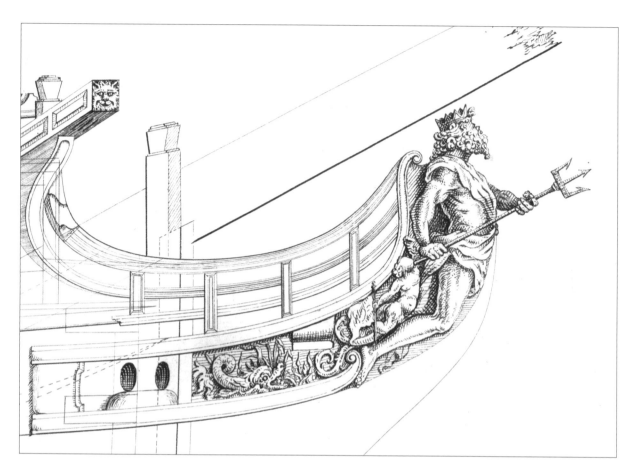

**5.13
Cumberland –
Ship plan detail.**
NATIONAL MARITIME MUSEUM

The twelve 'Labours of Hercules' made *Hercules* an appropriate name for a ship of the line and, when the French *L'Hercule* was captured in 1798, she became the second ship of the Royal Navy to have borne the name. A new figurehead was carved for her by James Dickerson of Plymouth and his design is amongst those in the Dickerson Archive in Australia [5.14]. Hercules is shown wearing the skin of the Nemean lion that he killed with his bare hands and his olive-wood club in the first of his Labours, wearing it thereafter. In the trailboard can be seen Cerberus, the three-headed watchdog that guarded the gate of Hades' realm and which he captured in his final Labour. An almost identical representation of the figurehead appears in the 'as fitted' plan for the 1798 ship except that the trailboard detail has been omitted.[18]

Another character from mythology that appeared as an eighteenth-century standing figure was Polyphemus, one of the Cyclops famous for having but a single eye. The 1782 *Polyphemus* (64) was built in Sheerness Dockyard, her figurehead having been carved by William Savage.[19] It is shown on her ship plan and, despite the fact that only the head of the carving has survived, it is

18 Ship plan NMM ZAZ0881.

19 Thomas, *British Figurehead & Ship Carvers*, p 98.

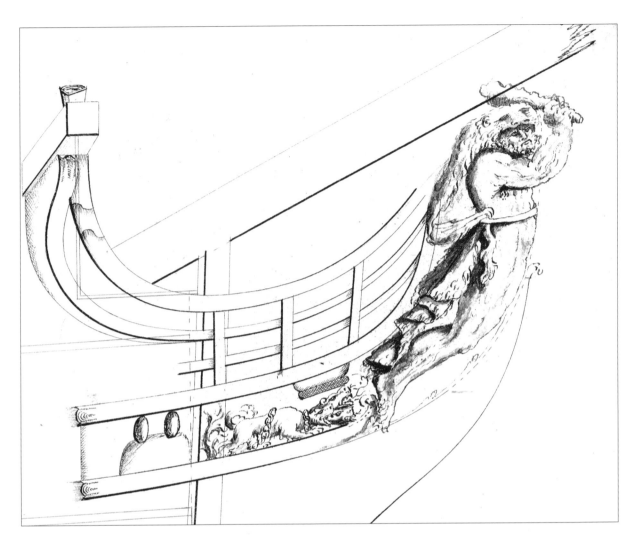

5.14
Hercules - **Dickerson design, undated.**
DICKERSON ARCHIVE

[20] Ship plan NMM ZAZ1496.

[21] Ship plan NMM ZAZ2114.

very special as it saw much action and the ship was awarded the battle honours 'Copenhagen 1801' and 'Trafalgar 1805'.[20] It is now in the National Maritime Museum, Greenwich.

Full-length figures were also carved for numerous smaller ships. The 1778 *Charon* (44) was built by Barnard of Harwich, the figurehead being the ferryman who carried the dead across the river Styx wielding his paddle [5.15]. Just as with *Hercules* mentioned above, Cerberus – the three-headed watchdog that guarded the entrance to the Underworld – can be seen in the trailboards.[21]

Hermes was not only the son of Zeus but his messenger and was thus a suitable subject for figureheads on smaller ships that played that role for the ships of the line. Depicted as a young man wearing a wide-brimmed winged hat and winged sandals, he carried a herald's staff – a caduceus – around which were entwined two snakes. Examples appear in both ship plans and ship models:

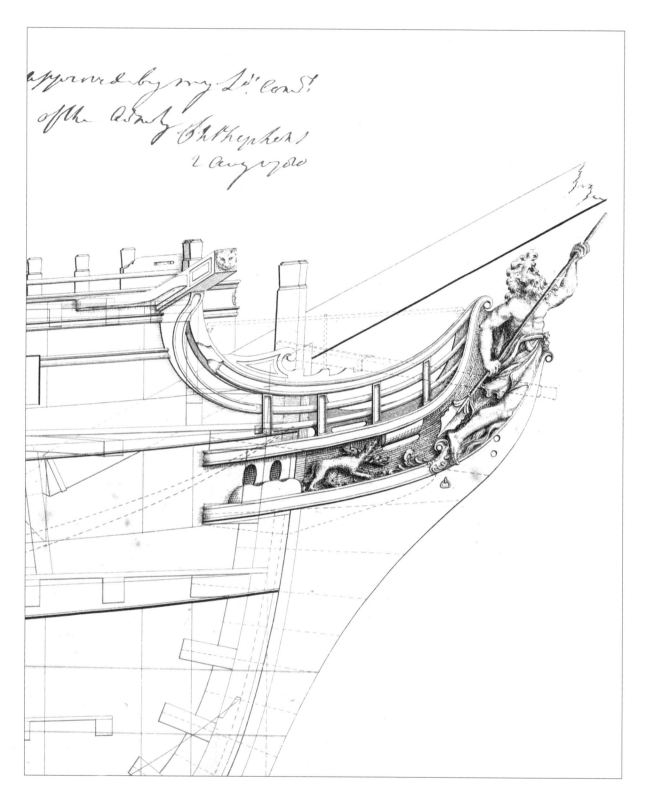

5·15
Charon – Ship plan detail.

5.16
Plymouth - Ship model detail.

the 1742 *Granado* bomb, built by Barnard of Ipswich and shown on her ship plan;[22] *Vigilant* (58), captured from the French in 1745 and shown on her ship plan;[23] the 1755 *Plymouth* yacht, built in Plymouth Dockyard and shown on her ship plan[24] and her contemporary ship model [5.16];[25] and the 1777 *Swift* (14) also built in Plymouth Dockyard and shown on her ship plan.[26]

The figurehead designs of several ships that were built by Henry Adams of Buckler's Hard on the Beaulieu River in Hampshire are now preserved in the archives of the Buckler's Hard Maritime Museum. They include those for the 1773 *Triton* (28) [5.17], the 1773 *Greyhound* (28), the 1779 *Brilliant* (28), the 1783 *Gladiator* (44) and the 1783 *Heroine* (32).[27] The form of each is described briefly in the Directory. There is no suggestion that these designs were submitted for approval but they form a valuable record of some of the figureheads that were carved in this small private shipyard.

5.17
Triton –
Henry Adams design.
BUCKLERS HARD MARITIME MUSEUM

IV. OTHER DESIGNS

Creatures from Greek and Roman mythology resulted in some most uncomfortable-looking figureheads. The *Centaur* (74) was captured from the French in 1759 and the carvers must have had great difficulty fitting the body and legs of a horse and the head, torso and arms of a man into the space available [5.18]. The drawing comes from the 'as taken' ship plan for the *Centaur* dated 1760.[28] The Sixth Rate *Sphinx* (20) built in Portsmouth Dockyard and launched there in 1775 presented a similar difficulty as, although a Sphinx was reputed to be a monster with a woman's head and the body of a winged lion, the ship plan for the *Sphinx* shows her with the lion's body and a female torso carrying her folded wings, making it all somewhat cramped.[29]

Home-grown myths and legends were also represented in the names of the eighteenth-century navy. When the French Fifth Rate *La Licorne* was captured in 1778, there appears to have been no move to change her name to the English equivalent 'Unicorn' and she became the *Licorne* (32). As shown in Chapter 1,

22 Ship plan NMM ZAZ5628.
23 Ship plan NMM ZAZ6874.
24 Ship plan NMM NPD0741 & 0742.
25 Ship model NMM SLR0494.
26 Ship plan NMM ZAZ4732.
27 Buckler's Hard reference BH/II/PD5 68.
28 Ship plan NMM ZAZ0730.
29 Ship plan NMM ZAZ3919.

5.18
Centaur – **Ship plan detail.**
NATIONAL MARITIME MUSEUM

5.19
Leviathan – **Dickerson design, undated.**
DICKERSON ARCHIVE

30   Ship plan NMM ZAZ3111.
31   J M C Toynbee, 'Roman Trophies', *The Classical Review* Vol 10, No 1 (1960).

her ship plan shows an elegant unicorn with spiral markings up its single horn.[30] When *Merlin* (18) was purchased on the stocks in 1780, rather than fitting her with a figurehead representing the wizard from the legends of King Arthur, she was given a full-length dragon breathing fire, an allusion to Merlin's prophesy of the struggle between the Britons and the Saxons based on his vision of dragons fighting each other.

A group of unusual designs from the very end of the eighteenth century provides a suitable conclusion to the period, each having been drawn by James Dickerson of Plymouth. The 1787 *Captain* (74) had been built by Baston of Limehouse and it was in her that the then Commodore Horatio Nelson had distinguished himself at the battle of Cape St Vincent in February 1797. Severely damaged in the battle, it is not surprising that *Captain* required a replacement figurehead [Colour Plate 6]. The design combined the union flag in a central shield, a plumed helmet above it and trophies of war and symbols of victory around it. This arrangement has its origins in ancient Greece and Rome when, after a battle, a cruciform manikin was created covered with carefully arranged arms and armour giving the appearance of a stylized human figure.[31] Perhaps

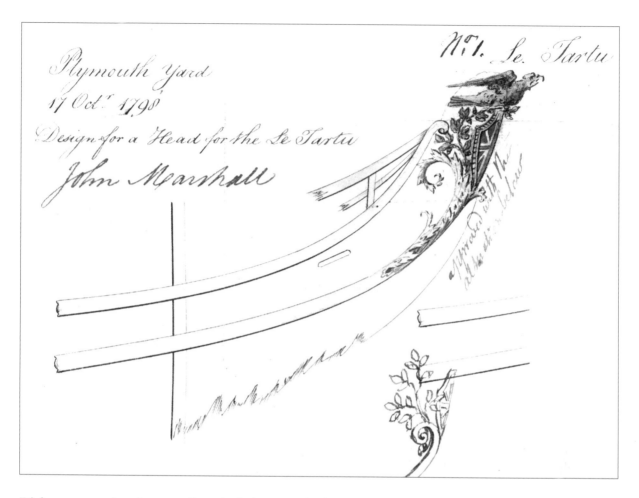

Plymouth Yard
17 Octr 1798
Design for a Head for the Le Tartu
John Marshall

N^o1. Le Tartu

Dickerson was drawing on a French design as a similar arrangement appears on the ship plan of the French ship *Revolutionnaire*, captured in 1794,[32] and in an undated Dickerson design [5.19] that has the pencil notation 'Leviathon' [*sic*]. Continuing the theme, but on this occasion with a face under the helmet, is a design offered in 1798 for a replacement figurehead for the 1785 *Castor* (32) [Colour Plate 7].

A design that shared many of the characteristics of these 'trophy' figureheads was submitted by James Dickerson later that year for the French *Le Tartu* (38) captured by *Polyphemus* off Ireland and renamed *Uranie*. Two designs were offered; No 1 being the union flag in a central shield surmounted by what appears to be an eagle [5.20], No 2 being in the form of a cannon surrounded by ensigns and branches of laurel. The first design was approved providing the alterations added to the drawing were incorporated. Whether the Surveyor's office intended that the eagle should be removed is not clear but that particular style of bird appeared in several of the Dickerson designs.

5.20
***Uranie** – Dickerson design 1798.*
DICKERSON ARCHIVE

[32] Ship plan NMM ZAZ2519.

CHAPTER 6

NINETEENTH-CENTURY FIGUREHEADS – BEASTS

1 TNA ADM 87/16 S9036 (1846).
2 Owen, 'Figureheads', p 326.
3 *A Record of the Figureheads in H M Naval Establishments under Plymouth Command* – undated – but created in response to an Admiralty instruction of about 1936 (Admiralty Library Ref Dh 20).

**6.1
HMS *Lion* – Hellyer design 1846.**
THE NATIONAL ARCHIVES

THE ships that were given the names of beasts were generally those that were the lighter and more nimble units of the fleet and were reasonably easy for the carvers to interpret, either designing a figurehead in the form of the animal itself or carving a male or female bust with the animal shown in the trailboards.

There were, of course, exceptions to the rule, the largest being the 1847 HMS *Lion* (80).[1] For this ship, building at Pembroke Dock, the Hellyers of Portsmouth offered to carve for £36 an uncrowned standing lion with its forepaws resting on an escutcheon bearing the royal arms. It was not approved.

A month later they submitted a second design with the lion now wearing a crown and this was accepted at £40 [6.1]. When the ship was sold in 1905 the figurehead was set up in Devonport Dockyard where, in 1913, Douglas Owen was suitably impressed, describing him as 'A magnificent crowned lion, painted white, 11ft 10ins, ... and two tails, one lashing either flank'.[2] Too large to be housed indoors, he eventually succumbed to rot and by *c*1936, when the Devonport muster of figureheads was made, sadly, he no longer existed.[3]

For animals that were not native to the British Isles, the carvers suggested this by carving a bust that was obviously a foreigner with a trailboard carving to identify the ship's name. Thus the 1860 HMS *Cameleon* wood screw sloop and the 1861 HMS *Rattlesnake* wood screw corvette each had the bust of a North American Indian wearing a feathered headdress with appropriate trailboard carvings

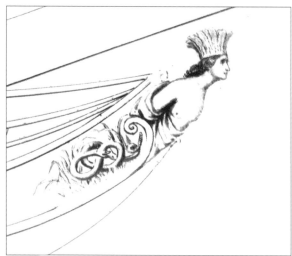

[6.2][6.3]. The Hellyers were allowed £10 for the former[4] and £27.10.0 for the latter,[5] a difference being explained by the larger size of the *Rattlesnake* carving.

When the 1849 HMS *Leopard* wood paddle frigate was building at Deptford Yard, the Hellyers of Portsmouth responded to a Deptford request for carved work with a design that consisted of a turbaned man with a spear and a leopard in the trailboards. The Surveyor of the Navy was not prepared to pay the £14 of the Hellyers' estimate and, as will be seen in the illustration, marked the arms of the design with lines (in red in the original) to indicate that a demi-head was not approved [6.4]. The resulting bust was approved for £13.[6] When in 1857 a replacement figurehead was required, Frederick Dickerson of Devonport submitted a design that clearly followed the original but did not include the image of the leopard [6.5].[7] He was allowed £10.[8]

The beast with the most far-flung origin was that carved for the 1852 HMS *Kangaroo* (12), launched in Chatham Dockyard. This design was submitted from the Hellyers' Blackwall workshop with an estimate of £6.10.0 [6.6].[9]

For ships named after our own native species, the carvers were able to use more familiar images. The 1829 HMS *Fox* was built in Portsmouth Dockyard as a sailing frigate but was first converted to screw propulsion and then to a store ship. Her figurehead was in the form of a huntsman and in all probability would have had a fox carved in the trailboards. When the ship was taken to pieces at Devonport in 1882, her figurehead was preserved in the fire-engine house collection where it was described in some detail by Douglas Owen.[10] In 1936 it was decided to move him to stand outside Admiralty House where he was photographed for the Plymouth Command archives [6.7].[11] The huntsman

6.2
HMS *Cameleon* - Hellyer design 1859.
THE NATIONAL ARCHIVES

6.3
HMS *Rattlesnake* - Hellyer design 1860.
THE NATIONAL ARCHIVES

4 TNA ADM 87/72 S5276 (1859).
5 TNA ADM 87/76 S4829 (1860).
6 TNA ADM 87/26 S2922 and 27 S3217 (1849).

7 TNA ADM 91/20 (1857).
8 TNA ADM 88/13 S968 (1857).

9 TNA ADM 87/39 S4508 (1852).

10 Owen, 'The Devonport Figureheads', p 146.
11 *A Record of the Figureheads in HM Naval Establishments under Plymouth Command* – undated – but created in response to an Admiralty instruction of about 1936 (Admiralty Library Ref Dh 20).

6.4
HMS *Leopard* – **Hellyer design 1849.**

12 TNA ADM 1/27846.
13 TNA ADM 87/18 S4001
(1847).

had survived when the 1957 muster of figureheads was made but in 1961 it was reported that he had disintegrated and the remains had been removed.[12]

The hunting theme was not a new one: the 1821 HMS *Reynard* (10), built in Pembroke Dockyard, had a full-length fox as her figurehead, carved by the Dickersons of Devonport [6.8]; while the 1848 HMS *Reynard* wood screw sloop, built in Deptford Dockyard, had the bust of a huntsman with a trailboard carving of a fox emerging from its den.[13]

The 1853 HMS *Squirrel* (12) was another Pembroke Dock ship. Her figurehead was carved by Frederick Dickerson of Devonport in 1851 who submitted his design on the Pembroke Dock outline and later developed his ideas in more detail [6.9]. When the ship was taken to pieces in Devonport in 1869, the figurehead was also preserved in the fire-engine house, after which its whereabouts can be tracked around the dockyard until, at some time in the 1950s, he was transferred to the WRNS quarters at St Budeaux to the north of Devonport. It was this move that sealed her fate as, left outside, she deteriorated and was eventually lost.

The figurehead of the 1830 HMS *Stag* (46) suffered a similar fate. It had been

6.5
HMS *Leopard* – **Dickerson design 1857.**

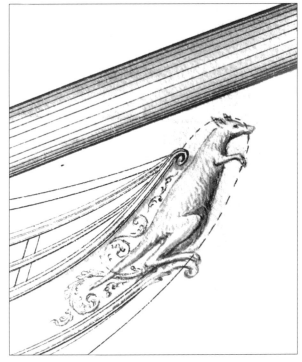

6.6
HMS *Kangaroo* – **Hellyer design 1852.**

6.7
HMS *Fox* –
Plymouth c1936.
CROWN COPYRIGHT

6.8
HMS *Reynard* –
Dickerson design 1820.
DICKERSON ARCHIVE

6.9
HMS *Squirrel* –
Dickerson design 1851.
DICKERSON ARCHIVE

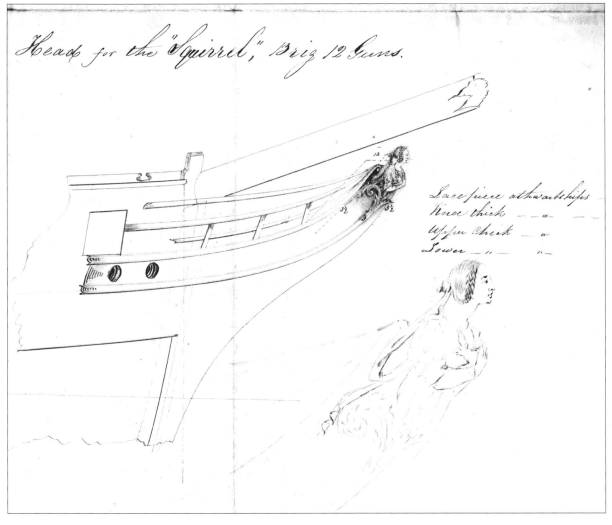

14   Owen, 'The Devonport
      Figureheads', p 146.
15   *A Record of the Figureheads in
      HM Naval Establishments
      under Plymouth Command* –
      undated – but created in
      response to an Admiralty
      instruction of about 1936
      (Admiralty Library Ref Dh
      20).
16   Ship plan NMM ZAZ4289
      (1789).
17   TNA ADM 87/11 S584 (1841).
18   *Figureheads in Dockyard,
      Royal Naval Barracks and
      Royal Naval Hospital,
      Chatham, 1938* – (Admiralty
      Library Ref Dh 23).

removed in 1866 before the ship was sold to Marshall of Plymouth for breaking up and had been added to the Devonport collection. Douglas Owen had described it as having 'spreading gilt antlers' in his article about the collection,[14] but when it was photographed for the Plymouth Command archives [6.10] it was said to be 'available for allocation'.[15] By 1947 it was recorded as being at the entrance to the RN Signal School, Glenholt, and later at the Royal Naval Camp, St Budeaux where, like the *Squirrel* figurehead, it was eventually lost.

There were five nineteenth-century ships named HMS *Serpent* and the carvers used both serpents and snake-charmers as the subjects of their figureheads. The 1789 *Serpent* had a male full-length figure with a snake spiralling up his body[16] while the 1832 *Serpent* had the head and forepart of a serpent as the figurehead with the rest of its body occupying the trailboards. When a replacement was required in 1841, J E Hellyer offered either a demi-head at £7.10.0 or a serpent at £8. The Surveyor of the Navy approved the latter but only allowed £6.10.0 [6.11].[17] The carving was added to the Chatham Dockyard collection, was photographed for their 1938 catalogue and was transferred to the National Maritime Museum in 1963.[18]

The 1887 torpedo cruiser HMS *Serpent* had a very short career with a tragic end. Built in Devonport Dockyard, she had been in reserve and only taken part in annual manoeuvres before heading south in November 1890 to join the 'West

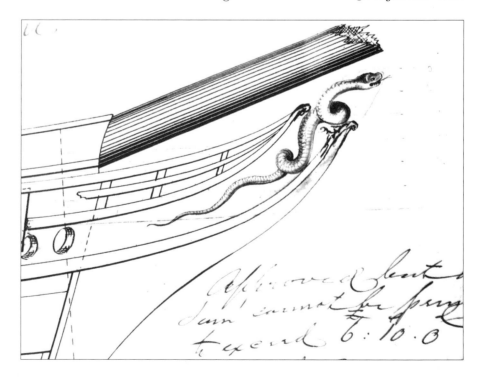

Coast of Africa and Cape of Good Hope Station'. In bad weather she ran aground on the rocky northern Spanish coast and all but three of the crew were lost. When the survivors were repatriated, they brought with them all that remained of the figurehead and this was mounted on a board in the fire-engine house at Devonport as a memorial to their lost shipmates. When Douglas Owen described the collection in 1913, he noted that it was 'the headless and handless three-quarter length male figurehead, 5ft high'.[19] It was in fact only the left half of the snake-charmer's body with his left arm outstretched and the serpent twined round both his body and arm. The relic was amongst the figureheads given to the National Maritime Museum by the Admiralty in 1936 and it is still in that collection.

It was not until 2003 that the other half of the figurehead was discovered and its identity confirmed by the author by careful measurement and comparison with the British half. Now in private ownership near the Costa de la Muerta where the ship had foundered, it had been recovered by local farmers after the storm, had been bought from them by a local doctor in the 1960s and is still in his family's ownership [6.12]. The head is at a peculiar angle, having been detached and re-connected with a metal strap, and the cap does not appear to be in keeping with a snake-charmer – perhaps a shipwright's repair before the storm.

Not surprisingly, domesticated animals also appeared in the list of ships' names. The 1846 HMS *Hound* (8) was given a figurehead by Hellyer & Son of Portsmouth in the form of the head and neck of a dog[20] for which they were allowed £5.15.0 while for the slightly larger 1845 HMS *Bloodhound* iron paddle

6.12
HMS *Serpent* – **Northern Spain 2003.**
AUTHOR'S COLLECTION

19   Owen, 'Figureheads', p 325.
20   TNA ADM 87/16 S6494 (1846).

6.13
HMS *Bloodhound* – **Hellyer design 1854.**
THE NATIONAL ARCHIVES

vessel, the Hellyers of Blackwall designed a full-length hound [6.13] and were allowed £6.10.0.[21]

The racing world was included with several ships named *Racehorse* or *Racer*. In 1816 the 1806 HMS *Racehorse* (18) was given a horse's head by Edward Hellyer of Portsmouth [6.14] for which he was allowed only £3[22] while Frederick Dickerson carved a jockey with his riding-crop in the trailboard [6.15] as an 1853 replacement for the 1830 HMS *Racehorse* (18).[23] As may be seen in the Directory, very similar alternative designs were offered for the 1833 HMS *Racer* (16). When Frederick Dickerson drew his design for the 1859 HMS *Greyhound* wood screw sloop, building at Pembroke Dock, he chose a racing greyhound [6.16] and, even though the drawing in the Dickerson Archive is undated, it has been marked with the register number of the Surveyor of the Navy's office

6.14
HMS *Racehorse* – **Hellyer design 1816.**
THE NATIONAL ARCHIVES

21   TNA ADM 87/50 S11,352 (1854).
22   TNA ADM 106/1888 (1816).
23   TNA ADM 91/16 (1853).

6.15
HMS *Racehorse* – **Dickerson design 1853.**
DICKERSON ARCHIVE

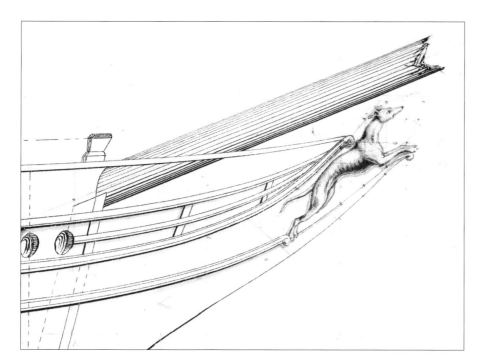

6.16
HMS *Greyhound* – Dickerson
design 1856.
DICKERSON ARCHIVE

6.17
HMS *Beagle* – Grayfoot and
Overton design 1819.
THE NATIONAL ARCHIVES

6.18
HMS *Bulldog* – **Hellyer design 1844.**
THE NATIONAL ARCHIVES

24   TNA ADM 88/11 & 12 S10,451 (1856).

25   TNA ADM 106/1795 (1819).

26   TNA ADM 87/14 S2432 (1844).

that identifies it as an 1856 letter.[24]

One of the better-known ships, because of her association with Charles Darwin, was the 1820 HMS *Beagle* (10). Built in Woolwich Dockyard, her figurehead was carved by Grayfoot and Overton whose 1819 design was approved but their estimate for £4.4.0 was reduced to £4![25] There has been much debate over the years whether the *Beagle* had a figurehead after she was converted for survey work in 1825. While this illustration does not answer that question one way or another, it does show that when building she was given the fore-part of a beagle as her figurehead [6.17].

Finally we have the 1845 HMS *Bulldog* wood paddle sloop that is depicted more as a symbol of Great Britain than as a domestic pet. Designed by Hellyer & Son of Portsmouth with an estimate of £9, it shows the bulldog with its forepaws resting on an oval escutcheon containing the union flag [6.18].[26] The figurehead was presented to the Royal United Services Institute (RUSI) that had its museum in the Banqueting House, Whitehall. The bulldog stood with the figurehead of the 1854 HMS *Orion* (80) on either side of the entrance to the Banqueting House and photographs of him there show that he was wearing a broad metal collar on which is engraved 'Cavecanem' (Beware of the Dog), but whether this was added before or after he came ashore is not clear. He was sold by RUSI to the National Maritime Museum in 1963 and is now in their collection.

CHAPTER 7

—◇—

NINETEENTH-CENTURY
FIGUREHEADS – BIRDS

AS with the ships given the names of beasts, those that were given bird names tended to be the lighter and more nimble units of the fleet rather than the heavyweights. The carvers usually used one of three devices to illustrate the ship's name: sometimes they carved the bird itself, sometimes they created a male or female bust with the bird in question in the trailboards and occasionally there was a bird perched on the hand of a demi-head.

The 1849 HMS *Buzzard* wood paddle sloop illustrates the first two styles as she had two different figureheads during her service, created by the two dominant figurehead carvers of the period, the Hellyers of Portsmouth and the Dickersons of Devonport. She was built in Pembroke Dockyard and her first figurehead was in the form of a standing buzzard designed by Hellyer & Son and drawn on the outline that had been sent to the Surveyor's office by Pembroke Yard [7.1].[1] The design shows this bird of prey with some strength, including

1 TNA ADM 87/19 S4474 (1848).

7.1
HMS *Buzzard* – Hellyer design 1848.

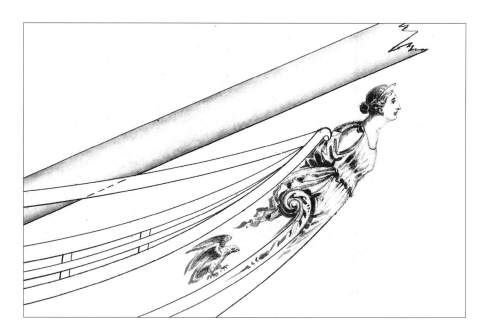

7.2
HMS *Buzzard* – **Dickerson design 1862.**
DICKERSON ARCHIVE

its large talons and hooked beak. The writing beside the bird shows the size of the adjacent timbers, more of which are listed elsewhere on the drawing. The notation 'App' to the right indicates the Surveyor's approval and the Hellyers were allowed £9.10.0 for the work.

A replacement was required in 1862 and Frederick Dickerson carved it at Devonport. Letters of approval are not included in the National Archives after 1860 so there is no explanation why the replacement was needed nor is the amount he was paid for the work given. However, the design is one of those preserved in the Dickerson Archive in Australia, dated 9 June 1862 with the Navy Board reference DM2570 [7.2]. Rather than carving a replacement for the earlier figurehead, he chose to provide a simple three-quarter-length female bust with a buzzard in the trailboards.

Other birds of prey had been at sea with the Royal Navy, like the 1854 wood screw sloop HMS *Falcon*, also built in Pembroke Dockyard [7.3]. The design is drawn on a large Pembroke Yard outline dated 31 January 1854 that includes the bow, stern and quarter views of the ship on which are also noted the sizes of the adjacent timbers. Although the subject is recorded in the appropriate letter books of the Surveyor's office, no price is quoted.[2] The drawing was retained by the carver and is now in the Dickerson Archive.

The 1843 HMS *Vulture* wood paddle frigate was also built in Pembroke Dockyard, her figurehead being another product of the Hellyer workshop at Portsmouth, for which he was allowed £9 [7.4].[3] While the above examples

[2]   TNA ADM 91/16 and 88/10 S6536 (1854).

[3]   TNA ADM 87/12 S1942 (1842).

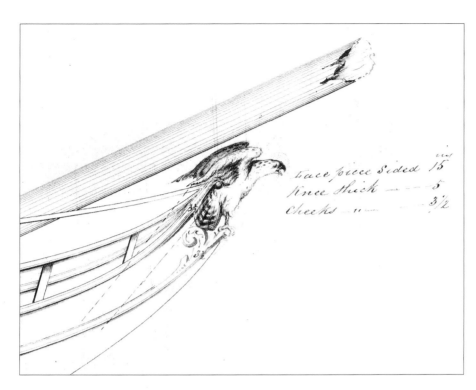

7·3
HMS *Falcon* – **Dickerson design 1854.**
DICKERSON ARCHIVE

7·4
HMS *Vulture* – **Hellyer design 1842.**
THE NATIONAL ARCHIVES

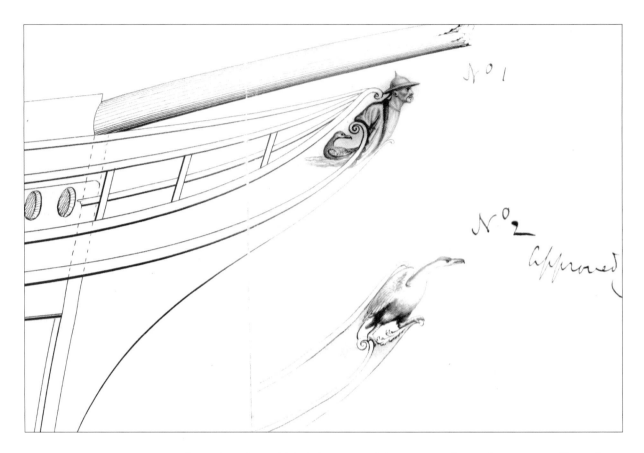

7.5
**HMS *Cormorant* – Hellyer
designs 1841.**
THE NATIONAL ARCHIVES

4   TNA ADM 87/13 S8175 (1843).

5   Surviving at the National
Maritime Museum.

6   TNA ADM 87/11 S649 (1841).

show the selected birds in reasonably accurate form, the carvers will not have
had access to the same reference books and illustrations as abound today and
the Hellyer portrayal of an osprey for the 1844 HMS *Osprey* (12) looks more
like a capercaillie,[4] while that by Frederick Dickerson for the 1857 HMS *Gannet*
wood screw sloop looks more like a goose![5]

   Having mentioned a sea-bird, there were others in the Fleet. When the 1842
HMS *Cormorant* wood paddle sloop was building at Sheerness, J E Hellyer of
Portsmouth offered two designs, the bust of a Chinese fisherman with his
cormorant in the trailboards at £7.10.0 or a standing cormorant at £6.10.0 [7.5].[6]
While the first design has a certain charm with its allusion to the skill of fishermen
in the Far East using their cormorants to dive for fish – their necks tied so that
they cannot swallow them – it proved too difficult for a Victorian administrator
in London to agree to such a design for a ship of the Royal Navy. The standing
cormorant was approved.

   Frederick Dickerson carved two very similar figureheads for wood screw
sloops during 1860: that for HMS *Peterel*, building at Devonport [7.6]; and
that for HMS *Shearwater*, building at Pembroke Dock. Each of the designs

7.6
HMS *Peterel* – **Dickerson design 1860.**
DICKERSON ARCHIVE

had a female three-quarter-length bust with the subject-bird in the trailboards. The designs and estimates for both figureheads were approved,[7] the carver being allowed £6.10.0 for each. The movements of the *Peterel* figurehead can be tracked over the years since the ship was sold for breaking up in 1901. In the 1911 Admiralty Catalogue, she was included amongst the Devonport collection, by 1936 she was standing by the cricket ground of the Royal Naval Barracks, by 1957 she was at HMS *Royal Arthur* (the leadership school at Corsham, Wiltshire), and when that establishment closed in 1992, she was stored at the MoD Foxhill, Bath. She was restored by the Royal Dockyard Historical Trust and is now on display at Portsmouth in 'The Dockyard Apprentice' exhibition. There is no equivalent record for the *Shearwater* figurehead after that ship was broken up at Sheerness in 1877.

Two water-bird examples, HMS *Cygnet* and HMS *Pelican*, take us close to the end of the figurehead era and the designs assume a new style. The 1874 HMS *Cygnet* composite gunboat [7.7] was built by William Doxford of Sunderland, far away from the Thames and the other figurehead carvers of the south coast. Her figurehead was probably carved by a local craftsman and

[7] TNA ADM 88/16 S2420 (1860).

7·7
HMS *Cygnet* – **unknown carver 1873.**

7.8
HMS *Pelican* – **unknown carver 1875.**

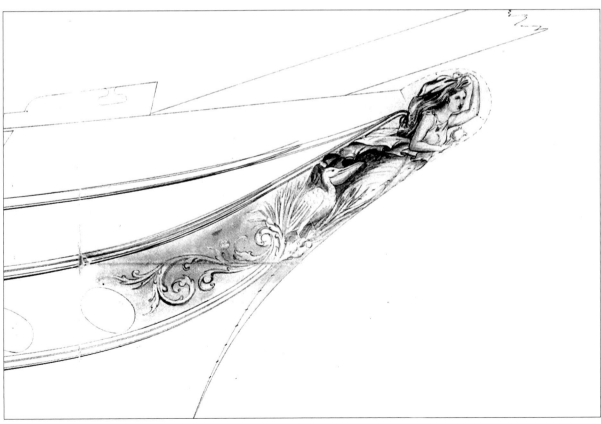

this would account for the free style of the design, but note the swan swimming in the trailboard. The design is amongst a small group preserved in the Admiralty Library, Portsmouth.[8]

The 1877 HMS *Pelican* composite screw sloop was built in Devonport Dockyard. Her figurehead design is a female full-length figure with a pelican and foliage in the trailboards but drawn by a different hand to Frederick Dickerson's designs [7.8].[9] After her service in the Royal Navy, *Pelican* was sold to the Hudson's Bay Company and, if the figurehead was still serviceable, it would probably have stayed with the ship.

From water-birds to waterfowl, the 1825 HMS *Sheldrake* (12) was built in Pembroke Dockyard, her figurehead being carved by James Dickerson of Devonport. Being only a brig with no carving at her stern or quarter, the Pembroke Yard outline dated 2 December 1824 is only a small one but the standing duck is neatly executed [7.9]. The design is amongst the documents that have been retained by the descendants of the Dickersons of Devonport and has a notation that the estimate for carving the head was £4. With no corresponding documents from The National Archives, it can only be assumed

[8] Admiralty Library Ref P1030.

[9] Ibid.

7.9
HMS *Sheldrake* – **Dickerson design 1824.**
DICKERSON ARCHIVE

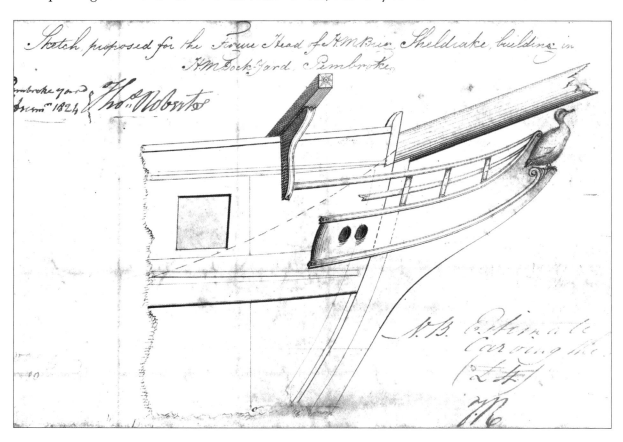

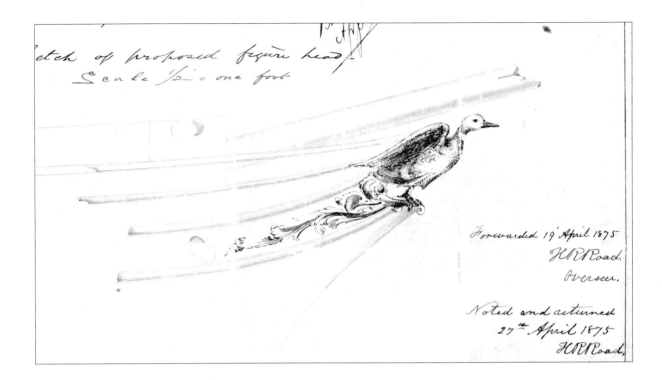

etch of proposed figure head
Scale ½ = one foot

Forwarded 19 April 1875
HRI Road.
Overseer.

Noted and returned
27th April 1875
HRI Road.

7.10
HMS *Mallard* – **unknown carver 1875.**
CROWN COPYRIGHT

that the design was approved; otherwise there would have been no reason to retain the drawing.

Fifty years later, the 1875 screw gunboat HMS *Mallard* was launched at Hull, having been built by Earl's Shipbuilding and Engineering Company. The design was prepared locally and was forwarded to the Surveyor's office by the overseer, who noted the approval a week later. No price is mentioned and it is assumed that this was included in the build contract for the ship [7.10]. The design is another of the small group preserved in the Admiralty Library, Portsmouth and is fortunate to have survived, having been drawn originally on tracing paper.[10]

Having shown how a figurehead carver could depict the particular bird by making it the subject of the figurehead or showing it in the trailboards, the two could be combined by perching the bird on a bust or a demi-head [7.11]. The detail of HMS *Sealark*'s original figurehead is not known but, as an eight-gun brig, it will not have been an elaborate one. After she had been fouled by the Southampton steam packet in early 1860, her figurehead was found to be rotten and the Hellyers submitted a three-quarter-length design with an estimate of £6.15.0.[11] The name 'sealark' being an alternative for the ringed plover, the carver made it an inconspicuous small bird.

The final example for this chapter encapsulates the whole figurehead approval process shown on one small framed document [7.12].[12] The bow structure was

10 Ibid.

11 TNA ADM 87/74 S1468 (1860).

12 TNA ADM 87/17 S290 (1847).

drawn and identified 'Chatham Yard Jan'y 21st 1847 Heron 12 Guns' showing the scale at the foot of the page and how the figurehead related to the datum of the ship. Hellyer and Son of Portsmouth added the drawing of the figurehead. The Surveyor's office registered the covering letter and gave it the letter-book entry 'S290'. The Surveyor examined the design and marked it 'Approved', after which it would have circulated once more to Devonport to be noted and would have been filed in London.

7.11
HMS *Sealark* – **Hellyer design 1860.**
THE NATIONAL ARCHIVES

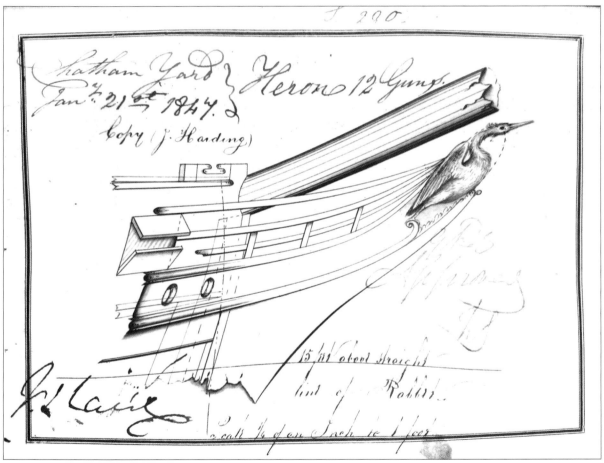

7.12
HMS *Heron* – **Hellyer design 1847.**
THE NATIONAL ARCHIVES

—◦—

CHAPTER 8

NINETEENTH-CENTURY FIGUREHEADS – FAMOUS PEOPLE

L EAVING the animal kingdom, and reviewing what famous people were depicted on the Royal Navy's warships, it is not surprising that high on the pecking order were admirals, famous for their great victories of the past, their importance being signalled in the size of the ship given their name.

Sir Walter Raleigh (1552–1618), although not actually an admiral, was an outstanding adventurer and explorer of his day and had no less than four nineteenth-century ships named after him. The 1806 HMS *Raleigh* was only a

8.1
HMS *Raleigh* – Hellyer design 1844.

8.3
HMS *Raleigh* – 1885-1905.

brig-sloop with a simple bust[1] but the 1845 HMS *Raleigh* (50) was given a stylish figurehead that included his famous cloak and scrolling decoration in the form of tobacco leaves [8.1]. By the time that the 1873 HMS *Raleigh* iron screw frigate was launched in Chatham Dockyard, her vertical bow was hardly suitable for a figurehead and the dockyard submitted a design for a bow decoration made up of the royal arms on each side of the bow, supported by winged cherubs.[2] This was not judged to be suitable and a bust of Sir Walter was approved in 1873, seen here amongst the chains and ropes of her iron hull [8.2].[3] When the ship was being prepared at Devonport in 1885 to become the flagship of the Cape and West Coast Squadron, her original figurehead was removed and a replacement was fitted, dressed in a leather jerkin heavily decorated with studwork [8.3]. This figurehead served her until she was broken up at

8.2
HMS *Raleigh* - 1873–85.
NATIONAL MARITIME MUSEUM

[1] TNA ADM 106/1943 (1817).

[2] Ship plan NMM NPB9660 (1872).

[3] Ship plan NMM NPB9659 (1873) – approved by Captain Chamberlain, Superintendent Chatham Dockyard.

Morecambe in 1905, after which the ship-breaker presented it to the sea cadets of Sheffield. This second figurehead was lost at some time in the 1970s but the original, having been preserved in the Devonport collection, was later transferred to the shore-training establishment, HMS *Raleigh*, where it remains to this day.

Admiral John Benbow (1653–1702) had a turbulent career, dying of his wounds in Jamaica after an action with a French squadron. The 1813 HMS *Benbow* (74) was named after him and this ship's figurehead is the first one that greets visitors to the Portsmouth Historic Dockyard, it having previously been in the Chatham collection. It was not, however, after Admiral Edward Vernon (1684–1757) that the 1832 HMS *Vernon* (50) was named but rather Lord George Vernon, politician and patron of the then Surveyor of the Navy, Captain Sir William Symonds.

The 1832 HMS *Vernon* had been built in Woolwich Dockyard but in 1849 Chatham Dockyard reported that her original figurehead had decayed and, as a result, Hellyer & Son of Portsmouth submitted a design showing the Vernon

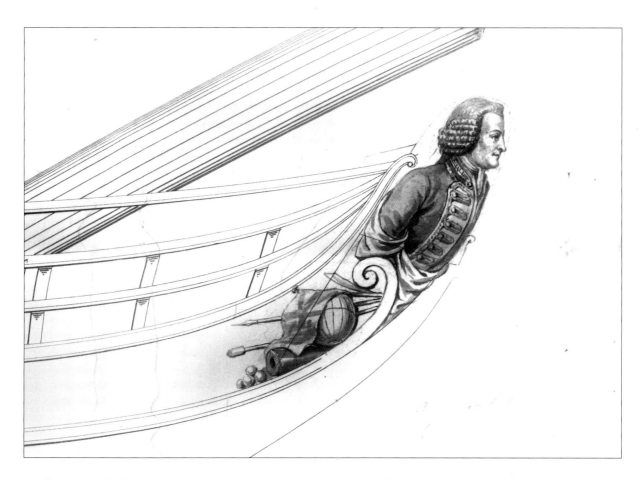

family arms with lion supporters and a crest consisting of a boar's head emerging from a baron's coronet. This was not approved and the carvers were instructed to produce one 'in the likeness of the late Lord Vernon'.[4] The resulting design [8.4] was a simple bust with the Vernon arms in the trailboards, incorporating the motto 'Vernon Semper Viret' (Vernon Always Succeeds), a feature that was later included in the arms of the shore establishment, HMS *Vernon*, that was the home of the post-war Torpedo and Anti-Submarine branch of the Royal Navy. The figurehead in the form of Lord Vernon now stands in Gunwharf Quays, the commercial development on the former shore establishment site.

Lord Anson (1697–1762), who is remembered for not only the circumnavigation of the world in HMS *Centurion* but also for other actions and for two spells as First Lord of the Admiralty, had a ship named after him in the eighteenth century and three in the nineteenth. The first of these, the 1812 HMS *Anson* (74) did not have a figurehead design submitted until 1819, probably because she was not commissioned but was laid up in Ordinary at Portsmouth.[5] Edward Hellyer of Portsmouth offered a standing figure wearing

8.5
HMS *Anson* – Hellyer design 1859.
THE NATIONAL ARCHIVES
4   TNA ADM 87/27 S3688 (1849).

5   TNA ADM 106/1889 (1819).

a bicorne hat and tail-coat holding a globe, for £36 or a bust for £21. The latter was approved. The second was the 1860 HMS *Anson* (screw 91), that was built in Woolwich Dockyard. The Hellyers of Portsmouth had again submitted a design, showing a bust of the admiral in uniform with a globe in the trailboards, again alluding to his circumnavigation of 1740–4 [8.5].[6] The figurehead was removed before the ship was sold for breaking up and was displayed at Chatham where it was recorded as being 15ft tall in the 1911 Admiralty Catalogue and in good condition in the 1938 and 1948 figurehead returns. It was probably in the 1950s that he, and several others, were sealed in a coating of fibreglass, a process that was no help in their long-term survival. He was transferred to HMS *Sultan* in 1983, prior to the closure of Chatham Dockyard but was found to be completely rotten within the fibreglass shell and was destroyed.[7]

Lord Hawke (1705–81) was another admiral renowned for his success in naval battles who rose to the position of First Lord of the Admiralty. The ship named after him was the 1820 HMS *Hawke* (74), that was also built in Woolwich

6   TNA ADM 87/73 S7974 (1859).

7   Commodore Admiralty Interview Board letter 527/1 dated 20 November 1984.

8.6
HMS *Hawke* – Hellyer design 1847.
THE NATIONAL ARCHIVES

8.7
HMS *Rodney* - Hellyer
design 1859.
THE NATIONAL ARCHIVES

Dockyard. Her first figurehead was carved by Grayfoot and Overton of London who offered a full-length figure of the admiral for £38 or a bust for £20. Neither design has survived but the full-length carving was commissioned although it was to be 'without arm outstretched as liable to accidents'.[8] By 1847 a replacement figurehead was required and a bust of the admiral in uniform [8.6], designed by the Hellyers of Portsmouth was approved. Their estimate for the work was £35.[9]

The career of Admiral Lord Rodney (1719–92) was celebrated in three nineteenth-century ships: the 1809 Third Rate built by Barnard of Deptford, the 1833 Second Rate built in Pembroke Dockyard and the 1884 battleship built in Chatham Dockyard. Nothing is known of the figurehead of the 1809 ship, nor the original figurehead for the 1833 HMS *Rodney*, but in 1859 when she

[8] TNA ADM 106/1795 (1818).

[9] TNA ADM 87/18 S3161 (1847).

8.8
HMS *Howe* – **Hellyer design
1859.**
THE NATIONAL ARCHIVES

10   TNA ADM 87/71 S2893
     (1858).

was being converted for steam propulsion at Chatham, the Hellyers of
Portsmouth designed a replacement [8.7] in the form of a uniformed bust for
which they were allowed £45.[10] The 1884 HMS *Rodney* was one of the most
inappropriate ships to have been fitted with a figurehead as she had a vertical
stem-post and no bowsprit so the half-length figure of Admiral Rodney sat
vertically with his head protruding over the level of the forecastle deck! The
figurehead is extremely lucky to have survived as, when the ship was sold for
breaking up in 1909 he was taken into the Chatham collection where he spent
many years standing in all weathers beside the 'Admiral's Walk' and later was
transferred to HMS *Warrior*, the then Headquarters of the Commander-in-Chief
Fleet, where again he stood outdoors. Happily he is now safely indoors in the
Museum of the Royal Dockyard at The Historic Dockyard, Chatham.

Admiral Lord Hood (1724–1816) was the best known of a family of distinguished naval officers and was commemorated in the screw Second Rate HMS *Hood* (91), built in Chatham Dockyard and launched there in 1859. Her figurehead was a bust of the admiral in uniform but, as the Hellyer & Son design was drawn on delicate tissue paper, it does not reproduce well. However, the figurehead was one of the six carvings mounted on the roof of the Millbank showrooms of Henry Castle & Son, ship-breakers, already seen in Chapter 3.

Admiral Lord Howe (1726–99) was remembered as both a great commander at sea and as a First Lord of the Admiralty and had two First Rate ships named after him, the 1815 HMS *Howe* (120) and the 1860 HMS *Howe* (110), figureheads from each of which have survived. The original figurehead for the 1815 ship was carved by George Williams of Chatham in the form of a bust of Lord Howe wearing the laurel wreath of a Roman senator and having a supporter on each side – one a sailor, the other a marine. Changes to the ship's bow were required by the Surveyor of the Navy and with these came the extra cost of modifying the figurehead. Williams justified this in an illustrated letter[11] and, after due consideration, Williams was allowed 120 guineas (£126) for his labours. The ship required a replacement figurehead in 1835 and Sheerness Yard forwarded a Hellyer design of a bust at £30; this offer was undercut by Robert Hall of Rotherhithe who submitted a bust design at £20.[12] Rather than making a decision in isolation, the Surveyor of the Navy called Messrs Hellyer and Hall to his office to receive instructions[13] and the Rotherhithe workshop of Hellyer & Browning were given the work for £26.8.0 – including the admiral's coat of arms in the trailboards.[14] Unfortunately, the designs from this negotiation are not filed amongst the Admiralty papers as they would have helped to authenticate the surviving figurehead. It was acquired by Mr Sydney Cumbers as part of his 'Long John Silver' collection, most of which was then transferred for display in the hold of the *Cutty Sark* at Greenwich. The figurehead attributed to HMS *Howe* was, however, presented to Lloyds of London by the widow of Sydney Cumbers for display outside their Chatham offices – now used by Medway Council.

There appear to have been modifications to the 1860 HMS *Howe* while she was building at Pembroke Dock as a letter in 1859 reported that the bow had been altered and that another figurehead was needed.[15] The Hellyers of Portsmouth submitted a design that showed the admiral in uniform [8.8] for which they were allowed £54. When the ship was sold for breaking up, she was

11   TNA ADM 106/1823 (1814).

12   TNA ADM 88/2 S3331 (1835).

13   TNA ADM 91/7 (1835).

14   TNA ADM 88/2 S3331 (1835).

15   TNA ADM 87/70 S1567 (1859).

bought by the Liberty family and her timbers were used in the structure of their Regent Street shop. The figurehead was taken to their family home near Great Missenden, Bucks where it was displayed in the garden. He remains there today under a shelter that has been created by the house's present owner.

Admiral Lord Duncan (1731–1804) had three nineteenth-century ships named after him but nothing is known of the figureheads of the first two – a Fifth Rate (38) and a Third Rate (74). In 1859, however, when HMS *Duncan* (101) was building in Portsmouth Dockyard, the resident carvers, Edward and James Hellyer, submitted their design for a bust of the admiral with trophies in the trailboards and with an estimate of £54 [8.9].[16] The ship saw various forms of harbour service before being renamed HMS *Pembroke* in 1890 and it was under this name that she became the receiving ship at Chatham and the forerunner to the barracks there. When the ship was broken up, the figurehead – complete

16 TNA ADM 87/72 S4794 (1859).

8.9
HMS *Duncan* – Hellyer design 1859.
THE NATIONAL ARCHIVES

with its trailboards – was sited at Chatham and subsequently at HMS *Camperdown*, the RNR drill-ship at Dundee [Colour Plate 8], and HMS *Caledonia* at Rosyth.

Admiral Jervis (1735–1823) was created Lord St Vincent after his success against the Spanish fleet in 1797 and, having later become First Lord of the Admiralty, was suitably honoured when the 1815 HMS *St Vincent* (120) was named after him. Built in Devonport Dockyard, her original figurehead was carved there in 1812 by James Dickerson for £35 but there is no clue from the correspondence on the form of the carving.[17] In 1851 the Superintendent at Portsmouth Yard informed the Surveyor that HMS *St Vincent*'s figurehead was defective and unfit for further service and forwarded a Hellyer & Son design for the replacement [8.10]. The Surveyor's office expressed some reservations about the design's resemblance to the admiral, presumably over the youthful

[17] TNA ADM 106/1941 (1812).

8.10
HMS *St Vincent* – **Hellyer design 1851.**
THE NATIONAL ARCHIVES

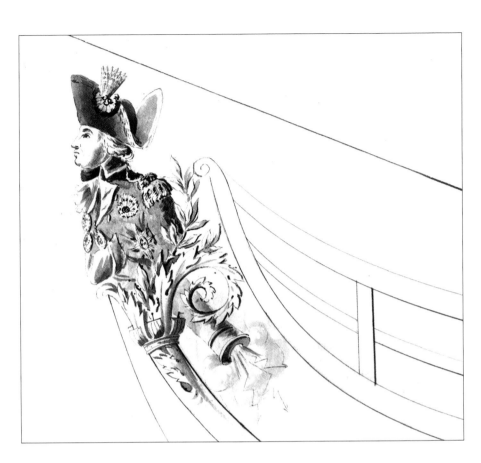

8.11
Horatio Nelson – Dickerson design *c*1806.
DICKERSON ARCHIVE

looks that had been given to the ageing admiral, but it was approved. Having become a training ship for boys at Portsmouth in 1862, it was appropriate that, when the ship was broken up in 1906, her figurehead was transferred to the newly-opened boys' training establishment, HMS *Ganges*, at Shotley, Suffolk where he stood just inside the main gate. By 1946 he was in a state of near collapse and a mould was made from the carving from which two plaster casts were made – the original falling to pieces in the process. The cast replicas went their separate ways, the first standing in the boys' training establishment HMS *St Vincent* in Gosport and then moving to HMS *Collingwood*, Fareham; the second stayed at Shotley and was destroyed there in about 1993. At about the same time, the owner of the Pusser's Rum company commissioned the figurehead carver Jack Whitehead of the Isle of Wight to carve a full-size replica of the *St Vincent* figurehead, after which it was shipped first to the British Virgin Islands and later to Charleston, South Carolina.

Not surprisingly, by far the most popular admiral who was remembered through figureheads was Lord Nelson (1758–1805). A local Plymouth paper of February 1806 records that Captain Pellew of HMS *Conqueror* (74) petitioned the Admiralty Board to have the figurehead of his ship replaced with one representing Lord Nelson, the original having been shot away at Trafalgar.[18] The report continues that the request was immediately complied with and a fine bust was carved in the dockyard and was gilded at the expense of Captain Pellew and his officers. While it would not be expected to find any record of such a spontaneous request in The National Archives, there is a design drawing in the Dickerson Archive in Australia that may well have been used to create the new *Conqueror* figurehead [8.11]. The drawing has neither a title nor a date but it is clearly of Lord Nelson as it shows the 'chelengk' in his hat (a plume of triumph presented to him by the Sultan of Turkey), the decorations on his chest and his empty right sleeve, despite the fact that it is a bust rather than a demi-head. The drawing has not passed through the approval process, as it bears no

18   *Plymouth Journal*, 11 February 1806.

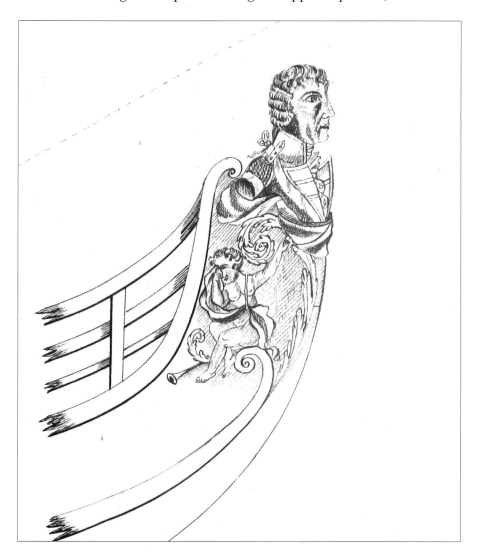

8.12
HMS *Victorious* – Hellyer design 1814.
THE NATIONAL ARCHIVES

Navy Board registration number, and it therefore bears all the hallmarks of a hastily-drawn design to fit the post-Trafalgar situation.

The earliest surviving representation of Horatio Nelson came from the 1807 HMS *Horatio* (38), built at Bursledon, with a figurehead carved in a style somewhat different from the standard busts of the period. There are exaggerated scrolls in front of the head and shoulders only of Nelson, shown with his right eye closed; an allusion no doubt to the loss of his sight in that eye. When the ship was broken up in 1865, the figurehead was put into the fire-engine house in Devonport Dockyard where it remained until it was transferred to the National Maritime Museum, Greenwich in 1936.

19   TNA ADM 106/1887 (1814).

In 1808 HMS *Victorious* (74) was launched at Bucklers Hard on the Beaulieu River in Hampshire. No records have been found that indicate the style of her original figurehead but, with the name *Victorious* only three years after Trafalgar, it would have been surprising if it did not depict Nelson. Certainly when she required a replacement figurehead in 1814, Edward Hellyer of Portsmouth proposed a bust that probably represents the admiral.[19] As it is only a bust, there is no evidence from his lost right arm but the cherub in the trailboard appears to be weeping as he points to the figurehead, suggesting his sorrow at the loss of the nation's hero [8.12].

20   W B Cooke from a drawing
     by L Francia dated 1814.
21   Ship model NMM SLR0680.

In 1814 HMS *Nelson* (120) was launched at Woolwich dockyard and a contemporary engraving of her launch[20] and a similar ship model at the National Maritime Museum show a bust of Nelson supported by two trumpeting figures.[21] Not needed in the post-Napoleonic period, the ship was laid up, unfinished, for forty years. In 1854 she was cut down to a two-decker and in 1860 was converted to steam propulsion. During this latter conversion at Portsmouth, the Hellyers submitted a design for a suitable replacement – a demi-head for £54 [8.13]. In approving the design and estimate, the Surveyor of the Navy observed '. . . it is objectionable to have a projecting arm as it is liable to be carried away.'[22] This may well have been his reason for objecting but it is also possible that he thought the carver was referring to Nelson raising his telescope to his blind eye at the battle of Copenhagen and such humour would not have been considered entirely proper. The ship spent her last years of service in Australian waters where the Government of Victoria used her as a colonial training ship. When her figurehead came ashore, it stood at first in the naval depot at Rushcutters Bay, Sydney before moving to the Australian National Maritime Museum, Sydney. It can be seen there still and Nelson is holding

22   TNA ADM 87/73 S7333
     (1859).

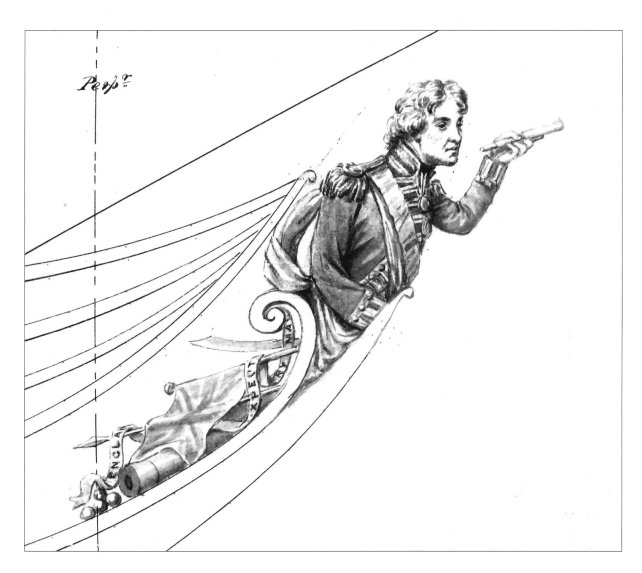

his telescope close to his chest, as instructed!

The first HMS *Trafalgar* (106) was launched in Chatham Dockyard in 1820 and, even though no figurehead designs have survived, sketches and estimate – probably by George Williams, the resident carver – were submitted in 1819.[23] His estimates were £126 for a standing figure or £52 for a bust but the Surveyor returned them, ordering that new designs be submitted without supporters and within a maximum fee of £46. It is assumed that a full-length figure was carved as a drawing of the ship laid up at Chatham in 1824 shows her under a roof that also covers the figurehead that has its legs protruding from the housing.[24]

HMS *Vanguard* (78) was built at Pembroke Dock and was launched there in 1835. Robert Hall of Rotherhithe and Frederick Dickerson of Devonport each submitted designs and, even though their drawings have not survived, the letter

8.13
HMS *Nelson* – Hellyer design 1859.
THE NATIONAL ARCHIVES

[23] TNA ADM 106/1824 (1819).

[24] Robert C Leslie, *Old Sea Wings, Ways and Words* (Chapman & Hall Ltd, 1890).

25 TNA ADM 88/1 S2650
(1833); TNA ADM 87/3
S2208 (1833).

books show that Hall was given the work for £30.[25] By the time the ship was taken to pieces at Chatham in 1875, she had been renamed HMS *Ajax* but her figurehead had not been changed and the 1911 Admiralty Catalogue records the 'figure of Nelson' amongst the Chatham collection. Fifteen feet tall with his left arm pointing forward, the figurehead was moved from the barracks to the dockyard after the Second World War but, when a fire destroyed No 2 Covered Slip in July 1966, the *Vanguard* figurehead was also lost.

HMS *Nile* (92) was launched in Plymouth Dockyard in 1839 and, even though details of her original figurehead are not filed in The National Archives, it was almost certainly in the likeness of Nelson. During the ship's conversion to steam in 1851, her figurehead was found to be rotten and Frederick Dickerson carved a replacement for £35 [8.14].[26] The ship retained this second figurehead when

26 TNA ADM 87/38 S3386
(1851).

8.14
HMS *Nile* – **Dickerson design.**
DICKERSON ARCHIVE

8.15
HMS *Trafalgar* – Hellyer &
Browning design.
THE NATIONAL ARCHIVES

she was renamed Training Ship *Conway* in 1876 but it was carried away when the ss *Bhamo* collided with her in June 1918 and for the next twenty years the cadets were trained on board without a figurehead. In 1937 the Conway Club of former cadets commissioned sculptor Carter Preston to carve a replacement and in 1938 this was unveiled by John Masefield, the Poet Laureate, himself an 'Old Conway'. The figurehead shows Nelson in the uniform of a rear admiral, his rank at the time of the Battle of the Nile – and, while the upper half is a traditional bust, the lower half has a modern look to it with the naval crown and Nelson's signal at Trafalgar [Colour Plate 9]. The figurehead was rescued when TS *Conway* was wrecked in the Menai Strait in 1953 and was eventually presented to HMS *Nelson*, the Royal Naval Barracks at Portsmouth, in 1974.

The second HMS *Trafalgar* (120) was launched at Woolwich in 1841, having been almost twelve years on the stocks. There must have been plans to launch

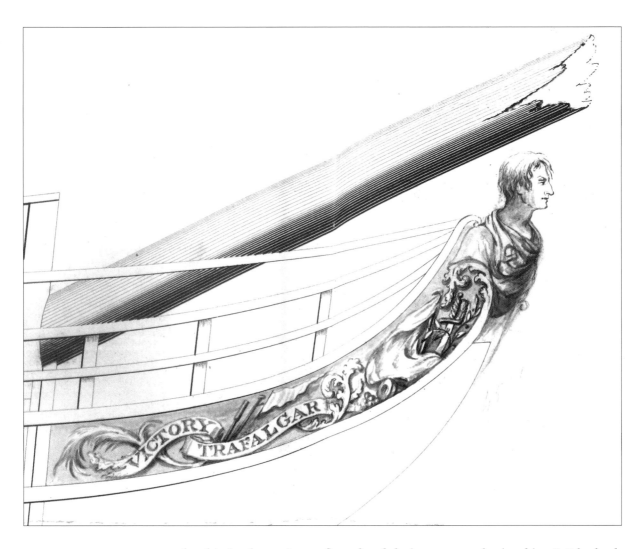

8.16
HMS *Trafalgar* – Robert Hall design.

27   TNA ADM 87/6 S5274
     (1836).

28   Portsmouth Museum Library
     Ref 450/81 – Letter dated 29
     October 1840.
29   TNA ADM 87/13 S7017
     (1843).

the ship in about 1837 as figurehead designs were submitted in 1836 by both Hellyer and Browning of Rotherhithe and Robert Hall of London.[27] The Hellyer and Browning design [8.15] is very similar to the figurehead carved for the *Vanguard* and was offered for £31.10.0, with an alternative in the form of a standing, winged figure of 'Fame' holding a medallion of Nelson in one hand while blowing a trumpet with the other. The Robert Hall design [8.16] was offered with an estimate of £45 for the bust-head plus a further £10 for the trailboards. Probably because of the delays in her building, no figurehead design seems to have been approved at this time and, in 1840, the Surveyor of the Navy commissioned a Mr Haydon, sculptor, to provide a bust of Lord Nelson from which the figurehead might be copied.[28] Whatever its form, the admiral must have been wearing a hat as in 1843 Hellyer & Son were allowed £5.15.0 to modify the figure as its hat was fouling the bowsprit.[29] The *Trafalgar* figurehead that now stands in the *Victory* area at Portsmouth was probably carved in 1859 when the ship was cut down to a two-decker and converted to steam. It remained on the ship's bow when she was renamed Training Ship *Boscawen* in 1873, came ashore to HMS *Ganges* when the ship was sold and moved to Portsmouth on the closure of HMS *Ganges* (see frontispiece).

The last example of ships named in memory of Lord Nelson is the 1848 HMS *Aboukir* (90), built in Devonport Dockyard. The resident carver, Frederick Dickerson, submitted a design in the form of a bust of a pharaoh [8.17][30] with an estimate of £40 but the contract was awarded to Edward Hellyer of Portsmouth who had submitted a design in the form of a bust of Lord Nelson

30 TNA ADM 87/17 S945 (1847).

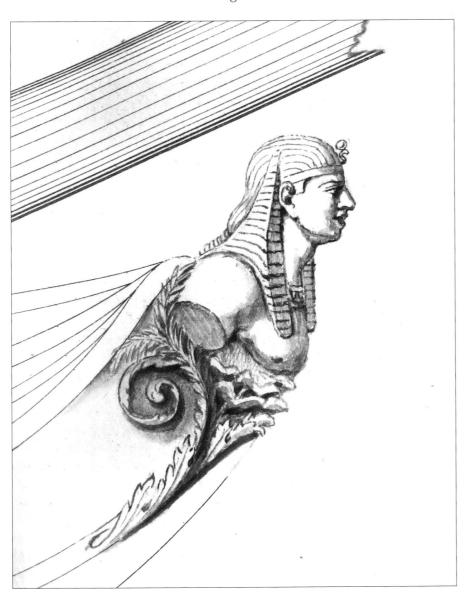

8.17
HMS *Aboukir* – **Dickerson design.**
THE NATIONAL ARCHIVES

for the same price. Dickerson appealed against the decision stating that, had he known that a bust of Nelson was required, he would have drawn one and asked for a change of heart as he had a young family entirely dependent on his work. The Surveyor of the Navy was persuaded and Dickerson was allowed to carve the figurehead to the Hellyer design [8.18]. As can be seen from the Surveyor's office deletions, the trailboard carvings were not allowed. After her active service, she became a floating battery and the receiving ship at Jamaica before being sold in 1878. Her figurehead was placed in the Dockyard at Port Royal, Jamaica but was reported in 1921 as having disintegrated.[31]

During its time ashore in Jamaica, the question was asked in a 1912 edition of *The Mariner's Mirror* whether the *Aboukir* figurehead represented Lord Nelson or General Abercromby as his uniform had been painted both blue and red over the years.[32] It was argued that Lord Nelson would have been an obvious candidate for the *Aboukir* figurehead but General Abercromby might also have been chosen as he commanded an expedition that landed at Aboukir Bay in 1801 but was mortally wounded in the engagement and his widow had been created Baroness Abercromby of Aboukir and Tullibody. While no conclusion

31   A W, 'Figure Heads in the West Indies', *The Mariner's Mirror* Vol VII, No 1 (1921).

32   'Figurehead of Aboukir', *The Mariner's Mirror* Vol II, No 2 (1912).

8.18
HMS *Aboukir* – **Hellyer design.**
DICKERSON ARCHIVE

8.19
HMS *Marlborough* - Hellyer
design 1854.
THE NATIONAL ARCHIVES

was reached in the 1912 correspondence, the evidence is now clear from the archives that it was the admiral and not the general who was so honoured.

Understandably, the Navy Board was less inclined to name its ships after the nation's generals, but there were exceptions. The Duke of Marlborough (1650– 1722) had several ships named after him, the largest of those from the 'sailing navy' being HMS *Marlborough*, built in Portsmouth Dockyard where she started life as a 120-gun sailing First Rate, only to be lengthened and converted to a 131-gun screw ship before being launched in 1855. Her figurehead was designed by J E Hellyer of Blackwall who offered a demi-head for £75 or a bust for £50. The bust was approved although there was some discussion whether it should be carved at the carver's Blackwall or Portsmouth workshops.[33] The Duke is shown wearing a wig and a formal jacket with a sash to show that he was a Knight

[33] TNA ADM 87/50 S10954 (1854).

of the Garter. The trailboards include military trophies and the word 'Blenheim' to celebrate his victory over the French and Bavarians in 1704 [8.19]. HMS *Marlborough* spent only a few years at sea and many more in various training roles in Portsmouth. Thus, in 1924 when she was sold for breaking up, her figurehead came ashore to continue the training tradition in HMS *Vernon*. Although the surviving figurehead is a bust of the Duke, it is very different from the original, being dressed in armour with the 'collar' of the Order of the Garter on his chest. No records have been found to explain when a replacement was found to be necessary but it was certainly before 1912 as an illustration of the surviving bust was included in a Player's Cigarette Card series of that date. In 2002 the figurehead was donated to the Portsmouth Gateway Project – regenerating the old *Vernon* site as the retail and residential Gunwharf Quays.

Another surviving bust of the Duke of Marlborough had been carved forty years earlier for the 1813 HMS *Blenheim* (74) built at Deptford Dockyard. The Duke is shown in uniform with the sash of the Order of the Garter, wearing a wreath of laurel leaves to signify 'victory' and bearing the arms of the Churchill family in the trailboards. The figurehead was in the Devonport collection when the Admiralty Catalogue was published in 1911 and was transferred to the National Maritime Museum in 1936.

After the defeat of Napoleon at the battle of Waterloo in 1815, the Duke of Wellington (1769–1852) was treated as another national hero and a number of ships were named in his honour. There had been ships with the name *Hero* since the middle of the eighteenth century but shortly after HMS *Hero* (74) was launched in Deptford Dockyard in 1816, her name was changed to HMS *Wellington*. Who carved the figurehead is not known but, when the ship was broken up in 1908, the figurehead was mounted at the south entrance of Devonport Dockyard where Douglas Owen recorded that it was a 'Bust; head laurel crowned; anybody's face with the Wellington nose. Military coat with aiguillettes'.[34] He remains at Devonport, very much as described except that he is now safely indoors.

HMS *Talavera* (80) had her keel laid in Portsmouth Dockyard in 1813, the ship being named to commemorate the victory of Lieutenant General Sir Arthur Wellesley (the future Duke of Wellington) in 1809. The ship was renamed HMS *Waterloo* in 1817, prompting Grayfoot & Overton of Woolwich to submit designs – a bust of the Duke of Wellington for £21 or a handsome standing figure of the Duke for £34.10.0. The Surveyor was clearly conscious of the need to

[34] Owen, 'Figureheads'.

(OPPOSITE)
8.20
HMS *Duke of Wellington.*
RICHARD HUNTER ARCHIVES

8.21
HMS *Brunswick* – **Hellyer design.**
THE NATIONAL ARCHIVES

[35] TNA ADM 106/1795 (1817).

[36] TNA ADM 91/4 (1818).

[37] TNA ADM 91/6 (1830).

have a true likeness and instructed that the bust should be carved to a sketch provided by him.[35] This does not appear to have been a success as in March 1818 the Surveyor instructed the Hellyers of Portsmouth to undertake the work.[36] In 1824 the ship was renamed HMS *Bellerophon*, and was given the helmeted and plumed figurehead that is now in the National Museum of the Royal Navy, Portsmouth.

Another HMS *Waterloo* (120) was built in Chatham Dockyard and launched there in 1833. The figurehead was carved in the dockyard, the Surveyor's office having sent the superintendent a plaster bust of the Duke of Wellington to ensure that his looks were captured.[37] Carved as a uniformed bust wearing a laurel

8.22
HMS *Watt* – **Hellyer design.**
THE NATIONAL ARCHIVES

wreath, the figurehead survived two changes of the ship's name (to *Conqueror* in 1862 and to *Warspite* in 1876), when she became the training ship for the Marine Society on the Thames. He survived a fire in 1918 and was eventually purchased by the owner of the Branson Line and was presented by him to the South Street Seaport Museum in New York.

By far the finest tribute to 'The Iron Duke' was the figurehead carved for the 1852 HMS *Duke of Wellington* (131). Built at Pembroke Dock as HMS *Windsor Castle*, she was launched on 14 September 1852 and, when Queen Victoria heard that the Duke of Wellington had died on the very day that the ship was launched, she ordered that the ship should be renamed in his honour. Hellyer

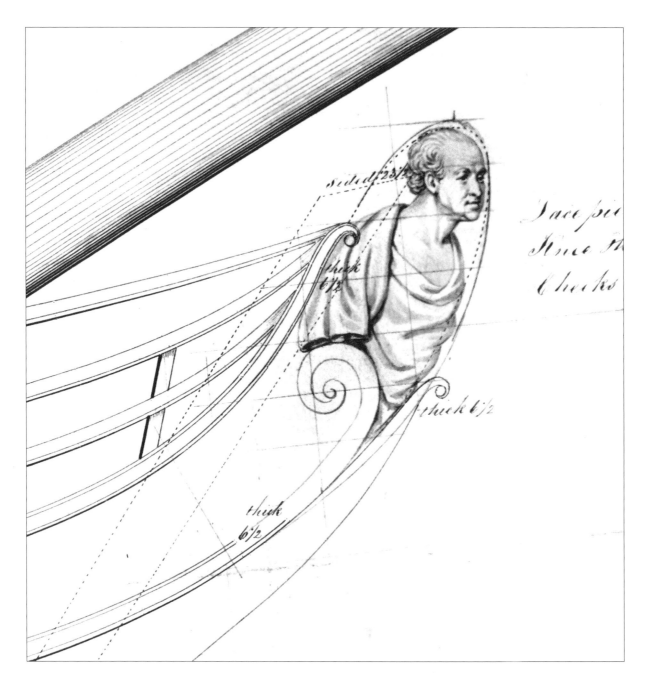

8.23
HMS *James Watt* – **Hellyer design.**
THE NATIONAL ARCHIVES

38   TNA ADM 91/15 (1852).

39   TNA ADM 87/42 S8503 (1852).

& Son were informed of the change and were invited to submit a design.[38] The response from their Blackwall workshop included an estimate for the very considerable sum of £250 but this was too much for the Surveyor to accept and only £100 was allowed.[39] The resulting bust of the Duke was huge; dressed in uniform with a gilt aiguillette, epaulettes and decorations he was a magnificent figure [8.20] and survived many years of harbour service before the ship was sold for breaking up in 1904. The figurehead was retained by the Castles

Shipbreaking Company who, after the figure's body had become rotten, placed its head and neck in their small museum in the early years of the twentieth century. What remained was lost in the London Blitz in 1941.

Other military figures are far less obvious candidates to appear on the bows of British warships. HMS *Brunswick* was named after the Duke of Brunswick (1735–1806) who commanded the Prussian and Austrian troops at Valmy in 1792.[40] Perhaps more significantly for the first ship of the name (launched 1790), the Duke was married to Princess Augusta, sister of George III. The name was, however, repeated in Queen Victoria's reign, the 1855 HMS *Brunswick* (80) being built at Pembroke Dockyard. The Hellyers of Portsmouth offered two designs, a simple bust at £14 or the rather more flamboyant demi-head with a plumed military hat [8.21].[41] The records appear to show that neither of these were accepted and that the work was undertaken by Nemiah Williams of London.

The introduction of the steam engine to the fleet was a slow and evolutionary process and, with old traditions dying hard, it is interesting to see that James Watt (1736–1819), a Scottish inventor and mechanical engineer, was amongst those commemorated in the names of the navy's warships. The first attempt was not successful as before HMS *Watt* wood paddle frigate was completed at Chatham Dockyard in 1844, her name was changed to *Retribution*. The Hellyers of Portsmouth had, however, forwarded a design[42] of a simple bust with a scroll in the trailboards saying 'WATT on Steam' and an estimate of £20, but whether this was ever carved is not recorded [8.22]. Ten years later, HMS *James Watt* (screw 80) – was launched at Pembroke Dock and the Hellyers again submitted a design, although this time he is portrayed as a rather older man [8.23].[43]

40　Manning and Walker, *British Warship Names*.

41　TNA ADM 87/48 S8331 (1850).

42　TNA ADM 87/12 S4944 (1842).

43　TNA ADM 87/41 S8463 (1852).

1   *A Record of the Figureheads in H M Naval Establishments under Plymouth Command –* undated – but created in response to an Admiralty instruction of about 1936 (Admiralty Library Ref Dh 20).

2   E A Hughes, *The Royal Naval College Dartmouth* (London, 1950), p 125.

3   TNA ADM 1/27846 (3 Feb 1961).

9.1
Bust of Britannia – lost Dartmouth 1961.
CROWN COPYRIGHT

CHAPTER 9

NINETEENTH-CENTURY FIGUREHEADS – GEOGRAPHIC

WITH the expansion of British interests around the world in the nineteenth century, it is not surprising that their lordships recognised this by including ship names that were representative of the United Kingdom and some of its more significant cities.

Britannia, the helmeted figure who first appeared on Roman coins, featured prominently both as the symbol of the nation and as a ship name. The 1820 HMS *Britannia* (100), the fourth warship of the name, was built in Plymouth Dockyard. She was adapted for use as the Royal Navy's cadet training ship and, after finding that neither Portsmouth nor Portland was suited to the task, arrived at Dartmouth in 1863 with the standing figure of Britannia as her figurehead. When, in 1869, she and her companion, HMS *Hindostan*, were found to be too small for the task, she was replaced by the larger HMS *Prince of Wales* (screw 121), which was renamed *Britannia* and was fitted with the Britannia figurehead. After the Royal Naval College was built in 1905, the cadets came ashore for their training and the figurehead joined them [Colour Plate 10]. She has occupied different sites over the years but today can be seen on the edge of the parade ground.

Another figurehead in the form of a bust of Britannia stood in the Royal Naval College grounds for many years. It is not clear when this carving was moved to Dartmouth as early photographs of the Royal Naval Barracks at Devonport show her in front of the drill-shed there. The pre-war photographic archive of the figureheads in the Plymouth Command identifies her as coming from the 1820 *Britannia* and records that she was then in the RN Barracks [9.1].[1] It is considered that this is a mis-identification and that she is a carving of Britannia rather than from HMS *Britannia*. A photograph of her also appears in *The Royal Naval College Dartmouth* where she is seen looking out over the river from the jetty at Sandquay.[2] While her true origin has yet to be discovered, her loss is well documented following a survey by HM Dockyard, Devonport in 1961 – the cause was dry rot.[3]

9.2
HMS *Albion* – **Dickerson
design 1860.**
DICKERSON ARCHIVE

The figure of Britannia was also carved for the figurehead of the 1842
HMS *Albion* (90), built in Plymouth Dockyard. Her original figurehead was a
demi-head of Britannia holding a trident in her right hand, as the Surveyor of
the Navy sent such a design to the Superintendent at Woolwich instructing that
figureheads at ½-inch and ¼-inch scales should be carved for ship models.[4]
When HMS *Albion* was converted for steam propulsion in 1860–1, she was given
a new figurehead carved by Frederick Dickerson for £35.[5] His design is now
preserved in the Dickerson Archive in Australia [9.2] while the figurehead itself
is in the Hull Maritime Museum.

Two nineteenth-century ships named HMS *Bulwark* had Britannia as their
figurehead, signifying the strength in defence that a bastion provided. When the
1806 HMS *Bulwark* (74) was building in Portsmouth Dockyard, Edward Hellyer
submitted a design in the form of a demi-head of Britannia holding a spear in one
hand and sprig of leaves in the other.[6] His estimate for carving it was £32 but this
was not approved and he was invited to resubmit his design as a bust. This he

4   TNA ADM 87/11 S7458 (1841).

5   TNA ADM 88/16 S5952
    (1860).

6   TNA ADM 106/1884 (1806).

9.3
HMS *Bulwark* - Hellyer
design 1806.
THE NATIONAL ARCHIVES

7   Ibid.
8   TNA ADM 87/76 S4852 and
    5499 (1860).

did [9.3] with an estimate of £25 and, while the design was approved, he was only allowed £21 for his efforts.[7] Fifty-four years later when the next HMS *Bulwark* was building in Chatham Dockyard, J E & J Hellyer were the resident carvers at Portsmouth and submitted a similar design but drawn in their rather more modern style [9.4], their estimate of £45 being accepted.[8] Work on the ship was suspended in 1861 and, while there were plans to convert her into a twin-turret monitor, these came to nothing and she was taken to pieces in 1873. Her figurehead was preserved in the Chatham collection where it was included in the Admiralty Catalogue of 1911 and where it has remained ever since.[9]

Britannia must also have been a candidate for the figurehead of the 1812 HMS *Briton* (38), built in Chatham Dockyard. No designs have been preserved but when the ship was broken up in 1860, her figurehead was taken into the Chatham collection [9.5]. She was photographed there for the 1948 muster, a matronly figure who was said to be at the armament depot at Upnor and in good condition.[10] No trace of her has been found since then.

Scotland, Ireland and Wales were included in the national theme of the nineteenth century, with HM Ships *Caledonia*, *Hibernia* and *Cambrian*.

The 1808 HMS *Caledonia* (120) was built in Plymouth Dockyard and, while

9   *Catalogue of Pictures, Presentation Plate, Figureheads, Models, Relics and Trophies at the Admiralty; on board H.M.Ships; and in the Naval Establishments at Home and Abroad* (London, April 1911).
10 *Figureheads at Chatham – 31.12.48.* An album on linen pages containing forty-seven figurehead photographs with descriptions (Chatham MCD No 13234).

9.4
HMS *Bulwark* – **Hellyer design 1860.**
THE NATIONAL ARCHIVES

9.5
HMS *Briton* – lost Chatham
*c*1950.

11 A 1:36 scale longitudinal
     sectional model – NMM
     SLR2908.
12 TNA ADM 87/15 S3628
     (1845).

no design drawings have been found for her, a contemporary ship model in the National Maritime Museum collection is in the form of a bust wearing a plate-mail tunic and a bonnet with a large feather.[11] Behind and below the bust are beautifully detailed huge thistles and leaves.

There are no surviving designs for the original figurehead of the 1804 HMS *Hibernia* (110), built in Plymouth Dockyard. However, when in 1845 she was commissioned as the flagship of the Commander-in-Chief Mediterranean, a new figurehead was required. Hellyer & Son of Portsmouth submitted two designs, 'Britannia supporting a harp' at £50 or 'a bard supporting a harp' at £47.[12] The latter was approved [9.6], although the Surveyor's office instructed that the winged figure forming part of the harp should not extend beyond the knee of the head (as shown on the dotted line) nor should the left arm extend beyond the line. The design is said to represent the Irish-Celtic god Dagda, holding the harp that he played each time the seasons changed. HMS *Hibernia* spent the last fifty years of her life as the receiving base ship at Malta and, having become something of a fixture in Grand Harbour, when she was sold for breaking up in 1902 her figurehead was landed and eventually located in Fort St Angelo. When the Royal Navy withdrew from Malta in the 1970s, the *Hibernia* figurehead was shipped back to the UK and was gifted to the Royal Naval Museum at Portsmouth [Colour Plate 11]. By 1994 discussions on the possible repatriation of the figurehead to Malta reached a mutually satisfactory conclusion and he returned to be displayed in the Malta Maritime Museum, Vittoriosa.

The Dickersons of Plymouth offered two designs for the 1841 HMS *Cambrian* (36), building in Pembroke Dockyard: the first a male bust wearing a trilby-style

9.6
HMS *Hibernia* – **Hellyer
design 1845.**
THE NATIONAL ARCHIVES

hat with perhaps a leek at its front, the second another bust but dressed in a plate-mail tunic with a coronet, each being offered for £10.[13] Neither designs were of good quality and that is perhaps why the Hellyers of Portsmouth were invited to submit an alternative design. They offered either a bust or a demi-head of a bearded bard, the latter being very similar to that submitted five years later for

[13] TNA ADM 87/10 S2847 (1840).

9.7
HMS *Gibraltar* – **Dickerson
design 1859.**
DICKERSON ARCHIVE

[14] TNA ADM 87/10 S3538
(1840).

[15] Ship plan NMM ZAZ0754.

Hibernia.[14] Only the design for the demi-head has survived at The National Archives, holding a harp, but it was the bust version that was approved and how the harp was incorporated is unknown, although probably in the trailboards.

In addition to these references to the United Kingdom, the names of overseas territories appeared as ship names, one example being the 1860 HMS *Gibraltar* (screw 101), built in Devonport Dockyard. She was the sixth ship to be given the name, her eighteenth-century immediate predecessor having a figurehead in the form of a full-length crowned lion, appropriate to a ship captured from the Spanish in 1780.[15] Frederick Dickerson's design for the 1860 ship was a uniformed bust of a naval officer [9.7] with a key in the trailboard – referring, no doubt, to Gibraltar being the 'Key to the Mediterranean' and Admiral Rooke who took Gibraltar in 1704. The design is one of the drawings retained by the carvers so that they could scale it up for the actual figurehead, their measurements being just visible on the drawing. Approval of the work at £35

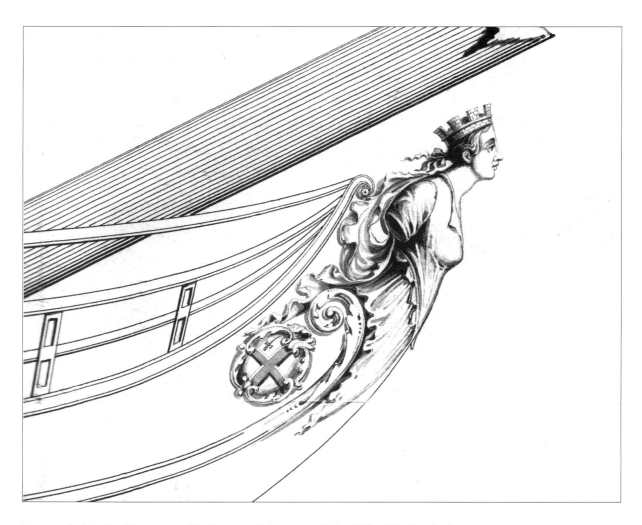

9.8
HMS *London* – Dickerson design 1857.
DICKERSON ARCHIVE

is recorded in the 'Register of In-Letters Relating to Ships',[16] while the design is amongst those preserved in the Dickerson Archive in Australia.

British cities featured – London, Liverpool and Bristol being fine English examples. The 1840 HMS *London* (92) was built in Chatham Dockyard having spent more than ten years on the stocks. Her figurehead was approved in 1830 as a bust and this was on her bow until she was converted to a screw ship (72) at Devonport in 1857–8.[17] During the conversion, the figurehead was reported as being rotten and a replacement was approved.[18] The rot cannot have been too severe as her original figurehead was landed and taken into the rigging house where it was included in subsequent reports.[19] The figure has a rectangular tower perched on her head, clearly representing the 'White Tower' of the Tower of London and was one of the figureheads transferred to the National Maritime Museum as part of its core collection in 1936. The 1857 replacement carving by Frederick Dickerson of Devonport had much more style, the Tower of London

16 TNA ADM 88/15 S6821 (1859).

17 TNA ADM 91/6 (1830).

18 TNA ADM 88/13 S822 (1857).

19 *Catalogue of Pictures, Presentation Plate, Figureheads, Models, Relics and Trophies at the Admiralty; on board H.M.Ships; and in the Naval Establishments at Home and Abroad* (London, April 1911); and Owen, 'The Devonport Figureheads', pp 145–7.

being suggested by a 'mural crown' and the City of London by the badge in the trailboards [9.8]. Dickerson was paid £35 for the work that then saw service in Zanzibar where the ship was eventually sold in 1884.

The 1860 HMS *Liverpool* wood screw frigate was built in Devonport Dockyard and given a figurehead carved by Frederick Dickerson that was very similar to that for the HMS *London* replacement. The female bust wears another mural crown but this time she is given a Liver Bird, the city's emblem, in the trailboard [9.9]. The design was approved and £18.10.0 was allowed – cheaper than that for HMS *London* as the carving was smaller.[20]

The 1861 HMS *Bristol* wood screw frigate was built in Woolwich Dockyard, her figurehead being carved by the Hellyers of Portsmouth, for £27.10.0.[21] The female three-quarter-length bust [9.10] has the arms of the City of Bristol in the trailboards, the ship and the castle signifying a strongly fortified harbour. When the ship was broken up by Castles in 1883, her figurehead was placed in their small museum and was one of the casualties of the London Blitz in April 1941. While most of the figureheads were totally destroyed, the head of HMS *Bristol*'s figurehead was salvaged and in 1963 was presented to the National

[20] TNA ADM 88/16 S2419 (1860).

[21] TNA ADM 87/74 S 2184 & 2394 (1860).

9.9
HMS *Liverpool* – Dickerson design 1860.
DICKERSON ARCHIVE

9.10
HMS *Bristol* - J E & J Hellyer
design 1860.
THE NATIONAL ARCHIVES

Maritime Museum where it is still preserved.

The 1811 HMS *Edinburgh* (74) was built at the private yard of Brent of Rotherhithe on the Thames and Edward Hellyer & Son of Portsmouth offered three designs in 1819, although no explanation is given in the letters why a new figurehead was required so early in the ship's life.[22] Their most expensive design at £44 was in the form of the arms of the city – a shield displaying the castle with supporters (dexter, a maiden and sinister, a doe) and an anchor above the shield. Next, with an estimate of £36, was a standing figure of a Scottish soldier in kilt and feather bonnet; and least expensive was a bust that he offered for £24. The first two designs are in The National Archives but that for the bust is missing, probably retained by the carver as it was approved for the reduced price of £21. When the ship was broken up by Castle & Beech in 1865, the

22 TNA ADM 106/1889 (1819).

9.11
HMS *Edinburgh* – Newport
News, Virginia 2011.

THE MARINERS' MUSEUM

23   TNA ADM 91/4 (1819).
24   *A Record of the Figureheads in
H M Naval Establishments
under Plymouth Command* –
Undated – but created in
response to an Admiralty
instruction of about 1936
(Admiralty Library Ref Dh
20).

figurehead was kept in their collection and was sold to an American field representative in 1939, almost certainly saving it from destruction during the London Blitz. It is now in the Mariners' Museum, Newport News, Virginia [9.11].

Ships were also given the names of counties. The 1798 HMS *Kent* (74) had been built in the private yard of Perry of Blackwall, but by 1819 she required a replacement figurehead and the Navy Board sent a drawing to Plymouth directing the officers there to have a figurehead carved for £35.[23] The design is of a standing longbowman and is unusual for the period being coloured [Colour Plate 12]. When she was taken to pieces at Devonport in 1881, the twelve-foot-tall figurehead was placed beside the road to the main gate where his presence was noted at each of the subsequent musters. Sadly, as was recorded in Chapter 3, he was destroyed by German bombing in 1941.

The first HMS *Cambridge* was built in 1666 but the nineteenth-century ship of the name was a Third Rate (80), launched in Deptford Dockyard in 1815. After her active service she was joined by HMS *Calcutta* to become the Devonport Gunnery School, and later still her name was given to the gunnery range at Wembury, near Plymouth. The 1815 HMS *Cambridge* had a figurehead of a seated lion with one fore-paw on the Royal arms, surmounted by his crown [9.12]. When the ship was taken to pieces in 1869, her figurehead stood beside the avenue leading up to the main gate of Devonport Dockyard but in the 1947 annual survey it was said to be in the advance stages of rot.[24] Over the years there has been much confusion between this figurehead and that from HMS *Lion* (80), also part of the early Devonport collection. As will be seen from Chapter 6, HMS *Lion's* figurehead was a lion rampant, wearing his crown and with both fore-paws on the Royal arms.

While it is not surprising to see British emblems and locations being promoted

9.12
HMS *Cambridge* – lost
Devonport 1947.
CROWN COPYRIGHT

in the ship names of the Royal Navy, the use of foreign nationals is not as easily understood. It is thought that the name of HMS *Arab* probably originated when the French ship *Arabe* was taken in 1791, even though she was not added to the Royal Navy.[25] The fifth ship of the name, a brig-sloop (16), was launched in Chatham Dockyard in 1847 but her keel had been laid down nine years earlier. Robert Hall and Hellyer & Browning, both of whose workshops were in Rotherhithe, bid for the work, Robert Hall submitting a suitable demi-head for £5 [9.13].[26] His design was not accepted, however, and Portsmouth Dockyard

[25] Manning & Walker, *British Warship Names.*
[26] TNA ADM 87/9 S7054 (1839).

9.13
HMS *Arab* – **Robert Hall
design.**

27 TNA ADM 91/9 (1838).
28 A *Record of the Figureheads in
H M Naval Establishments
under Plymouth Command* –
undated – but created in
response to an Admiralty
instruction of about 1936
(Admiralty Library Ref Dh
20).

was instructed to send the blocks to Messrs Hellyer & Browning for the work
to be done by them.[27]

In the same class of brig-sloops but built at Pembroke Dockyard, HMS *Grecian*
was employed in the fight against the slave-trade, capturing the slaver *Brazil* in
1848. When she was sold for breaking up in 1865, her figurehead was added
to the Devonport Dockyard collection [9.14] and was photographed there in
1936,[28] but was another of the collection lost during the bombing of the
Dockyard in 1941.

The 1810 HMS *Macedonian* (38) was built in Woolwich Dockyard and was
given a bust figurehead representing Alexander the Great, King of Macedonia
and the greatest general of ancient times, dressed in a finely tooled jerkin and
wearing a plumed helmet [9.15]. In 1812, the ship was captured in the Atlantic

by the American frigate *United States* and her figurehead now stands on a commemorative stone base, with four of her 18-pounder guns, in the central square of the US Naval Academy, Annapolis having been transferred there from New York Navy Yard in 1875.

When warships were named after rivers the carvers often illustrated this with some form of flowing water. The 1826 HMS *Tyne* (28) built in Woolwich Dockyard, was given a hirsute bust of a river god [9.16] carved by Overton & Faldo of Rotherhithe with water flowing from a large vessel in the trailboards,[29] while the 1860 HMS *Tweed* wood screw frigate laid down in Pembroke Dockyard

29   TNA ADM 106/1800 S326 (1826).

9.14
HMS *Grecian* – **lost Devonport 1941.**

CROWN COPYRIGHT

9.15
HMS *Macedonian* – **US Naval Academy, Annapolis.**

US NAVAL ACADEMY MUSEUM

9.17
HMS *Tweed* – **Hellyer design 1859.**

9.16
HMS *Tyne* – **Overton & Faldo design 1826.**

30   TNA ADM 87/73 S7714 (1859).

31   TNA ADM 106/1940 (1810).

but cancelled in 1864, was given a river maiden [9.17], designed by the Hellyers of Portsmouth, pouring water from a small jug.[30]

It is not known what figurehead the 1806 HMS *Shannon* (38) was given when she was built in the Brindley Yard at Frindsbury on the Medway but, in a submission by James Dickerson of Devonport in 1810, it was reported that it had been lost off Cadiz.[31] His replacement design was a female bust wearing a wreath of leaves in her hair and his estimate was £6. Drawn in the scroll of the trailboard was a sprig of shamrock leaves to give the design an Irish connection with the River Shannon. The ship became famous after she captured the American frigate *Chesapeake* off Boston in 1813 and, when she was broken up in 1859, her figurehead was presented to her captain, Philip Broke. It remained in the family, most recently at Shrubland Park, Suffolk [9.18], but was sold in 2006 and is now in a private collection in Florida.

9.18
HMS *Shannon* – Shrubland
Park, Suffolk 2003.
AUTHOR'S COLLECTION

CHAPTER 10

NINETEENTH-CENTURY FIGUREHEADS – MISCELLANEOUS

**10.2
HMS *Dragon* – Dickerson
design 1844.**
DICKERSON ARCHIVE

DRAGONS have featured in myths and legends for centuries and it is not surprising, therefore, that they appear on the bows of ships of the Royal Navy. There were four nineteenth-century ships called HMS *Dragon*, three of which were in the figurehead era and show the various ways in which the carvers could address a subject.

While the 1798 HMS *Dragon* (74) was technically an eighteenth-century ship, built by Wells at Deptford, it was in 1807 that the Superintendent at Portsmouth reported that her figurehead was too rotten to be repaired and forwarded a replacement design for approval. The bust of a knight in armour has a dragon as the crest on his helmet, while his lance and a shield bearing the cross of St George lie in the trailboard [10.1], opposite. The design was by Edward Hellyer with an estimate of £24 and, while the design itself was approved, only £21 was allowed.

When the 1845 HMS *Dragon* wood paddle frigate was launched at Pembroke Dockyard, Frederick Dickerson of Devonport had already submitted a design with an estimate of £7, the lower estimate being appropriate for the smaller ship.[1] He created a full-length winged dragon with its coiled tail running down the trailboards port and starboard [10.2], above. The design is not filed at the National Archives with the submission letter and estimate as it was retained by the carver for use while creating the finished product and is now preserved in the Dickerson Archive in Australia.

By the time that the third ship of the name – a composite screw sloop – was launched in Devonport Dockyard in 1878, the form of her bow was much blunter

[1] TNA ADM 87/14 S1278 & 1476 (1844).

10.1
HMS *Dragon* – Hellyer
design 1807.
THE NATIONAL ARCHIVES

and, while the head and neck of the dragon protruded forward, its wings were little more than surface decorations. A photograph of this figurehead appeared in the pre-war photographic archive of figureheads in the Plymouth Command [10.3], where it is noted as being in the garage of the Superintendent of Police![2] It was one of three figureheads that were moved to the WRNS quarters at St Budeaux, Plymouth, and it was there that it was lost to decay in the 1960s.

The theme of the dragon is continued in the 1840 HMS *St George* (120) built

2 *A Record of the Figureheads in H M Naval Establishments under Plymouth Command –* undated – but created in response to an Admiralty instruction of about 1936 (Admiralty Library Ref Dh 20).

10.3
HMS *Dragon* – lost Plymouth
*c*1967.

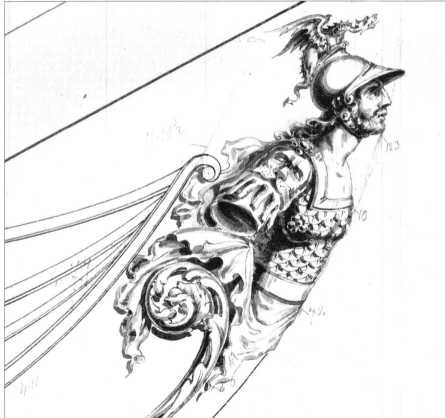

10.4
HMS *St George* – Dickerson
design 1858.

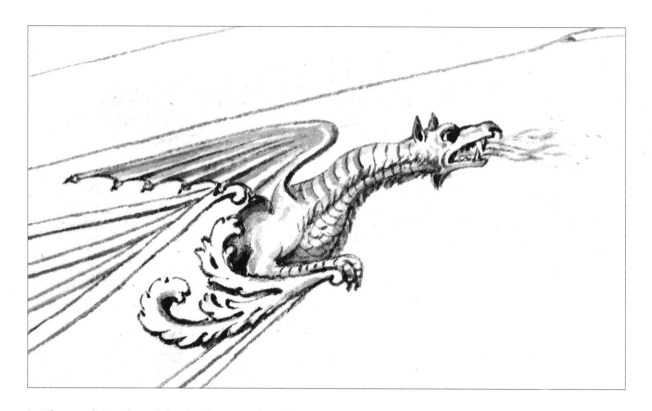

10.5
HMS *Spitfire* - **Hellyer design 1844.**
THE NATIONAL ARCHIVES

in Plymouth Dockyard, having been no less than thirteen years on the stocks. The yard had become Devonport Dockyard by the time that she returned there in 1858 to be converted to steam propulsion, a process that involved her being cut down from a three-decker to a two-decker. As has already been seen in Chapter 3, her original figurehead had been a standing figure of St George, resplendent in armour with the dragon at his feet being despatched with his lance; or, as Douglas Owen described the scene in 1913, 'With right arm on high, he is thrusting a spear into the dragon's mouth.' While suitable for a three-decker, the figurehead was too large for the cut-down ship and so was landed, only to be destroyed in the Blitz. For the newly emerging screw two-decker, Frederick Dickerson designed a warrior bust with a dragon as the crest on his helmet [10.4] and for this he was allowed £35.[3] The drawing is now preserved in the Dickerson Archive in Australia.

An interesting variation to the dragon theme was the figurehead designed for the 1845 HMS *Spitfire* wood paddle vessel, built in Deptford Dockyard. While the name today is associated with the fighter aircraft of the Second World War, spitting fire from its cannons, when the Hellyers of Portsmouth submitted a design for her figurehead, they offered the fore-part of a dragon spitting fire and were allowed £8.10.0 for the work [10.5].[4]

[3] TNA ADM 91/21 and 88/14 S4598 (1858).

[4] TNA ADM 87/14 S1896 (1844).

Moving from myths and legends to traditional pantomime, the name Harlequin is given to a mute character usually masked and dressed in a diamond-patterned costume. The 1836 HMS *Harlequin* (16), built in Pembroke Dockyard, had her original figurehead carved by Robert Hall of London,[5] but by 1845 a replacement was required and the Hellyers of Portsmouth submitted a design with an estimate for £6.15.0 [10.6].[6] *Harlequin* ended her service as a coal-hulk at Devonport but, before being sold for breaking up in 1889, her figurehead was added to the collection there. In 1936 she was one of the figureheads given to the National Maritime Museum as part of their core collection and he remains there today in his brightly-coloured tunic.

Turning to the skies we find references to a Meteor and the North Star. The 1823 HMS *Meteor* bomb was built in Pembroke Dockyard. The authorisation

5   TNA ADM 87/3 S2209 (1833).

6   TNA ADM 87/15 S5293 (1845).

10.6
HMS *Harlequin* – Hellyer design 1845.
THE NATIONAL ARCHIVES

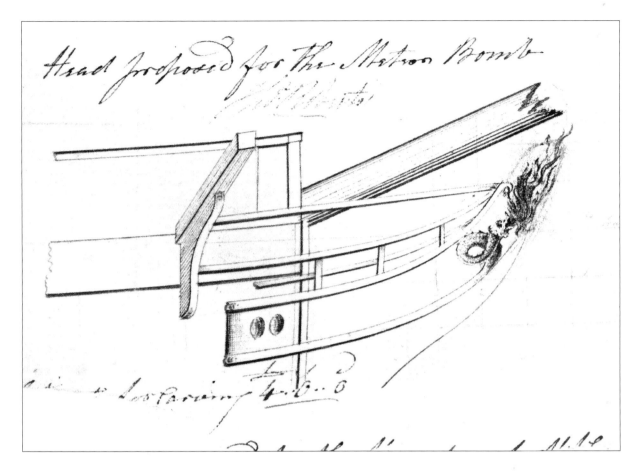

10.7
HMS *Meteor* - **Dickerson design 1823.**
DICKERSON ARCHIVE

letters are not amongst the papers at the National Archives but the design is one of those in the Dickerson Archive in Australia, the clue to the identity of which *Meteor* it was designed for coming from a reference to HMS *Hamadryad* which was building in Pembroke Dockyard at the same time as the 1823 bomb [10.7]. A serpent has been developed from the 'lower cheek' that frames the trailboard and is breathing flames in a manner suitable to a bomb vessel.

The 1824 HMS *North Star* (28) was built in Woolwich Dockyard, the figurehead carvers Greyfoot & Overton submitting an ingenious design in 1821 made up from 'A full-length figure of a bear with North Star on top of head' and an estimate of £10. The design was clearly intended as a play on words relating their carving to the 'Great Bear' constellation and showing the other stars of the constellation in the design [10.8]. The design was not approved and the carvers were instructed to carve 'a neat busthead of a naval officer for £5'.[7] A surviving figurehead of a three-quarter-length female bust that stands in the Ship Gallery of the Science Museum in London has a description saying that she was from this 1824 *North Star* but this is believed to be incorrect and that she came from

7 TNA ADM 106/1795 (1821).

10.8
HMS *North Star* – **Greyfoot & Overton design 1821.**

8   *Catalogue of Pictures,*
    Presentation Plate,
    Figureheads, Models, Relics
    and Trophies at the Admiralty;
    on board H.M.Ships; and in
    the Naval Establishments at
    Home and Abroad (London,
    April 1911).
9   Owen, 'Figureheads', pp 293.
10 'Figure-Head of HMS North
    Star', *The Sheerness Times* (17
    September 1931).

the later HMS *North Star* wood screw corvette, laid down in Sheerness Dockyard in 1860 but cancelled in 1865. She was included in the 1911 Admiralty Catalogue which described her as being at Sheerness and coming from the 1860 ship,[8] an identity that was confirmed in Douglas Owen's article of 1913.[9] In 1931 when she was installed at the main entrance to Sheerness Dockyard, an article in the local paper charted her movements over the years[10] and so it was not until 1948 that she was said to have come from the earlier *North Star* – a simple case of misidentification that has been perpetuated ever since.

Turning next to the sea, the 1857 HMS *Pelorus* wood screw corvette, built in Devonport Dockyard was the second ship of the name but, whether her name had its origin in the ancient name for Cape Faro, Sicily, or the name of Hannibal's pilot, is not clear. £10 was allowed for the design that was submitted from Devonport in 1856, a sum that would be appropriate for a bust so the carvers seem to have opted for Hannibal's pilot.[11] When the ship was taken to pieces at Devonport in 1869, her figurehead was added to the collection in the rigging house[12] and later his photograph appeared in the pre-war photographic archive of figureheads in the Plymouth Command [10.9].[13] He was said to be still in the rigging house but later manuscript notes record that he was moved to the RN Barracks in 1939 and that he was destroyed in the Blitz.

Grampus was the name given to the 1784 HMS *Tremendous* (74) when she was cut down to a 50-gun frigate in Woolwich Dockyard in 1845. While *Tremendous* had been a suitable name for a 74-gun ship, it would not have been appropriate for a frigate and with the grampus being a member of the dolphin family, it was selected. The Hellyers of Portsmouth offered a design that included a bust of King Neptune with a grampus in the trailboards, and an estimate of £5.15.0 [10.10].[14] This figurehead has survived and is now in the National Museum of the Royal Navy at Portsmouth but, as the trailboards were lost when the ship

[11] TNA ADM 91/19 (1856).
[12] Owen, 'Figureheads', p 325.
[13] *A Record of the Figureheads in H M Naval Establishments under Plymouth Command* – undated – but created in response to an Admiralty instruction of about 1936 (Admiralty Library Ref Dh 20).
[14] TNA ADM 87/15 S4271 (1845).

was sold for breaking up, it will never be known whether the carvings looked more like a grampus or a spouting whale.

The name *Flying Fish* was popular for small vessels and also gave the carvers plenty of artistic licence. The 1844 HMS *Flying Fish* (12) was built in Pembroke Dockyard, the Hellyers of Portsmouth having forwarded a design in the previous December.[15] The design was certainly unusual being a full-length fish appearing to fly from the bow of the ship [10.11]. All was not plain sailing thereafter as by 15 February 1844 the Hellyers were being hurried along: on 20 February they were told that the *Adventure* Transport bound for Pembroke had sailed from Woolwich and would call in for it on the way. By 26 March, however, the letters tell us that she was still at Devonport with *Flying Fish* due to

10.11
HMS *Flying Fish* – Hellyer
design 1843.
THE NATIONAL ARCHIVES

[15] TNA ADM 87/13 S8064
(1843).

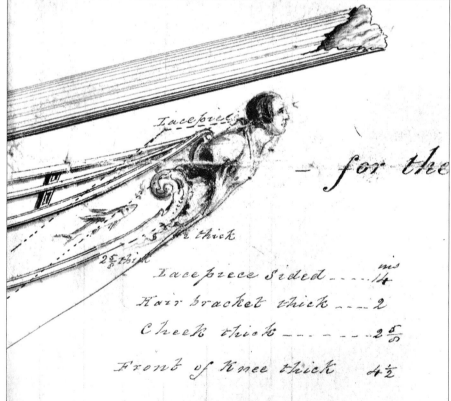

10.12
HMS *Flying Fish* – Dickerson
design 1855.
DICKERSON ARCHIVE

launch on 3 April. Whether she made it on time is not recorded but at the end of April the Hellyers were instructed to 'reduce the head and make it more comfortable'.[16]

When the next HMS *Flying Fish* wood screw dispatch vessel was launched at Pembroke Dockyard in 1855, Frederick Dickerson of Devonport followed the more conventional route and submitted a design with a standard female three-quarter-length bust and a flying fish in each trailboard [10.12]. The design was approved and £6.10.0 was allowed, but, as was their custom, the Dickersons retained the drawing as their carving guide and it is now preserved in the Dickerson Archive in Australia.[17]

Wings were not a new feature on figureheads as, when the 1809 HMS *Zephyr* (16) was built in Portsmouth Dockyard, the Hellyers had to devise a figure that would represent the 'west wind'. They gave their bust a pair of wings [Colour Plate 13] and were allowed £3 for their troubles.[18]

It is not too difficult to understand why the Navy Board should select the name *Minx* for one of their smaller vessels and a 'flirtatious young woman' might then be expected to appear as the figurehead. Much more difficult to fathom is why the 1846 HMS *Minx* iron screw gunboat was given a figurehead in the form of the bust of a warrior. She had been built in the yard of Miller, Ravenhill & Co of Blackwall so perhaps the normal controls did not apply or perhaps the warrior was a late replacement. In 1859 she was fitted out as a water-tank steamer and operated from the Royal William Yard at Devonport, presumably taking fresh water to the fleet. A photograph of the figurehead [10.13] appeared in the pre-war photographic archive of figureheads in the Plymouth Command where he is noted as being at the north end of the Cooperage Block.[19] A manuscript entry dated 1947 records that his condition was deteriorating and that he should be removed at once for survey and, if in a fit condition, repaired and re-sited under cover – a familiar story and the last that was heard of the carving.

The *Emerald* class of composite screw corvettes had ships named after both precious and semi-precious stones and the 1875 HMS *Tourmaline* was one of these. She became a coal hulk in 1899 and it was probably then that her figurehead was landed as it was recorded as being in the Chatham collection in the 1911 Admiralty Catalogue.[20] Photographed there for the 1938[21] and 1948[22] musters she was at first in the Dockyard Museum and then at the Armament Depot, Upnor [10.14]. The index of the latter has been annotated with the destinations of the figureheads when Chatham closed and, as there is no such

10.13
HMS *Minx* – lost Plymouth c1948.
CROWN COPYRIGHT

[16] TNA ADM 91/11 (1843).
[17] TNA ADM 88/11 S4163 and 91/18 (1855).
[18] TNA ADM 106/1885 (1809).
[19] *A Record of the Figureheads in H M Naval Establishments under Plymouth Command* – undated – but created in response to an Admiralty instruction of about 1936 (Admiralty Library Ref Dh 20).
[20] *Catalogue of Pictures, Presentation Plate, Figureheads, Models, Relics and Trophies at the Admiralty; on board H.M.Ships; and in the Naval Establishments at Home and Abroad* (London, April 1911).
[21] *Figureheads in Dockyard, Royal Naval Barracks and Royal Naval Hospital, Chatham 1938* (D 9270/38).
[22] *Figureheads at Chatham 31:12:48 Part I H.M.Dockyard Part II RN Barracks, St Marys, Collingwood, RN Hospital and RN Armament Depot Upnor.*

mark against *Tourmaline*, it must be assumed that she was in no condition to be moved.

As a postscript to this chapter, there were times when the decisions of the Surveyor of the Navy made the carvers think laterally. Examples of ordinary sailors being portrayed in warship figureheads will be found in Chapter 14, but they were also carved for two small ships called *Cruizer*. The first, a brig-sloop (13) built at Chatham Dockyard and launched there in 1828, had the bust of a sailor with crossed pistol and cutlass in the trailboards, a Hellyer & Son design offered for £7.[23] For the second HMS *Cruizer*, a wood screw sloop built in Deptford Dockyard and launched in 1852, the Hellyers of Blackwall offered a demi-head for £9.10.0 or a bust-head for £6.10.0 [10.15]. As can be seen in the illustration, the Surveyor's office indicated that only a bust was approved by drawing red lines across the sailor's arms. The figurehead has survived, despite being bombed in 1942 when he was ashore in Malta, and is now in the collection of the National Museum of the Royal Navy, Portsmouth. The carvers solved the problem of the amputated arms by putting the sailor's hat on his head!

10.14
HMS *Tourmaline* – lost Chatham *c*1948.
CROWN COPYRIGHT

23 TNA ADM 87/14 S1209 (1844).

10.15
HMS *Cruizer* – Hellyer design 1851.
THE NATIONAL ARCHIVES

CHAPTER 11

NINETEENTH-CENTURY FIGUREHEADS – FROM MYTHOLOGY

1 TNA ADM 87/68 S4040
   (1858).
2 TNA ADM 87/17 S613 (1847).
3 TNA ADM 87/16 S6465
   (1846).
4 *A Record of the Figureheads in
   H M Naval Establishments
   under Plymouth Command* –
   undated – but created in
   response to an Admiralty
   instruction of about 1936
   (Admiralty Library Ref Dh 20).

THE growth of the Royal Navy during the nineteenth century required the creation of a lot more ship names and many of these were chosen from Greek and Roman mythology. Whether the sailors who served in ships with such names knew the background to them is doubtful, but the carvers must have had access to reference books on the subject as they produced figureheads that ranged from beautiful women to fearsome monsters, many of which included in the trailboards subtle references to the myths.

Looking first at several of the beautiful women, Ariadne was the daughter of King Minos of Crete and, after her death, her wedding garland was placed in the sky as a constellation. When the 1859 HMS *Ariadne* wood screw frigate was launched at Deptford Dockyard, the Hellyers of Portsmouth carved a three-quarter-length bust with a coronet decorated with stars in the trailboards – still to be seen in the Historic Dockyard at Portsmouth.[1] Atalanta was a swift-footed huntress so, when the 1847 HMS *Atalanta* (16) was building at Pembroke Dock, the Hellyers of Portsmouth again carved a three-quarter-length bust but with a bow and arrow in the trailboards – still preserved in the National Maritime Museum's collection.[2] Arachne was skilled at weaving but challenged Athena, the patron goddess of weaving, to a competition and, for her presumption, was turned into a spider. With the 1846 HMS *Arachne* (18) building in Devonport Dockyard, Frederick Dickerson's design for her figurehead was approved and £5 was allowed.[3] The design has not survived, but when the ship was sold for breaking up the bust was taken into the Devonport collection and her photograph appeared in the pre-war photographic archive of figureheads in the Plymouth Command [11.1].[4] A post-war note in the album records that the figurehead was lost in the Blitz.

There were nine Muses, the daughters of Zeus – himself the supreme ruler of the Greek gods – each one being identified with one of the intellectual pursuits. The Admiralty used no less than six of them for ship names, five being in the

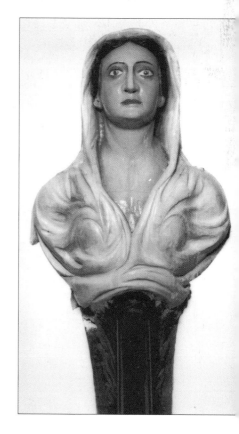

11.1
HMS *Arachne* – lost
Devonport 1941.

5   TNA ADM 87/7 – S91/8
    (1837).
6   TNA ADM 87/7 S781 & S917
    (1837).

7   TNA ADM 87/39 S5219
    (1852).

11.2
HMS *Calliope* – Robert Hall
design 1837.
THE NATIONAL ARCHIVES

nineteenth century. The first, Calliope, was the Muse of Epic Poetry and, when the 1837 HMS *Calliope* (28) was building in Sheerness Dockyard, designs were submitted by Robert Hall of Rotherhithe[5] and the Hellyers of Portsmouth.[6] Robert Hall had a loose style to his designs [11.2], offering that shown here for £7 with her book and horn, another with a lute and a third holding a book and a quill-pen. J E Hellyer submitted a rather more precise three-quarter-length figure with a wreath and a scroll [11.3] and it was his design that was approved, but only as a bust for £6. The second muse, Clio, was the Muse of History and, while it is known that the Hellyers carved a figurehead for the 1858 HMS *Clio* wood screw corvette for £20, the design has not survived. Melpomene was the Muse of Tragedy so the 1857 HMS *Melpomene* wood screw frigate was given a three-quarter-length crowned bust with a goblet and a dagger in the trailboards relating to the gruesome end of some tragedies.[7] Terpsichore was the Muse of Lyric Poetry or Dance and, having been built in the private yard of Wigram of Blackwall, the design for the figurehead of the 1847 HMS *Terpsichore*

11.3
HMS *Calliope* – J E Hellyer
design 1837.
THE NATIONAL ARCHIVES

8 *A Record of the Figureheads in H M Naval Establishments under Plymouth Command* – undated – but created in response to an Admiralty instruction of about 1936 (Admiralty Library Ref Dh 20).

9 'Old Figure-Heads', *The Navy and Army Illustrated* Vol 15 (1902–3).

10 TNA ADM 87/16 S4825 & 8034 (1846).

11.4
HMS *Thalia* – lost
Devonport c1947.
CROWN COPYRIGHT

(18) has not survived, but the figurehead – a demi-head holding a lyre – was initially in the Chatham collection but is now at HMS *President*, the headquarters of the London Division, Royal Naval Reserve [Colour Plate 14]. Last of the muses was Thalia, the Muse of Comedy, the figurehead for the 1869 HMS *Thalia* wood screw corvette being in the form of a three-quarter-length bust that was taken into the Devonport collection when the ship was sold for breaking up. As with HMS *Arachne* above, her photograph appeared in the pre-war photographic archive of figureheads in the Plymouth Command [11.4] but, in an additional note dated 1947, she was described as being in the advanced stages of rot and was destroyed.[8]

Sibyl was a mythical woman, said to express her oracles in riddles, and it was from a painting of Lady Hamilton dressed as a Sibyl that the figurehead of the 1847 HMS *Sybille* is claimed to have been based.[9] Designed by the Hellyers of Portsmouth in 1846,[10] the three-quarter-length bust was taken into the Devonport collection after the ship was taken to pieces there in 1866 but in the 1950s was transferred to HMS *Sea Eagle* in Londonderry. She remained there in what later became the army's Ebrington Barracks until 2003 when she returned to the Plymouth Naval Base Museum. The Hellyer design was only ordered by

11.5
HMS *Eurydice* - J E Hellyer design.
THE NATIONAL ARCHIVES

[11] TNA ADM 91/11 (1845).

the Surveyor of the Navy after an earlier figurehead carved by Frederick Dickerson of Devonport had been declared to be 'badly carved and out of all proportion'.[11] The design had been submitted in colour in 1844 but clearly the workmanship was not as good as the artistry [Colour Plate 15]. See also HMS *Constance* in Chapter 14.

One of the saddest stories told by the figurehead carvings is that of Eurydice, wife of Orpheus, the supreme minstrel of Greek mythology who played the lyre so beautifully that the whole of nature would listen entranced. One day Eurydice trod on a snake, was bitten and she died. Orpheus was heart-broken and found the passage to the Underworld where he charmed Charon, the ferryman, and Cerberus, the watchdog, with music and also Hades, god of the dead and ruler of the Underworld. Because of his music he was allowed to recover Eurydice providing he did not look back until he reached the upper air again. With the end of the tunnel in sight, Orpheus could not resist gazing at his wife's face and, having broken his promise, Eurydice was turned into a wraith of mist. The figurehead for the 1843 HMS *Eurydice* (24) was carved by J E Hellyer of Portsmouth, for which he was allowed £18.0.0.[12] He carved Eurydice reaching out for her husband with a look of despair on her face [11.5] and in the trailboards he told the rest of the story – a little imp grasps her dress to pull her back, while the snake that bit her makes good its escape.

Others who featured in the story of Eurydice also appeared in figureheads. Orpheus, her husband, was carved for the 1860 HMS *Orpheus* wood screw corvette by the Hellyers of Portsmouth as a bare-chested youth with a lyre in the trailboards.[13] They were allowed £20 for the work. Charon ferried the souls of the departed across the river Styx, so when the 1841 HMS *Styx* wood paddle sloop was launched at Sheerness Dockyard and the Hellyers submitted a design of a female bust, it was not approved and they were told to carve a figurehead representing the Devil. The figurehead that came ashore when the ship was broken up in 1866 was certainly one of the ugliest in the Devonport collection [11.6] as can be seen in the photograph that appeared in the pre-war photographic archive of figureheads in the Plymouth Command.[14] As with others in the collection, this also has a note saying that it was destroyed in the Blitz. As for Cerberus, the three-headed watchdog, when the 1827 HMS *Cerberus* was building in Plymouth Dockyard, the Dickersons submitted a design that showed the monster [11.7]. Despite it being a design that would have been a

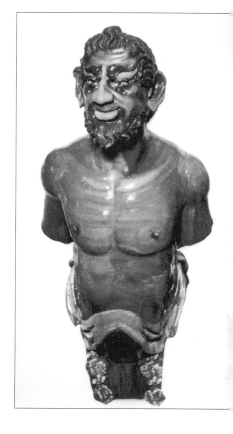

11.6
HMS *Styx* – lost Devonport 1941.
CROWN COPYRIGHT

[12]   TNA ADM 87/12 S5003 (1842).

[13]   TNA ADM 87/74 S1181 (1860).

[14]   *A Record of the Figureheads in H M Naval Establishments under Plymouth Command* – undated – but created in response to an Admiralty instruction of about 1936 (Admiralty Library Ref Dh 20).

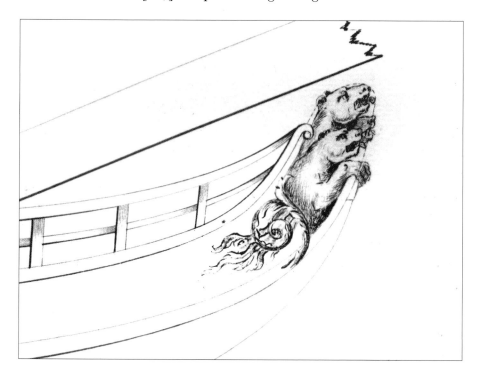

11.7
HMS *Cerberus* – Dickerson design 1822.
THE NATIONAL ARCHIVES

11.8
HMS *Belzebub* – Hellyer
design 1842.
THE NATIONAL ARCHIVES

15   TNA ADM 106/1946 (1822).

strong focus for the ship's company, the Surveyor's office did not approve it and instructed that a bust be carved in its place.[15] Finally, while there was no ship actually named Hades, the Admiralty got pretty close when, in 1842, it named a wooden paddle vessel building in Portsmouth Dockyard HMS *Belzebub*. The Hellyers of Portsmouth offered a bust design of the devil with horns and a set of pan-pipes in the trailboards for £8.10.0 that was accepted [11.8]. A month later, however, the ship's name was changed to HMS *Firebrand* and, presumably, the figurehead was changed to suit her new name.

Although the Dickersons were not allowed to carve a likeness of Cerberus as a figurehead, they included him in 1801 in the trailboard carvings of the figurehead for HMS *Hercules* (74) captured from the French three years earlier [11.9]. Hercules, the most popular of all the Greek heroes, is shown brandishing his olive-wood club and wearing the skin of the Nemean lion that he killed in the first of his twelve 'labours' and wore during the rest of his super-human tasks. The three-headed Cerberus with his restraining chain can be seen in the trailboard carving.

When Hercules was set the task of catching the huge Erymanthian boar, he came across the tribe of Centaurs who had the body and legs of a horse and the head, arms and torso of a man. The 1797 HMS *Centaur* (74) was built in Woolwich

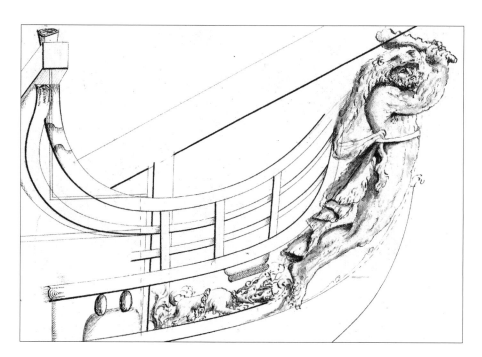

11.9 HMS *Hercules* – Dickerson design.

11.10 HMS *Centaur* – Dickerson design.

Dockyard but it was not until 1800 that James Dickerson of Devonport designed the full-length figurehead of the centaur brandishing his club [11.10]. The figurehead of the much smaller 1845 HMS *Centaur* wood paddle frigate is in the Plymouth Naval Base Museum collection.

As might be expected, a large number of the heroes from classical mythology were depicted as warriors in their figureheads. The Hellyers carved them to represent Agamemnon, Mars and Orestes, each with armour and a plumed helmet. Agamemnon was the commander of the Greek army at the siege of Troy and for the 1852 HMS *Agamemnon* (91) he was shown in a plate-mail tunic holding a scimitar and shield; £35 being allowed for the carving.[16] Mars was the Roman god of war and for the 1848 HMS *Mars* (80) he was shown in traditional armour, £36 being allowed [11.11].[17] Orestes was drawn for the 1860 HMS *Orestes* wood

16   TNA ADM 87/39 S1094
     (1851).

17   TNA ADM 87/17 S1293
     (1847).

**11.11
HMS *Mars* – Hellyer design
1847.**
THE NATIONAL ARCHIVES

11.12
HMS *Jason* – Dickerson design 1858.
DICKERSON ARCHIVE

screw corvette as a bust with a shield, spear and swords in the trailboards.[18] Two warrior figures are included in the Dickerson Archive in Australia depicting Jason and Perseus. The 1859 HMS *Jason* wood screw corvette was built in Devonport Dockyard and Frederick Dickerson submitted a warrior bust for approval, for which he was allowed £12 [11.12].[19] A light pencil grid has been drawn on the original design so that its detail could be scaled up for the figurehead itself, a technique that explains why the drawings were retained in Devonport rather than being returned to London with the letters of approval. The 1861 HMS *Perseus* wood screw sloop was given a similar bust of a warrior for which Frederick Dickerson was allowed £6.10.0.[20]

At the other end of the scale from the beautiful Muses were the Furies, hideous female spirits of justice and vengeance. An odd choice, perhaps, for warship names but both Alecto and Megaera appeared on the bows of Queen Victoria's navy. The 1839 HMS *Alecto* wood paddle sloop, built in Chatham Dockyard with a three-quarter-length snake-haired bust and a severed male head – also with

[18] TNA ADM 87/74 S2352 (1860).

[19] TNA ADM 88/14 S1919 (1858).

[20] TNA ADM 88/16 S2629 (1860).

21 TNA ADM 87/9 S630 (1839).

22 TNA ADM 87/7 S850 (1837).

snakes as his hair – in the trailboards, all carved by Hellyer and Browning of Portsmouth.[21] HMS *Megaera* wood paddle sloop had been launched two years earlier at Sheerness and was also fitted with a Hellyer and Browning figurehead but this one was carved in their Rotherhithe workshop.[22] For this ship they showed her as a demi-head holding a burning torch in one hand and a handful of snakes in the other [11.13].

Half-a-dozen surviving bust figureheads whose origins are in classical mythology deserve a mention. That from the 1809 HMS *Ajax* (74), carved as a bearded warrior with heavily-plumed helmet is in the collection of the National Maritime Museum. That from the 1805 HMS *Apollo* (38) – a sun god – shown stripped to the waist and wearing a wreath of laurel leaves, is in the collection of the National Museum of the Royal Navy. Those from the 1861 HMS *Aurora* wood screw frigate – the goddess of dawn, naked to the waist – and the 1856 HMS *Cadmus* wood screw corvette – the king of Thebes – crowned and wearing a plate-mail tunic [Colour Plate 16] are both in the collection of the Plymouth Naval Base Museum. That from the 1848 HMS *Leander* (50) [Colour Plate 17] is at HMS *Collingwood* in Hampshire. That from the 1844 HMS *Flora* (36) – the goddess of springtime and flowers – three-quarter-length with flowers in her hair, is in the collection of the South African Naval Museum, Simon's Town. The photograph of another figurehead attributed to HMS *Aurora* was included

11.13
HMS *Megaera* – Hellyer & Browning design 1837.
THE NATIONAL ARCHIVES

in the Devonport pre-war photographic archive [11.14].[23] The accompanying notes acknowledged that there was another figurehead in the album from HMS *Aurora* and sought clarification. This figurehead appears to have been lost soon after the war.

Involvement with water was evident in some of the myths, three examples being Amphitrite, Arethusa and Calypso. Amphitrite was the wife of Poseidon, principal Greek god of the sea so when the 1816 HMS *Amphitrite* (26) was cut down to a corvette in 1846, she was given a three-quarter-length female bust with a sea-shell in her hair and a dolphin in the trailboards, the Hellyers of Portsmouth being allowed £14 for the work.[24] Arethusa was a wood-nymph who was turned into a spring so the 1849 HMS *Arethusa* (50) was given a three-quarter-length female bust with the spring-water flowing in the trailboards [11.15]. For this, the Hellyers of Portsmouth were allowed £24.[25] Calypso was a sea-nymph who lived on the mythical island of Ogygia on which Odysseus was shipwrecked when returning home from Troy. When the 1845 HMS *Calypso* (20) was built in Chatham Dockyard she was given a naked female bust rising from a base of bulrushes and also with a sea-shell in her hair. The Hellyers were allowed £12 for the work.[26]

11.14 (ABOVE)
Attributed to HMS *Aurora* – Devonport *c*1936.
CROWN COPYRIGHT

11.15 (ABOVE LEFT)
HMS *Arethusa* – Hellyer design 1847.
THE NATIONAL ARCHIVES

[23] *A Record of the Figureheads in H M Naval Establishments under Plymouth Command –* undated – but created in response to an Admiralty instruction of about 1936 (Admiralty Library Ref Dh 20).

[24] TNA ADM 87/15 S5009 (1845).

[25] TNA ADM 87/17 S613 (1847).

[26] TNA ADM 87/13 S7017 (1843).

CHAPTER 12

NINETEENTH-CENTURY FIGUREHEADS – OCCUPATIONS

1 Andrew Lambert, *Warrior – Restoring the World's First Ironclad* (Conway Maritime Press, 1987).
2 TNA ADM 88/16 S5187 (1860).
3 TNA ADM 91/24 (1860).
4 J G Wells, 'The *Warrior*'s Figureheads', *The Mariner's Mirror* Vol 69 (1983), p 268.

**12.1
Figurehead of a warrior – lost Devonport 1941.**

I N a book that is analysing the figureheads of warships, it is not surprising that warriors in one form or another appear in several of its chapters. Under the heading of 'Mythology' for example, the figurehead for HMS *Mars* – the God of War – was a prime candidate, and HMS *Defiance* will be found amongst other warriors in the chapter on 'Qualities'.

The only nineteenth-century HMS *Warrior*, however, is the iron-hulled armoured ship now fully restored and open to the public in the Historic Dockyard, Portsmouth.[1] Built at Blackwall on the Thames by the Thames Iron Shipbuilding Co and launched in 1860, her figurehead was carved by James Hellyer & Son who had a workshop in Blackwall and had offered the shipbuilder alternative designs for her figurehead.[2] The design was only approved four months before the ship was launched so there must have been some urgent work to meet the date.[3] It appears that the original figurehead was destroyed in a collision with HMS *Royal Oak* off Portland in 1868 and a replacement was carved again by the Hellyers.[4] This second figurehead was brought ashore in 1900, before *Warrior* became part of the torpedo school as *Vernon III,* and was placed immediately inside the main entrance to Portsmouth Dockyard where he stood for the next sixty years. In 1963 when the fleet headquarters at Northwood was named HMS *Warrior*, the figurehead was moved there but by then it was in the final stages of decay and it was destroyed. When the ship herself was handed over to the Maritime Trust in 1979, a third figurehead was commissioned. Carved at Cowes on the Isle of Wight by Jack Whitehead and Norman Gaches, it can now be seen mounted on the ship's bow.

While figureheads are normally known by the name of the ship for which they were carved, there are occasions when the ship's identity has been forgotten and the figurehead is given the descriptive name of what it looks like. This is probably what happened to the next warrior figurehead [12.1]. His photograph appeared in the photographic archive of figureheads in the Plymouth Command in which he is referred to as 'Warrior' but a pencil note states that no records are available.[5] He was only 1ft 6in tall and was sited in the Captain of the Dockyard's Boatswain's Store. A further post-war pencil note records that he was 'lost in the Blitz'.

As the commander in the Roman army of 100 men, the 'centurion' had a particular role in life and two nineteenth-century ships were named after his occupation. First was the 1844 HMS *Centurion* (80), built in Pembroke Dockyard. The records show that the Hellyers of Portsmouth carved the figurehead but neither the design drawing nor the estimate is filed with the letters of approval.[6] There is, however, in the Topsham Museum on the Exe estuary the bust of a warrior in plumed helmet and decorated armour that has always been understood to have come from the 1844 ship [Colour Plate 18]. He was mounted for many years on the end of a house in Topsham that had once been the sail-loft of a local shipbuilding yard and was saved in the early years of this century when it was evident that his condition was deteriorating. A fibreglass replica was made for the house so that the original could be restored by the museum. The second HMS *Centurion* battleship was built in Portsmouth Dockyard and launched there in 1892, by which time the capital ships of the Royal Navy were being built of steel in a very modern style and looked very uncomfortable with a figurehead. However, *Centurion* and her sister-ship HMS *Barfleur* were each given one until their mid-life reconstruction, the bust of the centurion in a helmet and a plate-mail tunic standing vertically just in front of the jack-staff. When removed from his ship, the centurion was taken into the then Dockyard Museum at Portsmouth and is now on display at the National Museum of the Royal Navy there.

Another ship's name that recognised the fighting skills of old was the 1844 HMS *Gladiator* wood paddle frigate, built in Woolwich Dockyard. Hellyer & Son of Portsmouth offered to carve a demi-head for £12.10.0 or a bust for £8.10.0, the design for the latter being a strapping young man, stripped to the waist. The bust was approved.[7] A replacement must have been required during the ship's thirty-five years service as the figurehead that was preserved in Devonport after she was broken up was entirely different, being a bust in the form of a warrior in a heavily-plumed helmet and a plate-mail tunic [12.2]. Early photographs of the Royal Naval Barracks at Keyham show the figurehead under the mast there and this would explain why this carving was not included in the 1911 Admiralty Catalogue, it being separated from the bulk of the collection in the dockyard. His photograph also appeared in the pre-war photographic

5   *A Record of the Figureheads in H M Naval Establishments under Plymouth Command* – undated – but created in response to an Admiralty instruction of about 1936 (Admiralty Library Ref Dh 20).
6   TNA ADM 87/13 S6098 (1843).
7   TNA ADM 87/14 S503 (1844).

12.2
HMS *Gladiator* – lost **Devonport 1947.**
CROWN COPYRIGHT

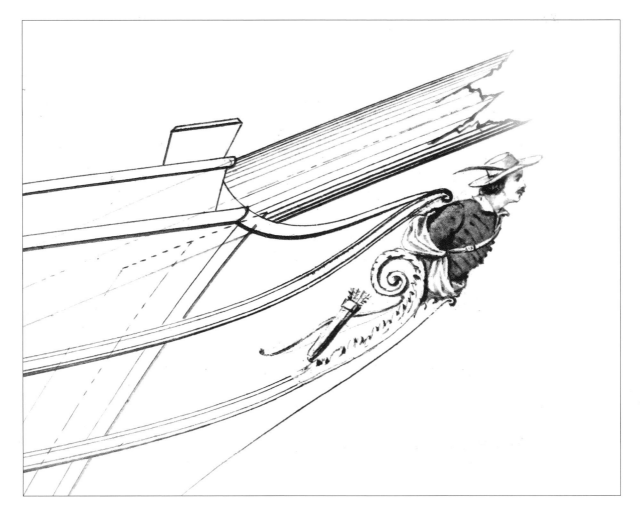

12.3
HMS *Archer* – Hellyer design
1848.

8   *A Record of the Figureheads in*
    H M Naval Establishments
    under Plymouth Command –
    undated – but created in
    response to an Admiralty
    instruction of about 1936
    (Admiralty Library Ref Dh
    20).
9   TNA ADM 87/21 S6220
    (1848).
10 TNA ADM 87/15 S5009
    (1845).

archive of figureheads in the Plymouth Command.[8]

Everyday occupations were represented in the names of small ships. The 1849 HMS *Archer* wood screw sloop was built in Deptford Dockyard with the bust of man wearing a stylish hat and a quiver full of arrows in the trailboard [12.3], the design having been submitted by Hellyer & Son of Portsmouth with an estimate of £8.10.0.[9] The 1846 HMS *Rifleman* wood screw gunvessel was built in Portsmouth Dockyard, the Hellyers of Portsmouth again offered a design [12.4] and, even though it was unusual for such a small ship to have a standing figure as its figurehead, the drawing shows that it was 'Approved' on 2 September on behalf of the Surveyor.[10] The reference number 'S5009' refers to the line in the Surveyor of the Navy's 'Register of In-Letters relating to ships' and it can also be seen that in addition the Hellyers hoped that the design might be approved for HMS *Sharpshooter* iron screw gunvessel then building at the yard of Ditchburn & Mare at Blackwall on the Thames. The suggestion has been

12.4
HMS *Rifleman* – Hellyer
design 1845.
THE NATIONAL ARCHIVES

deleted in the Surveyor's office, probably because the cost of the figurehead for a ship building in this private yard would have been included in the overall contract for building the ship,

Two ships of the nineteenth century were named *Driver* and their figureheads show how the nation's transport developed over the first half of the century. The 1797 HMS *Driver* sloop was built in Bermuda but the design submitted by Edward Hellyer & Son of Portsmouth was not offered until 1814 and was thus, presumably, a replacement.[11] It is a bust of a uniformed driver with the royal cipher 'GR' on his hat and a cutlass and pistol in the trailboards [12.5], combining the formality and the potential hazards of the stage-coach. It would only have been a small carving as the estimate for its creation was only £4. The next ship to bear the name was the 1840 HMS *Driver* wood paddle sloop launched in Portsmouth Dockyard. It was again the Hellyers who offered a design, but on this occasion it was a male bust wearing a formal hat and cape, reminiscent of the hansom cab drivers, by then very popular in the streets of London [12.6].[12] The estimate for this work was £6. Amongst the ships that

[11] TNA ADM 106/1887 (1814).

12.5
HMS *Driver* – Hellyer design 1814.

12.6
HMS *Driver* – Hellyer design 1840.

12.7
HMS *Pilot* – Dickerson design 1836.

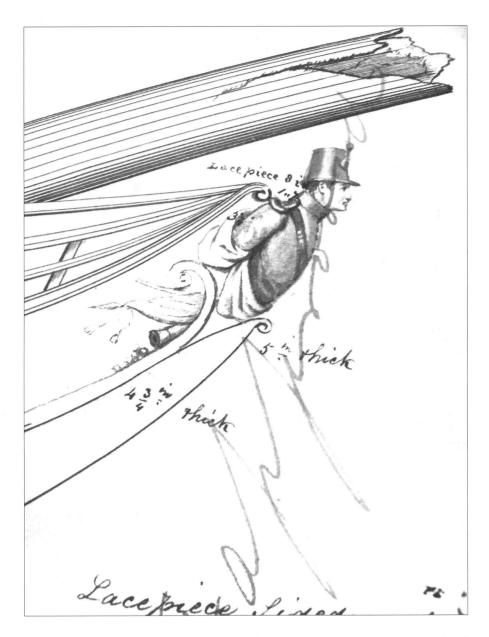

12.8
HMS *Scout* – Hellyer design
1855.
THE NATIONAL ARCHIVES

were building at the time and for which figurehead designs were being offered was HMS *Growler* wood paddle sloop building in Chatham Dockyard. The 'growler' was the name given at the time to the four-wheeled heavier version of the hansom cab, so the carvers could well have offered another bust representing its driver. However, they volunteered either a dog's head at £9 or a demi-head of a sailor at £8 and the latter wearing a boater with the name 'GROWLER' across his chest was approved.[13]

There were three nineteenth-century small ships named *Pilot* as this was a role on which every captain relied. The first was built in a private yard at

12 TNA ADM 87/10 S5644 (1840).
13 TNA ADM 87/10 S5101 (1840).

12.9
HMS *Scout* – lost
HMS *Cambridge* c1960.

14   TNA ADM 87/6 S5246
     (1836).
15   TNA ADM 87/56 (1855).
16   *Catalogue of Pictures,
     Presentation Plate,
     Figureheads, Models, Relics
     and Trophies at the Admiralty;
     on board H.M.Ships; and in
     the Naval Establishments at
     Home and Abroad* (London,
     April 1911).
17   *Figureheads in Dockyard,
     Royal Naval Barracks and
     Royal Naval Hospital,
     Chatham 1938* (D 9270/38).
18   *Figureheads at Chatham
     31:12:48 Part I H.M.Dockyard
     Part II RN Barracks, St
     Marys, Collingwood, RN
     Hospital and RN Armament
     Depot Upnor.*

Northam in 1807 and it is not, therefore, surprising that no records exist on her figurehead. The second HMS *Pilot* (16) was launched in Plymouth Dockyard in 1838, her design being one of Frederick Dickerson's early submissions, forwarded in 1836 with an estimate of five guineas 'as that had been allowed for HM Ships *Ringdove* and *Sappho* in 1832'.[14] That for *Pilot* showed the demi-head of a pilot holding a lead-line [12.7]. The third HMS *Pilot* (training brig 8) was built at Pembroke Dock in 1879 and had a demi-head dressed in a peak cap and gold-buttoned uniform jacket that shows just how far uniform had progressed during the century. The figurehead is in the collection of the Vancouver Maritime Museum, British Columbia.

Scout was another appropriate name for small and agile vessels and so when the 1855 HMS *Scout* wood screw corvette was building in Woolwich Dockyard, the superintendent forwarded two Hellyer designs.[15] The first was a bust in military uniform with a cannon and colours in the trailboards [12.8] but the endorsement across the drawing shows that it was 'Not Approved'. The second was a female bust with her right breast exposed and flowing hair but with no particular reference to the ship's name; despite this, the design was approved for £10. When the ship was taken to pieces at Chatham in 1877, her figurehead was added to that collection where it was included in the 1911 Admiralty Catalogue.[16] Photographed there for the 1938[17] and 1948[18] musters [12.9], she was at first in the Dockyard Museum and then at the RN Hospital, being transferred to HMS *Cambridge*, the gunnery range near Plymouth in 1960, this being her last move before being lost.

CHAPTER 13

NINETEENTH-CENTURY FIGUREHEADS – PRIZE AND COMMEMORATIVE NAMES

I N the latter part of the eighteenth century, numerous enemy ships were captured and, if they were fit for further service, they were added to the Royal Navy's strength. If a prize name was not too difficult to pronounce in English and, if the name was not already in use in the fleet, it was usually left unchanged. Thereafter, the name was treated as an ordinary British ship's name, being passed on to her successor when she had completed her active service. Thus there were many nineteenth-century ships that bore unusual names, creating in their turn challenges to the figurehead carvers tasked with interpreting them.

13.1
HMS *Arrogant* – **Hellyer design 1846.**
THE NATIONAL ARCHIVES

The 1848 HMS *Arrogant* wood screw frigate was built in Portsmouth Dockyard, her name coming from a French prize captured in 1705. The Hellyers of Portsmouth submitted a design in 1846 of a three-quarter-length female figure, the allusion to arrogance being a peacock in the trailboards [13.1].[1] They were allowed £24 for the work.

The 1855 HMS *Chesapeake* wood screw frigate was built in Chatham Dockyard, her name coming from the famous 1813 single-ship action between the two fairly evenly-matched vessels, HMS *Shannon* (38) and the American *Chesapeake*, in which the *Chesapeake* was taken within sight of Boston. It was again the Hellyers of Portsmouth who carved her figurehead, submitting a design that represented the Chesapeake tribe of North American Indians [13.2].[2] When she was sold for breaking up in 1867, her figurehead was mounted just inside the main gate

[1] TNA ADM 87/16 S7691 (1846).

[2] TNA ADM 87/52 S1861 (1855).

13.2
HMS *Chesapeake* – Hellyer design 1855.
THE NATIONAL ARCHIVES

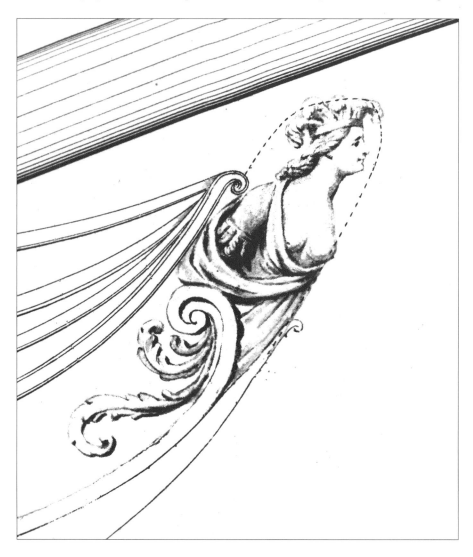

of Sheerness Dockyard[3] and later was listed in the 1911 Admiralty Catalogue.[4] Attempts to protect the Sheerness figureheads with small individual roofs were not successful and by the time *Chesapeake* was in the care of the Medway Ports Authority she was in a state of collapse. A replica has been carved by Andrew Peters of Maritima Woodcarving that incorporates as many pieces of the original as was possible, intended for Blue Town Museum, Isle of Sheppey.

The 1845 HMS *Creole* (26) was built in Devonport Dockyard, her name coming from a French prize captured in the West Indies in 1803. The figurehead for the 1845 ship is known to have been carved by Frederick Dickerson but neither his design nor his estimate has survived.[5] The ship was taken to pieces in Devonport in 1875 and her figurehead was placed in the Rigging House collection.[6] Her photograph appears in the pre-war photographic archive of

3 'Sheerness Dockyard', *The Navy & Army Illustrated* Vol 13 (1901).

4 *Catalogue of Pictures, Presentation Plate, Figureheads, Models, Relics and Trophies at the Admiralty; on board H.M.Ships; and in the Naval Establishments at Home and Abroad* (London, April 1911).

5 TNA ADM 88/5 S7018 and 91/11 (1843).

6 Owen, 'Figureheads', p 325.

13.3
HMS *Creole* – lost at Devonport 1941.
CROWN COPYRIGHT

13.4
HMS *Espoir* – Dickerson design 1859.
DICKERSON ARCHIVE

13.5
HMS *Magicienne* – lost at
Devonport 1941.
CROWN COPYRIGHT

7   *A Record of the Figureheads in
    H M Naval Establishments
    under Plymouth Command* –
    undated – but created in
    response to an Admiralty
    instruction of about 1936
    (Admiralty Library Ref Dh 20).
8   TNA ADM 88/15 S2447 (1859).
9   TNA ADM 106/1886 (1812).
10 TNA ADM 87/19 S4474 (1848).
11 *Catalogue of Pictures,
    Presentation Plate, Figureheads,
    Models, Relics and Trophies at
    the Admiralty; on board
    H.M.Ships; and in the Naval
    Establishments at Home and
    Abroad* (London, April 1911).
12 *A Record of the Figureheads in
    H M Naval Establishments
    under Plymouth Command* –
    undated – but created in
    response to an Admiralty
    instruction of about 1936
    (Admiralty Library Ref Dh 20).

figureheads in the Plymouth Command, a useful record as a manuscript addition states that she was 'Destroyed in the Blitz' [13.3].[7]

The 1860 HMS *Espoir* wood screw gunvessel was built in Pembroke Dockyard, her name coming from the French brig-sloop captured by HMS *Thalia* in the Mediterranean in 1804. When Frederick Dickerson of Devonport submitted his design for the 1860 ship's figurehead he made the connection between the French 'espoir', the English 'hope' and the tradition of Hope with her anchor – proposing a three-quarter-length female bust with an anchor in the trailboards [13.4]. The design was approved, the carver was allowed £6 and his very small drawing now resides in the Dickerson Archive in Australia.[8] Reference is also made to Hope and her anchor in Chapter 14.

The 1812 HMS *Lacedaemonian* (38) was built in Portsmouth Dockyard. Her predecessor was a French privateer, *Lacedemonienne*, that had been captured by HM Ships *Pique* and *Charon* in the West Indies in 1796 and, despite the difficulty that the ship's company must have had with the name, it was continued with this the second ship in 1812. With Lacedaemonian being an alternative to Spartan, the carvers – Edward Hellyer & Son – chose the bust of a warrior as the figurehead with trophies of war in the trailboards, using colour in their design [Colour Plate 19]. The estimate for the work was £7 but only £6 was allowed.[9]

The 1849 HMS *Magicienne* wood paddle frigate was built in Pembroke Dockyard, her name coming from the French frigate *Magicienne*, captured by HMS *Chatham* in North American waters in 1781. The design for the 1849 ship was submitted by the Hellyers of Portsmouth in 1848, being a female three-quarter-length bust with an open book in the trailboards for which they were allowed £9.10.0.[10] The ship was sold for breaking up in Plymouth in 1866 but her figurehead was removed and was placed in the Devonport collection.[11] As with the *Creole* figurehead, her photograph appears in the pre-war archive,[12] another fortunate record as a manuscript addition states that she was 'Destroyed in the Blitz' [13.5].

Moving now to 'Commemorative Names', the 1858 HMS *Donegal* (screw 101) was built in Devonport Dockyard, her name being a tribute to an action off the Donegal coast in 1798. The French had been attempting to land troops in Ireland to take advantage of unrest there but were intercepted by the Royal Navy. Several French ships were taken, the largest being the *Hoche* and it was she who became the first HMS *Donegal*. It was again the Dickersons who offered two alternative designs for the 1858 ship, a female three-quarter-length bust with flowers and

13.6
HMS *Donegal* – **Dickerson design 1855.**
DICKERSON ARCHIVE

shamrock leaves in her hair or a male bust in naval uniform [13.6]. The latter was approved and the carvers were allowed £35 for the work.[13] There are no clues in the design that would help to identify the figure but it is probably intended to represent Commodore Sir John Warren who commanded the British squadron in 1798. Both designs are now preserved in the Dickerson Archive in Australia.

The 1815 HMS *Java* (50) was built in Plymouth Dockyard, the third ship of the name. The first two ships called *Java* were prizes – the Dutch *Maria Reijgersbergen*, taken off the Java coast in 1806, and the French *Renommée*, taken off Madagascar in 1811. A figurehead design for the 1815 ship was submitted from Plymouth in 1814 with an estimate of £14; James Dickerson was the resident carver at the time.[14] The design has not survived but references to it have: the Surveyor only allowed £8, saying that the *Java* approximated to the 30-gun frigates for which only £6 was allowed. In 1832 a replacement was required and a design, submitted by Portsmouth, was approved.[15] By 1846 another replacement figurehead was called for and the Hellyers of Portsmouth forwarded a design [13.7] that was approved at £18 and it is assumed that this survived for

13 TNA ADM 88/11 & 12 S3081 (1855).

14 TNA ADM 106/1942 (1814).

15 TNA ADM 91/6 (1832).

13.7
HMS *Java* – **Hellyer design 1846.**
THE NATIONAL ARCHIVES

[16] TNA ADM 87/16 S7060 (1846).

[17] TNA ADM 106/1886 (1812).

the rest of her service.[16] The report of the 1840 fire in Devonport Dockyard that destroyed the Adelaide Gallery and all its relics records that the figurehead of HMS *Java* was amongst those lost – presumably the original figurehead of the 1811 ship. See Chapter 3 for a brief account of the fire.

When the French frigate *Néreide* was captured in 1811 she had to be given a new name as there was already an HMS *Nereide* in the Royal Navy, her name having its origin in an action of 1797. As the 1811 capture took place off Tamatave on the island of Madagascar, she was taken into service as HMS *Madagascar* (38). In 1812, Edward Hellyer & Son of Portsmouth forwarded a design for her figurehead in the form of a bust of an African male with a cornucopia of tropical fruits in the trailboards [Colour Plate 20]. The design was approved, the carver being allowed £6 for the work.[17] The second HMS *Madagascar* (46) was built in Bombay Dockyard in 1822 and probably had a very similar figurehead, part of which has survived. The ship had spent the last ten years of her life as the receiving ship at Rio de Janeiro and it was there that she was sold in 1863. The donor who gave the head of this figurehead to the Royal Naval Museum in 1995 understands that one of his ancestors who lived in Brazil at the time found the figurehead being burned on a bonfire and was only able to save the

13.8
HMS *Meeanee* – Hellyer
design 1859.
THE NATIONAL ARCHIVES

head! When it returned to the UK is not known but it was restored in 1996 by Allan Mechen of Southampton, who confirmed that the figure is carved in teak – supporting evidence of her Indian origin.

The 1848 HMS *Meeanee* (80) was built in Bombay Dockyard. Originally laid down as HMS *Madras*, she was renamed in 1843 to commemorate Sir Charles Napier's subjugation of the Indian province of Sindh that year. Her original figurehead, when the ship was still named *Madras*, was one of four that were carved by the Hellyers of Portsmouth as was described in Chapter 2. In 1859, the Superintendent at Sheerness reported that *Meeanee*'s figurehead was rotten and that Messrs Hellyer had asked for the defective parts to be sent to them as a guide for the replacement.[18] The resulting design [13.8] was approved and the estimate of £40 was accepted, the similarity between it and that for *Madras* being evident despite the passing of fifteen years.[19]

The 1810 HMS *Minden* (74) was also built in Bombay Dockyard, named to commemorate the victory of the British and Prussian armies over the French in 1759, according to Manning and Walker.[20] *Minden* was the ship that was in dock in Plymouth Yard, immediately astern of HMS *Talavera* when the latter was destroyed in the 1840 fire – see Chapter 3 for details. While *Minden* herself

[18] TNA ADM 88/15 S6151 (1859).

[19] TNA ADM 87/72 S7467 (1859).

[20] Manning and Walker, *British Warship Names*.

13.9
HMS *Minden* – Dickerson
design 1841.

21   TNA ADM 87/11 S5824
(1841).

22   TNA ADM 91/14 and 88/9
S5368 (1852).

was saved, her figurehead was lost and a replacement design was submitted by Frederick Dickerson in 1841.[21] The design shows a warrior figure of ages past [13.9] and not of the 1750s so perhaps the carver understood the name to commemorate the much earlier battle of Minden during the Roman Empire's Germanic Wars. The design is preserved in the Dickerson Archive in Australia.

Another design in the Dickerson Archive is that for the figurehead of the 1853 HMS *St Jean d'Acre* (screw 101), built in Devonport Dockyard, her name commemorating the bombardment and capture of Acre on the shores of the eastern Mediterranean in 1840 [13.10]. The city had been called 'St Jean d'Acre' by the crusaders under King Richard I who, in 1191, had captured it and it is that event to which the carver alluded in his design. The design was approved and Dickerson was allowed £36 for the work.[22]

The 1819 HMS *Seringapatam* (46) was built in Bombay Dockyard, her name commemorating the victory of Sir Arthur Wellesley, governor-general of India, over Tipu Sultan, the ruler of Mysore, in 1799. It is not clear how the figurehead

13.10
HMS *St Jean d'Acre* –
Dickerson design 1852.
DICKERSON ARCHIVE

from this ship came to be in the Devonport collection as she became the coal depot and receiving ship at the Cape of Good Hope and was broken up there in 1883. However, a photograph of part of the Devonport collection in the fire-engine house taken in 1897 shows Tipu Sultan, complete with his umbrella, beside that of HMS *Black Prince*.[23] The figurehead was listed in the 1911 Admiralty catalogue, and in 1936 was one of the figureheads given by Their Lordships as part of the core collection of the National Maritime Museum, Greenwich [Colour Plate 21].[24] Riding on the back of a mythical bird, a 'roc', he adds a splash of Indian colour to that collection.

[23] 'The Figurehead and its Story', *The Navy & Army Illustrated* (1897).
[24] *Catalogue of Pictures, Presentation Plate, Figureheads, Models, Relics and Trophies at the Admiralty; on board H.M.Ships; and in the Naval Establishments at Home and Abroad* (London, April 1911).

CHAPTER 14

——◆◇◆——

NINETEENTH-CENTURY FIGUREHEADS – QUALITIES

PERHAPS the most telling ship names in the nineteenth century were those that defined the qualities that Lords of the Admiralty required in the fleet. Some of them were admirable qualities and some had interesting interpretations by the carvers.

We have seen in Chapter 5 that the 1765 HMS *Victory* was fitted with a group figurehead of some complexity. The question that has caused much debate over the years is what was the figurehead that was fitted at the time of Trafalgar and, in particular, was it similar to that seen today except that a marine and a sailor were the 'supporters' rather than the two cherubs? That such a design existed was given credibility by articles that circulated in the London newspapers in 1806 reporting that, as a result of the action at Trafalgar, the sailor supporter lost an arm and the marine supporter lost a leg. The articles continued that 'all men who lost arms on board the *Victory* were sailors and those who lost legs were marines' and, with such fascinating coincidence, the story was given credibility.[1] As will be seen in the Bibliography and Sources, the contested design was illustrated in one of the cigarette cards issued by John Player & Sons in 1912 but, in a report to the Victory Technical Committee in 1924, it was stated that 'the preponderance of evidence is in favour of the cupids having been given to the ship in 1803'.[2] Letters that were seen by the Curator of the Dockyard Museum in 1969 confirm that cherubs supported the royal arms at the time of Trafalgar and finally disproved the suggestion of 'sailor and marine' supporters.[3]

The 1845 HMS *Active* (36) was built in Chatham Dockyard. Frederick Dickerson of Devonport submitted a design in the form of a bust of Hermes, messenger to Zeus the supreme king of the gods, wearing the distinctive winged helmet.[4] A pencil addition beside the design shows the herald's staff with its entwined snakes that Hermes used to carry and a note that it could be added in the trailboards. Although this would appear to be a suitable representation for the name *Active*, the Surveyor did not give his approval and invited the

[1] Edward Fraser, 'HMS *Victory*', *The Mariner's Mirror* Vol VIII (1922), p 299.

[2] L G Carr Laughton, 'Report to the *Victory* Technical Committee of a search among the Admiralty records', *The Mariner's Mirror* Vol X (1924), pp 197–201.

[3] A J Pack, 'The figurehead of HMS *Victory* at the time of Trafalgar', *The Mariner's Mirror* Vol 55 (1969), pp 451–2.

[4] TNA ADM 87/14 S2602 (1844).

14.1
HMS *Active* **- Hellyer design**
1845.

Hellyers of Rotherhithe to submit a design. The Hellyer design was a bust of the young Queen Victoria [14.1] and, even though the estimate was for £16, and thus £6 more than that offered by the Dickersons, it was approved.[5] As will be seen from the Directory, a figurehead from this ship survives, having been removed when she was broken up at Bo'ness. It is a female three-quarter-length figure holding a rose in her right hand but when this figure replaced that of

5 TNA ADM 91/11 (1845).

Queen Victoria is not known.

The name *Constance* was given to four nineteenth-century ships, the one that was launched in Pembroke Dockyard in 1846 being a Fourth Rate (50). The design that was offered by Frederick Dickerson of Devonport was unusual in that it was submitted in colour, a feature that was presumably intended to help the Surveyor of the Navy to approve it [Colour Plate 22].[6] The design was approved, but a year later – and well before the ship was launched – it was reported that the figurehead was 'badly carved and out of all proportion', so the Admiral Superintendent at Devonport was ordered to return the designs and to report who had examined the bust on its completion.[7] Mr Hellyer at Portsmouth was ordered to carve a replacement and it is this carving that is today at HMS *Excellent* on Whale Island, Portsmouth [Colour Plate 23].

The 1864 HMS *Enterprise* ironclad sloop was built in Deptford Dockyard and, as can be seen from the design drawing [14.2], had a bow profile that would only just accommodate a figurehead. Enterprise has been interpreted as requiring force as the warrior is well protected and carries a hefty weapon. The design was submitted by Frederick Dickerson in May 1863 and, although the Navy Board records for the period do not exist, the drawing in the Dickerson Archive in Australia carries the reference 'DM 3803'.

Urgent iron screw troopship was bought in 1855 whilst on the stocks at the

[6] TNA ADM 87/14 S1278 & 1476 (1844).

[7] TNA ADM 91/11 (1845).

14.2
HMS *Enterprise* – Dickerson design 1863.
DICKERSON ARCHIVE

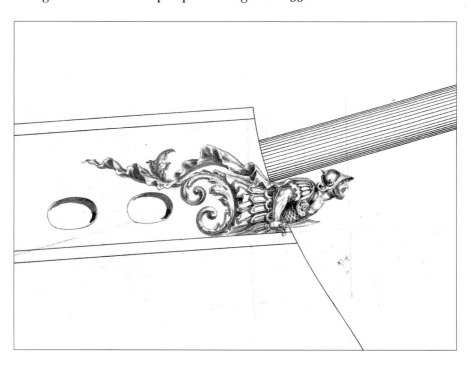

**14.3
HMS *Urgent* - at Bermuda,
date unknown.**
RICHARD HUNTER ARCHIVES

C J Mare shipyard of Blackwall. After twenty years of active service, she became the depot ship at Jamaica in 1876 and it was there that her figurehead was landed when she was sold in 1903. Soon after that the figurehead was transferred to the Royal Dockyard, Bermuda where she can be seen to be in good condition [14.3]. The Chief Constructor, Bermuda Yard produced an annotated photograph album of the local figureheads in 1948 that showed how much the figurehead had deteriorated; her right arm being completely missing as was much of her left hand.[8] When the Bermuda dockyard was closed in 1952 the *Urgent* figurehead, with three others, were shipped to Canada, *Urgent* being sent to HMCS *Cornwallis*. She succumbed to rot in the late 1960s.

Not surprisingly, many of the qualities that were used in ship names demanded a fearsome figurehead. The 1847 HMS *Dauntless* wood screw frigate, built in Portsmouth Dockyard, was given a very realistic standing lion, his fore-paws resting on the Royal arms with a rose, thistle and shamrock in the trailboards. The design by Hellyer & Son was approved for £18.[9]

[8] *Figureheads – H M Dockyard Bermuda (1948)* – Admiralty Library Dh 21.

[9] TNA ADM 87/16 S7691 (1846).

The 1861 HMS *Defiance* (screw 81) was built in Pembroke Dockyard for which the Hellyers of Portsmouth had submitted a design in the form of a warrior bust [14.4] with an estimate of £40.[10] The Surveyor's office was reluctant to approve this warrior figure as a similar one had been carved in 1855 for HMS *Repulse* but had not been fitted when her name was changed to *Victor Emanuel*. The Hellyers were asked how much it would cost for the *Repulse* carving to be altered to fit *Defiance* and their estimate of £4 was accepted. The rather softer design [14.5] that had been submitted in 1855 wearing a beard and with a shield in the trailboards was fitted and still survives in the Plymouth Naval Base Museum.

The 1825 HMS *Formidable* (84) was built in Chatham dockyard from frames that had been captured on the stocks in Genoa in 1814. After her sea-service she was employed as a training ship at Portishead until she was broken up by

10   TNA ADM 87/71 S2097 &
2348 (1859).

14.4
HMS *Defiance* – **Hellyer design 1859.**
THE NATIONAL ARCHIVES

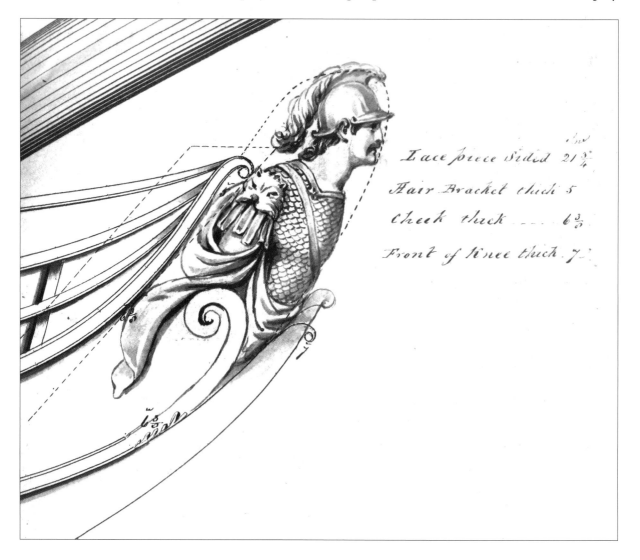

Castles' Shipbreaking Company in 1906. Her figurehead was kept in their collection and was sold to an American field representative in 1939, almost certainly saving it from destruction during the London Blitz. It is now in the Mariners' Museum, Newport News, Virginia [14.6].

HMS *Irresistible* was laid down in Chatham Dockyard in 1849, was re-ordered in 1854 and was eventually launched there as a screw Second Rate (80) in 1859. With such a name, Hellyer & Son of Portsmouth submitted a powerful representation of Zeus, the supreme ruler of the Greek gods and always associated with the weather, crowned and holding in his right hand a thunderbolt [14.7]. The design was approved, as was his estimate of £35.[11] After various duties in home waters, *Irresistible* became the depot ship at Bermuda in 1868 and was broken up there in 1894. On coming ashore, the figurehead stood for

11 TNA ADM 87/39 S4795 and
    91/14 (1851).

14.5
HMS *Repulse* – Hellyer design 1855 – fitted to HMS *Defiance*.
THE NATIONAL ARCHIVES

14.6
HMS *Formidable* – Newport News, Virginia 2011.
THE MARINERS' MUSEUM

14.7
HMS *Irresistible* – **Hellyer design 1851.**
THE NATIONAL ARCHIVES

12 A W, 'Figure Heads in the West Indies', *The Mariner's Mirror* Vol VII (1921), p 25.

many years at Clarence Cove, his photograph appearing in the 1921 *Mariner's Mirror*.[12] Having lost both arms he was given new ones and, probably for the first time, a trident. Thus it was that he was thought of as a representation of Neptune. In 1974 he was moved to the Keep in Bermuda Dockyard that subsequently became the Bermuda Maritime Museum but because of his gradual deterioration a decision was made to have a stone replica made for the museum. The figurehead was shipped back to the UK where in his Bristol studio the sculptor Laurence Tindall carved the replica for Bermuda, after which the remains of the original were sent to Chatham Historic Dockyard for a long programme of restoration.

HMS *Vengeance* could equally have been included in the chapter on Prize Names as the first British ship of that name had been the French privateer *La Vengeance*, captured in 1758. However, as there are certain similarities between *Vengeance* and *Irresistible* (above) the subject is better assessed here. The nineteenth-century HMS *Vengeance* (84) was built in Pembroke Dockyard but, for some reason not explained in the surviving documentation, the Surveyor of the Navy's office informed the Plymouth officers that a drawing for the figurehead of HMS *Vengeance* had been sent to Plymouth and that it should be used before the carving was forwarded to Pembroke. The carver was to be allowed £21 for the work.[13] The drawing has survived in the Dickerson Archive in Australia where it is identified as being for 'Vengeance', even though it has none of the notations normally found when a design has passed through the approval process [14.8]. With the symbols of a thunderbolt in the trailboards, the crowned figure was probably intended to represent Zeus and the similarity with that of *Irresistible* can be seen. A photograph of the ship being broken up shows the figurehead still on the bow, complete with his trailboard carvings.[14] By 1926 the figurehead had found its way to the Upper Thames Sailing Club at Bourne End where it stood on the club lawn for many years, thought to be a representation of Neptune. In the 1990s the figurehead disintegrated but his remains were preserved and, from these and old photographs, a replica was carved for the club by Andrew Peters of Maritima Woodcarving.

The 1812 HMS *Surprise* (38) was built at Milford Shipyard in South Wales before Pembroke Dockyard was operational. The ship was sold in 1837 but what happened to her figurehead is not evident as it is not included in the 1911 Admiralty Catalogue.[15] A photograph of her figurehead does, however, appear in the pre-war return of figureheads in the Plymouth Command [14.9].[16] Seen to be a neatly cut three-quarter-length figure, she is identified as coming from the 1812 *Surprise*, is said to be in the Constructive Manager's Mould Loft, South Yard and a later note says that she was 'Destroyed in the Blitz'.

There were two ships called HMS *Hope* during the nineteenth century whose figureheads appear in the records: the first was a brig-sloop (10) built by Bailey of Ipswich in 1808, the second in Plymouth Dockyard in 1824. The anchor has been associated with Christianity from its earliest days when it was used in place of a cross and its connection with a faithful wife waiting for her husband's

14.8
HMS *Vengeance* - **Surveyor of the Navy design 1821.**
DICKERSON ARCHIVE

13 TNA ADM 91/5 (1821).
14 *The Navy & Army Illustrated,* Vol 7 (1899).
15 *Catalogue of Pictures, Presentation Plate, Figureheads, Models, Relics and Trophies at the Admiralty; on board H.M.Ships; and in the Naval Establishments at Home and Abroad* (London, April 1911).
16 *A Record of the Figureheads in H M Naval Establishments under Plymouth Command* – undated – but created in response to an Admiralty instruction of about 1936 (Admiralty Library Ref Dh 20).

return has resulted in the symbolism of the 'Hope and Anchor'. Edward Hellyer & Son offered to carve a standing figure for the 1808 HMS *Hope* for £4 [Colour Plate 24] but only a bust was approved.[17] It must be assumed that this would have included an anchor in the trailboards, as did the figurehead for the 1824 ship when the Dickersons of Devonport submitted their design and an estimate for £3.[18] The officials in the Surveyor's office were less than impressed with this submission (linked with a similar one for HMS *Mutine*) as there is a note on the reverse of the document asking 'Did you ever see two such monsters?' The 'Hope and Anchor' theme will also be found in Chapter 13 under the 1860 HMS *Espoir* wood screw gunvessel.

Members of the Navy Board were clearly proud of the sailors who served in the Fleet as they appeared on the bows of several ships whose names did them great credit. The 1844 HMS *Daring* (12) was given a demi-head of a sailor with his arms crossed and the ship's name embroidered on his chest [14.10]. With the brig building in Portsmouth Dockyard, the design was submitted by the Hellyers in 1843 with an estimate of £7 and was approved.[19]

The 1845 HMS *Inflexible* wood paddle sloop was building in Pembroke Dockyard and the Superintendent at Devonport was invited to 'call upon the carver to transmit a design for the Figure Head and an Estimate for the Carve Work'.[20] The design that Frederick Dickerson submitted is drawn in a very different style and he used colour to enhance the image [Colour Plate 25]. The design was approved and he was allowed £6 for the carving, the artwork that he produced for approval now being preserved in the Dickerson Archive in Australia.[21]

The 1861 HMS *Undaunted* wood screw frigate was built in Chatham Dockyard. As in the *Daring* figurehead, the Hellyers offered a design that had a sailor with crossed arms [14.11] but the ship was larger and the carver had included a rose and a White Ensign in the trailboards, making the estimate much more expensive at £27.10.0.[22] Despite this, the design was approved.

A more modern sailor was approved as the figurehead of the 1877 HMS *Firm* composite screw gunboat built by Earles Shipbuilding & Engineering Co of Hull. As she was building in a private yard rather than a royal dockyard, the figurehead would have been included in the overall contract but, nevertheless, the overseer forwarded the design for approval of the Surveyor [14.12]. The design is amongst a small collection in the Admiralty Library.[23]

Last in the A-to-Z of qualities comes HMS *Zealous*; laid down in 1859 as a screw two-decker in Pembroke Dockyard, she was approved for conversion

14.9
HMS *Surprise* – lost Devonport 1941.
CROWN COPYRIGHT

17 TNA ADM 106/1886 (1811).
18 TNA ADM 106/1949 (1824).
19 TNA ADM 87/13 S8175 (1843).
20 TNA ADM 91/11 (1844).
21 TNA ADM 87/14 S1476 (1844).
22 TNA ADM 87/74 S1307 (1860).
23 Admiralty Library Ref P 1030.

14.10
HMS *Daring* – Hellyer
design 1843.

14.11
HMS *Undaunted* – Hellyer
design 1860.

14.12
HMS *Firm* – **Shipbuilder's design 1876.**
CROWN COPYRIGHT

24 TNA ADM 87/73 S7715 (1859).
25 TNA ADM 87/73 S1594 (1860).
26 DM 6388/64.

to an ironclad in 1861, and was eventually launched in 1864. The Hellyers of Portsmouth submitted their first proposals for her figurehead in 1859 – a demi-head for £45 or a bust for £40.[24] These were not approved, the Surveyor asking for another design without the protruding arm. Early in 1860 the Hellyers submitted several further designs, a military bust being approved at £40 [14.13].[25] It would appear, however, that the figurehead was no longer suitable for the converted ship as the Dickerson Archive contains a fine bow decoration dated 1863 with a lion's head in both the forward-facing escutcheon and those on the port and starboard bows [14.14]. It was clearly approved as it carries the departmental reference number.[26]

14.13
HMS *Zealous* – Hellyer design 1860.
THE NATIONAL ARCHIVES

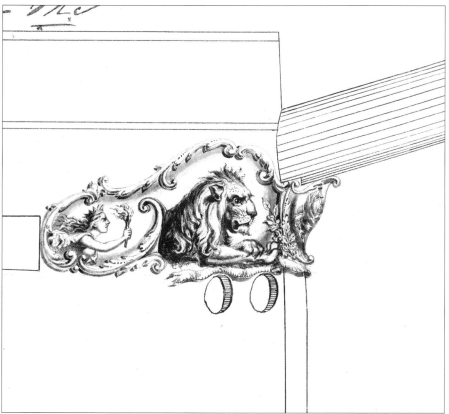

14.14
HMS *Zealous* – Dickerson design.
DICKERSON ARCHIVE

CHAPTER 15

NINETEENTH-CENTURY FIGUREHEADS – ROYALTY

GEORGE III had been on the throne for forty years at the start of the nineteenth century so it is not surprising that, when the 1803 HMS *Illustrious* (74) was launched at Randall & Brent's yard in Rotherhithe, she was given a figurehead in the likeness of the king. Perhaps a figurehead was carved for her while she was building at Rotherhithe, but the first surviving design was submitted by Edward Hellyer of Portsmouth in June 1808 [15.1], a crowned bust with an estimate of £24.[1] The design was approved but only £21 was allowed, that being the rate then allowed for 74-gun ships. In 1813 she was taken in hand at Portsmouth for a Large Repair and in June 1816 Edward Hellyer submitted another design of a bust showing the king in a more formal crown and an ermine cape [15.2] and an estimate for £21.[2] There is some evidence that a shield for £16 was approved in lieu of this design but none of this explains why the surviving figurehead for this ship is a magnificent bust, now in the Portsmouth collection, of the king wearing a wig of flowing curls and a wreath of laurel leaves – a late replacement, perhaps, during Queen Victoria's reign when HMS *Illustrious* became the first training ship for officer cadets, five years before HMS *Britannia* assumed that role.

The figurehead of the eighteenth-century HMS *Queen Charlotte* (100), named after King George III's consort, has already been described in Chapter 5. By the time the next ship to be named after her was built, the 1810 HMS *Queen Charlotte* (104), full-length figureheads were no longer in fashion and she was given a large bust of the crowned Queen [Colour Plate 26]. She now stands in HMS *Excellent*, Portsmouth.

The 1794 HMS *Prince of Wales* (90) had been built in Portsmouth Dockyard but by 1809 she required a replacement figurehead. The Superintendent at Chatham Dockyard made the request, forwarding a design by Edward Hellyer and his estimate for £35.[3] The design [15.3] includes much interesting detail, particularly the coronet and 'collar' that he is wearing. The former includes the

[1] TNA ADM 106/1885 (1808).

[2] TNA ADM 106/1888 (1816).

[3] TNA ADM 106/1821 (1809).

15.1
HMS *Illustrious* – Hellyer
design 1808.
THE NATIONAL ARCHIVES

Prince of Wales feathers while the latter is almost certainly that of the Order of the Garter. The ribbon running through the trailboard carries the Prince's motto 'Ich Dien'. What is also unusual is that the drawing is initialled and dated 'C.W. 1809' – perhaps the artist in the Hellyer workshop who actually drew the design.

HMS *Prince Regent* (120) was ordered in 1815 in the middle of the last decade of George III's reign when the Prince of Wales had been given full powers to act as sovereign. As a First Rate her original figurehead would probably have been a standing figure representing the future George IV, but when she was cut down to a Second Rate (92) in 1847 she would have required a smaller figurehead and Hellyer & Son of Portsmouth were instructed to carve it.[4] The Prince Regent [15.4] is shown wearing an ermine cape and the three 'collars' of the orders of chivalry: the Scottish Order of the Thistle, the Irish Order of St Patrick and the English Order of the Garter, below which can be seen hanging the 'George' in the form of St George slaying the dragon. The deletion marks over the Prince

4   TNA ADM 87/17 S1265 (1847).

15.2
HMS *Illustrious* **– Hellyer design 1816.**

15.3
HMS *Prince of Wales* –
Hellyer design 1809.
THE NATIONAL ARCHIVES

of Wales feathers in the trailboard indicate that, while the bust was approved, the trailboard carvings were not; this decision was taken in the Navy Board offices because the ship was being named in his honour as the Prince Regent and not as the Prince of Wales, even though they were one and the same man. The price allowed was £40 rather than the carver's estimate of £45.

Two different ships were laid down as HMS *Royal Frederick*, intended to be named in memory of George III's second son, Frederick, Duke of York, but each in turn was renamed before her launch. The first was laid down in 1833 in Portsmouth Dockyard but was renamed *Queen* in 1839 only weeks before her launch, to honour the new Queen Victoria. The second was laid down, also at

Portsmouth, in 1841 and by 1846 the Hellyers had submitted a design in the likeness of the late Duke of York with an estimate of £45. Unfortunately, by the time she was launched in 1860, her name had also been changed to HMS *Frederick William* to commemorate the marriage of the Princess Royal to Prince Frederick William, later to become the German emperor. The figurehead was never used, was taken into the Portsmouth Dockyard Museum and its fate will be found later in this chapter with that of HMS *Royal Sovereign*. Designs for HMS *Frederick William* were hastily produced and may be found in Chapter 1.

HMS *Royal George* (120) was launched in 1827, in the middle of George IV's reign, and again would probably have been given a standing figure of the king. In this case, part of the carving has survived – the head and shoulders – the king

15.4
HMS *Prince Regent* – Hellyer design 1847.
THE NATIONAL ARCHIVES

wearing Roman armour and a laurel wreath. It is preserved at the National Maritime Museum and, as this part measures 4ft 10in, some idea of the size of the whole can be visualised. In 1854 HMS *Royal George* was converted to a screw ship and, having been cut down, a smaller figurehead was required. It was not, however, until 1860 that Frederick Dickerson of Devonport offered two alternative designs.[5] The first [15.5] shows King George IV in military uniform with the Garter sash and a neck decoration; this was not approved. The second [15.6] shows King George III crowned with the sash, collar and star of the Order of the Garter; this design was approved, £35 being allowed. There is no trace of this figurehead after the ship was broken up at Castle's Charlton Yard in 1875.

William IV was known as 'The Sailor King' as he had served in the Royal Navy

[5]   TNA ADM 91/23 and 91/24 (1859-60).

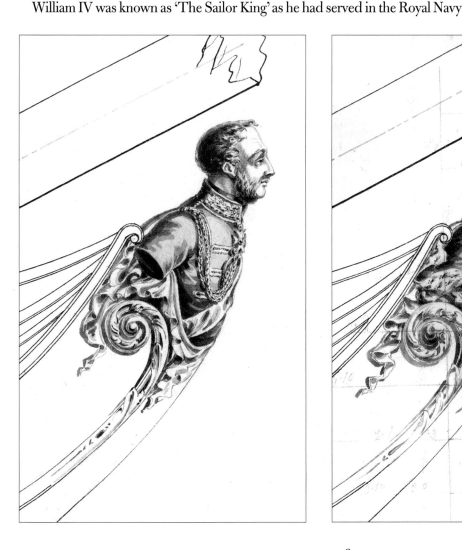

15.5
HMS *Royal George* – Frederick Dickerson design 1860.
DICKERSON ARCHIVE

15.6
HMS *Royal George* – Frederick Dickerson design 1860.
DICKERSON ARCHIVE

15.7
HMS *Royal Adelaide* c1938.
AUTHOR'S COLLECTION

15.8
HMS *Royal William* –
**Frederick Dickerson design
1859.**
DICKERSON ARCHIVE

as a young man between 1779 and 1790. Before he came to the throne in 1830, a First Rate (104) that had been building at Plymouth since 1819 as HMS *London*, was renamed HMS *Royal Adelaide* to honour his wife, then the Duchess of Clarence. The standing full-length figurehead survived for many years but was presumably carved after William IV's coronation as she is wearing a crown rather than a ducal coronet [15.7]. HMS *Royal Adelaide* spent most of her career at Plymouth in various roles; first she was the Port Admiral's flagship, then the guardship, the depot ship for reserves and finally a receiving hulk. She was moved to Chatham in 1890 and it was there that her figurehead was landed before the ship was sold for breaking up in 1905. As will be seen, she was far too tall to be housed with the rest of the Chatham collection and this resulted in her eventual loss. She survived the Second World War, was included in the 1938[6] and 1948[7] musters but the latter recorded that she was broken up in July 1949.

When William IV became king in 1830, HMS *Royal William* (120) was already

6   *Figureheads in Dockyard,
    Royal Naval Barracks and
    Royal Naval Hospital,
    Chatham.* D9270/38 (1938).
7   *Figureheads at Chatham –
    1948.* MCD 13234 (1949).

15.9
HMS *Queen* – **Hellyer design**
1858.

8   TNA ADM 88/1 S1100 (1832).

building at Pembroke Dock. She was launched in 1833 and, although no design drawings have been found, it is known that her figurehead was carved at Devonport as its delivery was hastened in November 1832 [Colour Plate 27].[8] The King is crowned and wearing ceremonial robes of the Order of the Garter with beautifully detailed 'collars' of the orders of chivalry; the uppermost is the Scottish Order of the Thistle, in the centre is the Irish Order of St Patrick (including the Irish harp) and the lowest of the three the English Order of the Garter (below which can be seen hanging the 'George' in the form of St George slaying the dragon.)

This figurehead saw only a little sea-service in the Baltic fleet during the Crimean War and in 1858 *Royal William* was taken in hand at Devonport to be cut down and converted to a screw line-of-battle ship (72), thus making this standing figure too large for her bow. He was landed and set up at the extreme southern point of the South Yard, looking out over Plymouth Sound where he

15.10
HMS *Superb* – **Hellyer design
1842.**
THE NATIONAL ARCHIVES

stood for over 140 years. In late 2000 he was found to be rotting internally and, as there were strong local feelings that 'King Billy' should continue to serve the fleet as he had for so many years – wishing units well on their deployment from Devonport and greeting them on their return – a fibreglass replica was made to stand looking out to the Sound while the original carving was brought into the safe environment of one of the ropery buildings.

With the ship in hand for conversion to steam, Frederick Dickerson submitted his design for a replacement [15.8] with an estimate of £35.[9] As with the successful replacement for HMS *Royal George*, the Dickerson design was a formal bust that was approved by the Surveyor of the Navy but he instructed that the crown should be made larger and brought down lower on the head. He also asked that the carver should send a rough sketch of the alteration. It can be seen on the original design that Dickerson has made some pencil marks where the crown should then sit and he submitted a tracing-paper amendment that was

9   TNA ADM 88/15 S1758
    (1859).

subsequently approved. This drawing is filed in The National Archives while the original design was retained by the carver and is therefore in the Dickerson Archive in Australia. The replacement bust did not survive, it having been lost in 1899 when the ship (renamed *Clarence*) burnt by accident in the Mersey.

When Queen Victoria came to the throne in 1837, the growth of the Royal Navy and a dutiful Navy Board ensured that there were numerous ships that carried her likeness in their figureheads. First came HMS *Queen* (110), that had

15.11
HMS *Sans Pareil* – **Dickerson design 1849.**

been building in Portsmouth Dockyard as HMS *Royal Frederick* since 1833. With her name changed to *Queen* in 1839, a design was submitted, but there was some debate on the size of the head and face in proportion to the bust and an extra charge of £5 to carve a tiara.[10] When the ship was taken in hand at Sheerness in 1858, to be cut down and reduced to 86 guns, her figurehead was found to be decayed and a replacement was ordered from Portsmouth [15.9].[11] This three-quarter-length bust of the young queen was probably a direct copy of the

[10] TNA ADM 88/4 S2775 (1840).

[11] TNA ADM 87/69 S4492 (1858).

15.12
HMS *Majestic* – **Hellyer design 1851.**
THE NATIONAL ARCHIVES

12 TNA ADM 87/12 S3405
    (1842).

13 TNA ADM 91/13 (1849).

14 TNA ADM 87/36 S766
    (1851).

15.13
HMS *Royal Sovereign* c1930
at HMS *St Vincent*, Gosport.
NATIONAL MUSEUM OF THE ROYAL NAVY

15 TNA ADM 87/25 S274
    (1849).

one that was being replaced and £44 was allowed.

In 1842, HMS *Superb* (80) was launched at Pembroke Dock and was given a three-quarter-length bust of the young queen carved by the Hellyers of Portsmouth.[12] It is a sensitive design showing a feminine rather than regal character [15.10], even though it is difficult to see how the queen's veil would be carved with such delicacy. £35 was allowed.

The 1851 HMS *Sans Pareil* (screw 81) was built in Devonport Dockyard, and, as she took her name from the French Third Rate captured in 1794 at the Battle of the First of June, she might well have appeared in Chapter 13 under 'prize names'. However, Frederick Dickerson submitted a delicate design, that was probably in the likeness of the young Queen Victoria [15.11]. Although she is not shown with any symbols of the monarch, she does appear to be wearing a sash and the design was approved 'without the crowns', suggesting that these were listed separately in the estimate of cost.[13] The design is now preserved in the Dickerson Archive in Australia.

In 1853 HMS *Majestic* (74) was launched at Chatham Dockyard, who had asked for a figurehead to be provided during her build. The Hellyers of Portsmouth offered two designs of which this rather more formal three-quarter-length bust [15.12] was approved.[14] The queen is wearing the sash and 'collar' of the Order of the Garter, a coronet and an ermine trimmed cape. Her crown, sceptre and sword of state are in the trailboards. Hellyer's estimate of £35 was approved.

In 1857 HMS *Royal Sovereign*, originally ordered as a First Rate (121) but re-ordered as a screw battleship, was launched at Portsmouth and again the Hellyers' design for her figurehead was approved. In 1864 she was cut down to an ironclad with gun turrets and her figurehead was no longer required and was landed [15.13]. The figurehead was initially placed indoors at the entrance to the Dockyard Museum at Portsmouth opposite a matching bust from HMS *Royal Frederick*. Unfortunately, in about 1930, the two carvings were transferred to the newly-opened boys' training establishment in Gosport, HMS *St Vincent*, where they stood on the parade ground beside the saluting dais. This was, no doubt a well-intentioned move to encourage esprit in the navy's youth but it resulted in their loss due to rot; *Royal Sovereign* was destroyed in 1946 and *Royal Frederick* in 1957.

In 1858 HMS *Windsor Castle* (116) was launched at Pembroke Dock. She had been laid down in 1844 as HMS *Victoria* and it was for that ship that Hellyer & Son of Portsmouth designed her figurehead.[15] The most formal of the

15.14
HMS *Victoria* renamed
Windsor Castle – Hellyer
design 1849.
THE NATIONAL ARCHIVES

representations of the queen, she again is crowned and wears the sash and 'collar' of the Order of the Garter and, on this occasion, holds the orb and sceptre [15.14]. Roses, a shamrock and a thistle can be seen around the base of the figurehead. She saw no sea service and in 1869 she became part of the *Cambridge* gunnery training ship at Devonport. When gunnery training moved ashore in 1907, the figurehead was set up in the RN Barracks at Devonport and later at the Royal Naval Engineering College at Manadon. Somewhere in this process her identity became confused and she was given a shield naming her

15.15
HMS *Victoria* – Hellyer
design 1859.

16   TNA ADM 87/71 S3263
(1859).

as HMS *Royal Adelaide* – a mistake that was eventually discovered and rectified. When the Engineering College closed in 1994, the figurehead went to the shore-based gunnery range, HMS *Cambridge* at Wembury [Colour Plate 28] until its closure in 2001. It was then moved to the Plymouth Naval Base Museum in the South Yard of HM Naval Base, Devonport.

By 1859 when HMS *Victoria* (screw 121) was launched in Portsmouth, the cost of carving figureheads seem to have inflated: when the Hellyers submitted their design [15.15] the estimate had increased to £70 and the Surveyor of the Navy accepted it without any reduction.[16] This was the last figurehead to be carved in the likeness of Queen Victoria as, when Prince Albert died in 1861 and the Queen went into mourning, the Navy Board no longer used ship names that might have suggested her presence on the bow.

Prince Albert had himself featured on one of Her Majesty's ships: the 1854

15.16
HMS *Royal Albert* - Hellyer
design 1853.
THE NATIONAL ARCHIVES

HMS *Royal Albert* (screw 121). Built in Woolwich Dockyard, the figurehead was a three-quarter-length in robes with an intricate sleeve to his coat; he carries a field-marshal's baton and is wearing, amongst other orders, the Spanish Order of the Golden Fleece. The design was submitted by Hellyer and Son from their Blackwall workshop [15.16] with an estimate of £150 that included the Royal Arms on one side and those of Prince Albert on the other. As will be seen from the deletions on the trailboards, this detail was not allowed and the cost was reduced to £100. It was this figurehead that, as was mentioned in Chapter 3, was given to the Dockyard Museum at Portsmouth in 1913 by Philip Castle of the ship-breaking family. Unfortunately, at over 16ft tall, he was too big to fit into the museum so he stood outside it on a plinth. No trace has been found of exactly when he succumbed to rot but, by the time the commands were instructed to report their holdings of figureheads in 1957, he was not listed.

15.17
HMS *Prince of Wales* –
Hellyer design 1853.
THE NATIONAL ARCHIVES

17   TNA ADM 87/42 S9692
       (1852).

Several of Queen Victoria's children featured on the bows of her warships, the two largest ships being the 1860 HMS *Prince of Wales* and the 1853 HMS *Princess Royal*. HMS *Prince of Wales* was laid down in Portsmouth Dockyard in 1848 as a sailing First Rate (120) but in 1856 – and before she was ever launched – she was ordered to be converted to a screw ship (121). Two designs for her figurehead were offered during her period on the building slip: an 1852 design in the form of the Royal Arms was rejected and an 1853 design of the young prince in a sailor suit [15.17] met with some resistance because of the estimate being £70.[17] The design is most unusual for a warship with the young prince looking ahead, the ribbon in his hat and his silk blowing in the wind. Britannia sits with her shield in the trailboard holding onto a princely crown around the Prince of Wales feathers. Hellyer wrote to the Surveyor of the Navy explaining

15.18
HMS *Princess Royal* –
Hellyer design 1852.
THE NATIONAL ARCHIVES

that a good likeness would be expected and this required workmen of the highest talent. He concluded that, if the estimate was still considered too high, he would submit a less costly design. When the ship was eventually completed, the figurehead that was fitted was a bust of a much older prince dressed in military uniform with crowns denoting his rank on his collar and the sash and star of the Order of the Garter. It has been suggested that this is intended to show him as the ADC to his mother, Queen Victoria.

It was this ship that replaced HMS *Britannia* as the training ship for naval cadets at Dartmouth in 1869 and, to allow this to happen, her name was changed to *Britannia*. As part of her conversion to a training ship at Devonport, her figurehead was removed so that the carving of Britannia could be installed and the Prince of Wales was landed and added to the collection in the fire-engine house there. When Douglas Owen inspected the figureheads in 1913 – see Chapter 3 – there was some confusion about his identity, probably caused by a small tally that had been screwed to his base naming him as 'HMS *Clive*', but how this happened is a mystery. It was under this name that the figurehead was transferred to the Clyde Division of the RNR, HMS *Graham*, in 1938 but it was not until after HMS *Graham*'s closure that an explanation for this 'mistaken identity' was set out in *The Mariner's Mirror* of May 1995 and the error was corrected. The figurehead was transferred to the Scottish Maritime Museum, Irvine where it is now correctly identified.[18]

The 1853 HMS *Princess Royal* (screw 91), was built in Portsmouth Dockyard and named in honour of Queen Victoria's eldest daughter, Princess Victoria. The design [15.18] by Hellyer & Son of Portsmouth shows a surprisingly mature young woman as she was only twelve years old when the figurehead was approved.[19] For this design with her hair in fashionable ringlets and her left hand holding a light shawl that then drifts down the trailboards to the royal arms, the Hellyers were allowed £35. The ship was broken up in 1872 by Castles at their Charlton yard and her figurehead was mounted above one of the gates at Baltic Wharf – see Chapter 3. Whether the then survivor was the original figurehead is hard to tell as there are certainly differences from the design and she has lost both arms at some stage. Whatever the case, she was lost in the Blitz in 1941 so she will never now tell us the answer.

18   A Query by James S Warren 'The Original Figurehead of HMS Britannia?', *The Mariner's Mirror* Vol 81 (1995), p 219.

19   TNA ADM 87/42 S5364 (1852).

———◦◦◦———

CHAPTER 16

BOW DECORATIONS AND TWENTIETH-CENTURY FIGUREHEADS

A
S ship design developed during the second half of the nineteenth century and the bows of the Royal Navy's ships became unsuitable for figureheads, those who wished to preserve the old traditions resorted to 'bow decorations', most of which were in the form of the royal arms in a cartouche with carved scroll-work flowing back on each side of the bow. Some of the decorations were made to represent the ship's name and, as these are a continuation of the spirit of the figurehead, they are included in the Figurehead Directory.

16.1
HMS *Lord Clyde* – Dickerson design 1864.
DICKERSON ARCHIVE

Just as for the nineteenth-century figureheads, these can be considered in categories. 'Famous People' included the 1864 HMS *Lord Clyde* ironclad battleship [16.1] named after the field marshal who played a prominent part in the Crimean War; 'Geographic' included the 1881 HMS *Canada* screw corvette that carried the dominion coat of arms surrounded by a border of gilded maple leaves; 'Mythological' included the 1892 HMS *Theseus* cruiser incorporating a Greek Cross with supporters; while 'Qualities' included the 1870 HMS *Hotspur* armoured ram – this was the nickname of Henry Percy, eldest son of the Earl of

Northumberland, who was killed at Shrewsbury in 1403 and so bears the Percy family arms. 'Royalty' were given appropriate recognition: the 1875 HMS *Alexandra* battleship was named after HRH the Princess of Wales and carried the Prince of Wales feathers; the 1864 HMS *Prince Albert* iron screw turret ship was named in the memory of Queen Victoria's consort who had died in 1861, his bust being surrounded by a wreath of laurel and oak branches [16.2].

Queen Victoria had three royal yachts named *Victoria and Albert*. The first two, launched in 1843 and 1855 had bow decorations in the form of an escutcheon bearing the royal arms facing to the starboard bow and Prince Albert's arms facing to the port bow. Prince Albert's arms were omitted from the decoration of the third *Victoria and Albert* in 1899, the royal arms being carved with elaborate surrounds but pointing straight ahead.

Very few ships of the Royal Navy were launched after the turn of the century with bows that were suitable for figureheads. Two classes of screw sloops did, however, have bows in the traditional 'clipper' shape with a prominent bowsprit – the *Condor* class and the *Cadmus* class.

While two of the *Condor* class had been launched in 1898, four were launched in 1900 – HM Ships *Shearwater*, *Vestal*, *Mutine* and *Rinaldo*, each of which were suitable for a figurehead. No evidence of such detail has been found to date.

The six *Cadmus* class sloops were all built in Sheerness Dockyard and launched between 1900 and 1903 with similar bows and appropriate figureheads.

16.3
HMS *Espiegle* c1920.
RICHARD HUNTER ARCHIVES

HMS *Espiegle* was launched in 1900, her name being a prize name dating from the capture of a French brig in 1793. She had a three-quarter-length female figurehead that had a domino mask across her eyes [16.3]. When the ship was sold on 7 September 1923 she had the distinction of being the very last ship of the fleet, afloat and in commission, to carry a figurehead.[1] Despite the fact that she was sold at Bombay, her figurehead found its way to the Portsmouth Dockyard Museum collection and is now in the National Museum of the Royal Navy, Portsmouth.

The three ships of the class that were launched in 1901 were HMS *Fantome* with a three-quarter-length female figurehead, HMS *Odin* with an unidentified figurehead, while HMS *Merlin* had the bearded Arthurian magician on her bow. The last two ships of the class were launched in 1903: HMS *Clio*, the muse of history, had a female bust while HMS *Cadmus*, King of Thebes, had the three-quarter-length figure of a warrior with a sword in his hand. As *Cadmus* was the last of the class, she has the distinction of being the last ship of the Royal Navy to have been built with a figurehead.[2] In the 1920s both HMS *Merlin* and HMS *Cadmus* were sold in Hong Kong and their figureheads were mounted on buildings near the dockyard entrance.[3] Neither carving appears to have survived the huge changes that occurred when the dockyard closed in 1959.

[1] A B Sainsbury and F L Phillips, *The Royal Navy Day by Day* (Sutton Publishing, 2005), p 379.

[2] Sainsbury and Phillips, *The Royal Navy Day by Day*, p 175.

[3] Kathleen Harland, *The Royal Navy in Hong Kong 1841-1980* (The Royal Navy, 1980), p 42.

CHAPTER 17

CONCLUSIONS

IT is hoped that this book will have provided a sufficiently wide range of examples to show how the art of the carver served the Royal Navy over the centuries and will have offered enough references for any reader who wants to delve deeper into a particular facet of the subject. It is estimated that over the centuries about 5,000 ships of the Royal Navy were given a figurehead so the 200 surviving examples only represent 4 per cent of the total and, even when all the information contained in the Directory is added to the equation, details are known of only about 20 per cent of the whole.

When Douglas Owen toured the royal dockyards before the First World War and made notes on the figurehead collections, he praised the individuals who had created local museums but could not disguise his regret that so much of the nation's naval history had been lost.[1] He wrote:

[1]   Owen, 'Figureheads' and 'The Devonport Figureheads'.

If only the Society for Nautical Research had been founded 100 years, 50 years ago! How many priceless relics of our naval history and achievements, even in late years, [would] have not been lost to the nation through failure to recognise their value until too late! And amongst these relics what more priceless than the figureheads of ships which took a glorious part in our epoch-making sea-fights.

He was writing long before the National Maritime Museum or the Royal Naval Museum were created but the historians of the day were clearly thinking along those lines with his concluding remarks: 'All such splendid relics should, of course, be in a great Naval Museum; but this, to our shame, we still lack', and 'so far, however, as they serve to stimulate the public interest or stir the national patriotism, most of them might almost as well be at the bottom of a mine.'

In 2008 the present author analysed what had happened to the figureheads that had been included in Owen's articles of 1913 and 1914. As we have already seen in Chapter 3, we now have well-cared-for collections in which conservation is addressed professionally but the sad facts are that, of the figureheads that were described by Owen in 1913–14, one-third has been lost, six in the Blitz but many more because they were left out of doors and, despite the best intentions of their custodians, decayed and were eventually destroyed.[2] Even today there are about twenty warship figureheads that are 'at risk' because they are not properly housed but their custodians lack either the funds or the inclination to correct the situation.

And so to the future: the NMM has a plan to create an illustrated database of all figureheads in the country from both ships of the Royal Navy and from merchantmen, accessible on the Internet – a huge task but a worthy research project. The National Museum of the Royal Navy, launched in September 2009, has a long-term plan to gather together as many naval figureheads as possible to create an impressive 'National Figurehead Collection'. Perhaps if both schemes were achieved, Douglas Owen's wishes of 1913 would at last be satisfied!

[2] David Pulvertaft, 'Warship Figureheads from the Royal Dockyards: Towards a National Collection?', *The Mariner's Mirror* Vol 95 (2009).

FIGUREHEAD DIRECTORY

INTRODUCTION

This Directory is comprised of four principal components:

Figureheads that are still surviving – including their present whereabouts. For these 'survivors' the ship's name is printed in bold type.

Figureheads that have been lost since they were brought ashore – including the date and place of their last sighting.

Carvers' design drawings – including their reference numbers and thus where they may now be found.

Ship plans and ship models where they provide extra figurehead information – including their reference numbers. Those that simply duplicate what is known from the actual figurehead have not been included.

The Admiralty records at The National Archive also include numerous references to named carvers creating the figurehead for a particular ship but, if these do not indicate the form of the carving, they too have been omitted.

Entries that are illustrated in the colour plates are indicated ‡.

Entries that have additional information in the Notes at the foot of the table are indicated †.

Ship Dates The dates given are generally the year of launch and the year of sale/breaking-up/taking-to-pieces. If the ship's name was changed, the second date shows the date of that change. If a ship's conversion required the figurehead to be changed, the ship is shown with two entries; one pre-conversion and one post-conversion.

Quoted prices If the carver's estimated price was approved, that is the value shown. If the estimated price was reduced, the lower 'allowed' value is shown. If the quoted price is not found in the quoted reference, it will generally have been found in the appropriate register or letter-book – ADM 88 or ADM 91.

ABBREVIATIONS

ADM	Admiralty archives
BRNC	Britannia Royal Naval College
IWM	Imperial War Museum
NMRN	National Museum of the Royal Navy
NRS	Navy Records Society
TNA	The National Archives

SHIP	DATES	SHIP TYPE	FIGUREHEAD/ORIGIN/DATE/COST	LOCATION/REF.
Abercrombie	1809-1817	Third Rate 74	Full-length horse with wings – ship plan	NMM ZAZ0734
Aboukir	1848-1877	Second Rate 90	Bust of a pharaoh – Dickerson design 1847 – £40 Bust of Lord Nelson – Hellyer design 1847 Bust of Lord Nelson – Last seen Port Royal, Jamaica	TNA ADM 87/17 Dickerson Archive Lost *c*1921
Achates	1808-1810	Brig-sloop 10	A stylised bird – ship plan 1809	NMM ZAZ4499
Achilles	1757-1784	Fourth Rate 60	Full-length Greek warrior – Georgian ship model	Science Museum 1881-31
Achille	1798-1865	Third Rate 74	Full-length male warrior – 1794 (French)	NMM ZAZ0803
Acorn	1838-1869	Brig 12	Female 3/4-length – Dickerson design 1836 – £5.5.0	TNA ADM 87/6
Actaeon	1775-1776 1831-1889	Sixth Rate 28 Sixth Rate 26	Full-length male with spear – ship plan Replacement figurehead – Dickerson of Devonport 1844 Male bust – Surviving	NMM ZAZ2924 TNA ADM 91/11 NMRN Portsmouth
Active	1845-1867	Fifth Rate 36	Bust of Hermes – Dickerson design 1844 – £10 Bust of Queen Victoria – Hellyer design 1845 – £16 Female 3/4-length holding a rose – surviving	TNA ADM 87/14 TNA ADM 87/15 & 91/11 HMS *Caledonia* Rosyth
Adventure	1691-1704 1857-1877 1857-1877	Fourth Rate 44 Troopship Troopship	Full-length crowned lion – gilt – Navy Board model Female head & neck with a blue shawl – surviving Female head & neck with a crown of stars – surviving	Kriegstein Collection USA NMM FHD0124 NMM FHD0119 †
Africaine	1801-1816	Fifth Rate 38	Female demi-head – ship plan (French)	NMM ZAZ2717
African	1825-1862	Paddle vessel	Bust of an African – carved by Overton & Faldo 1824	*Ship Carvers* – P Thomas
Agamemnon	1852-1870	Second Rate 91	Demi-head of a warrior – Hellyer design 1851 – £35	TNA ADM 87/39
Agincourt	1865-1904	Iron screw ship	Bow decoration with lion & unicorn supporters	*Figureheads* – P Norton
Aigle	1801-1870	Fifth Rate 36	Male bust – Grayfoot & Overton design 1818 – £12	TNA ADM 106/1795
Ajax	1767-1785 1809-1864	Third Rate 74 Third Rate 74	Full-length warrior – Navy Board model Bust of a warrior – surviving	NMM SLR0311 NMM FHD0120
Alarm	1845-1904	Sixth Rate 28	Bust of a warrior – Hellyer design 1844 – £12 Standing cock with tail-feathers in trailboard – gilt – design model of ship's bow	TNA ADM 87/14 NMM SLR2186
Albacore	1804-1815	Sloop 18	Female 3/4-length holding a fish – ship plan	NMM HIL0032
Albatross	1842-1860	Brig 16	A standing bird – Hellyer design 1839 – £5.16.0	TNA ADM 87/9
Albemarle	1779-1784	Sixth Rate 28	Full-length crowned lion – ship plan	NMM ZAZ3377
Alberta	1863-1912	Wood paddle yacht	Crown over royal arms – Dickerson design 1863 Crown over royal arms in cartouche – surviving	Dickerson Archive NMRN Portsmouth
Albion	1842-1884	Second Rate 90	3/4-length demi-head – Robert Owen design 1841 3/4-length bust – Dickerson design 1860 – £55 3/4-length demi-head – white – ship model 3/4-length bust of Britannia – surviving	TNA ADM 87/11 Dickerson Archive Science Museum 1849-230 Hull Maritime Museum
Alceste	1806-1818	Fifth Rate 38	Female bust – Hellyer design 1815 – £6 Helmeted standing figure – ship plan	TNA ADM 106/1889 NMM ZAZ2294
Alcmene	1779-1784	Fifth Rate 32	Full-length female – ship plan (French)	NMM ZAZ3391
Alderney	1757-1783	Sloop 12	Full-length griffin – ship plan – 1756	NMM ZAZ4663
Alecto	1839-1865	Wood pad. sloop	Female bust – Hellyer & Browning design 1839 – £6	TNA ADM 87/9
Alert	1856-1884 1894-1906	Wood screw sloop Sloop	Female 3/4-length bust – Dickerson design 1855 – £6.10.0 Escutcheon holding Garter Star & wreath – ship plan	Dickerson Archive NMM NPA5211
Alexandra	1875-1908	Battleship	Bow decoration – Crown over Prince of Wales feathers – surviving	Newport News, Virginia

SHIP	DATES	SHIP TYPE	FIGUREHEAD/ORIGIN/DATE/COST	LOCATION/REF.
Alfred	1778-1814	Third Rate 74	Full-length crowned king – ship plan	NMM ZAZ0563
	1819-1865	Third Rate 74 – 50	Crowned male bust – sketchbook 1848	NMM Picture Library
Algerine	1895-1919	Sloop	Male 3/4-length – Sam Trevenen design 1894 – £15	NMM NPN0336
Alliance	1795-1802	Storeship	Full-length uncrowned lion – ship plan (Dutch)	NMM ZAZ2918
Amazon	1745-1763	Sixth Rate 26	Full-length uncrowned lion – ship plan	NMM ZAZ4027 & 4028
	1773-1794	Fifth Rate 32	Female full-length – Georgian ship model	NMM SLR0315
	1799-1817	Fifth Rate 38	Full-length female warrior – ivory – Georgian ship mod.	USNA Museum Annapolis
	1799-1817	Fifth Rate 38	Amazon with dagger – lost in 'The Great Fire', Devonport 1840	See Chapter 3.I
	1821-1863	Fifth Rate 46	Female bust – surviving	HMS *Dryad* site †
Ambuscade	1773-1798	Fifth Rate 32	Male full-length – gilt – Navy Board model	Science Museum Pictorial
	1746-1762	Fifth Rate 40	Full-length male warrior – ship plan	NMM ZAZ2265
	1798-1804	Fifth Rate 40	Female standing figure – ship plan	NMM ZAZ2507
America	1810-1827	Third Rate 74	American female with plume of feathers – lost in 'The Great Fire', Devonport, 1840	See Chapter 3.I
Amethyst	1844-1869	Sixth Rate 26	Female 3/4-length bust – ivory – sailor-made ship model	Plymouth Mus. & Art Gal.
Amphion	1780-1796	Fifth Rate 32	Full-length figure holding a jar – ship plan	NMM ZAZ2956
	1846-1863	Wood screw frigate	Male bust – Hellyer design 1845 – £18	TNA ADM 87/15
			Male bust in uniform – ship plan – 1848	NMM ZAZ5380
Amphitrite	1804-1805	Fifth Rate 38	Original bust carved by Overton & Co 1813 – £6	TNA ADM 106/1794
			Female full-length with dolphin in trailboards – ship plan	NMM HIL0007
			1816-1862 Fifth Rate	Female bust – Hellyer
			design 1845 – £14	TNA ADM 87/15
Andromache	1781-1811	Fifth Rate 32	Full-length female holding child – ship plan	NMM ZAZ2905
Anson	1781-1807	Third Rate 64	Full-length male warrior – ship plan	NMM ZAZ1397
	1812-1844	Third Rate 74	Male standing fig. – Hellyer design 1819 – £36 (not approved)	TNA ADM 106/1889
			Male bust – Hellyer proposal 1819 – £21	TNA ADM 106/1889
	1860-1904	Screw ship 91	Bust of Admiral Anson – Hellyer design 1859 – £45	TNA ADM 87/73
			Bust of Adml Anson – Moved Chatham/HMS *Sultan* 1983	Destroyed 1984
Ant	1797-1815	Schooner 8	Female standing figure – ship plan (French)	NMM ZAZ6097
Antelope	1703-1783	Fourth Rate 54	Full-length crowned lion – ship plan	NMM ZAZ1700
	1802-1845	Fourth Rate 50	Female demi-head holding deer's head – ship plan	NMM ZAZ 1744
Apollo	1805-1856	Fifth Rate 38	Male standing figure – Hellyer design 1817 – £15	TNA ADM 106/1889
			Male bust – Hellyer design 1817 – £6 (approved)	TNA ADM 106/1889
			Male bust – surviving	NMRN Portsmouth
Aquilon	1786-1815	Fifth Rate 32	Male bust – Hellyer design 1810 – £8	TNA ADM 106/1885
Arab	1798-1810	Sixth Rate 22	A sea monster's head & neck – ship plan	NMM ZAZ3795 & 3796
	1847-1879	Brig-sloop 16	Male demi-head – Robert Hall design 1839 – £5	TNA ADM 87/9
Arachne	1809-1837	Brig-sloop 18	Female bust – Hellyer design 1815 – £3	TNA ADM 106/1888
	1847-1866	Sloop 18	Female bust – Last recorded Devonport c1936	Lost in Blitz 1941
Archer	1849-1866	Wood screw sloop	Male bust – Hellyer design – £8.10.0	TNA ADM 87/21
	1885-1905	Torpedo cruiser	Male 3/4-length with a bow – Kay & Reid design 1885	NMM NPA5625
Ardent	1841-1865	Wood pad. sloop	Bust of a warrior – Hellyer & Browning design 1839 – £7	TNA ADM 87/9
Arethusa	1817-1844	Fifth Rate 46	Female standing figure	Missing †
	1849-1934	Fourth Rate 50	Female 3/4-length bust – Hellyer design 1847 – £24	TNA ADM 87/17
			Female bust, gilt – design half-block model	NMM SLR0835
			Female 3/4-length bust – surviving	Lower Upnor †
Arethuse	1793-1795	Fifth Rate 38	Oval crowned & winged – ship plan (French)	NMM ZAZ3450
Argus	1849-1881	Wood pad. sloop	Female 3/4-length – Hellyer design 1849 – £10.12.0	TNA ADM 87/25
Ariadne	1776-1814	Sixth Rate 20	Full-length female with thread – ship plan	NMM ZAZ3940
	1859-1922	Wood screw frigate	Female 3/4-length bust – Hellyer design 1858 – £24.10.0	TNA ADM 87/68
			Female 3/4-length bust – surviving	HM Naval Base Portsm'th

SHIP	DATES	SHIP TYPE	FIGUREHEAD/ORIGIN/DATE/COST	LOCATION/REF.
Ariel	1854-1865	Wood screw sloop	Male bust – Dickerson design 1854	Dickerson Archive
Armide	1806-1815	Fifth Rate 38	Female bust – Dickerson design 1809 – £6	TNA ADM 106/1940
Arrogant	1761-1810	Third Rate 74	Female full-length with crown, key & lion	Design drawing in NMM†
	1848-1867	Wood screw frigate	Female 3/4-length – Hellyer design 1846 – £24	TNA ADM 87/16
Arrow	1823-1852	Cutter 10	Male bust – Hellyer & Browning design 1837 – £3	TNA ADM 87/7
			Arm with arrow – H & B design – not approved	TNA ADM 87/7
			American Indian demi-head with arrow – H & B design – not approved	TNA ADM 87/7
Asia	1824-1908	Second Rate 84	Male bust – surviving	NMRN Portsmouth
	Uncertain	?	Male demi-head – surviving (attributed to HMS *Asia*)	Mystic Seaport Mus.
Assurance	1646-1698	42-gun ship	Crowned lion – Van de Velde drawing *c*1671	NMM W737
Atalanta	1775-1781	Sloop 16	Full-length female – ship plan	NMM ZAZ4485
			Female full-length with bow – Georgian ship model	NMM SLR0340
	1847-1868	Brig 16	Female 3/4-length bust – Hellyer design 1847	TNA ADM 87/17
			Female 3/4-length bust – surviving	NMM FHD0062
Atalante	1797-1807	Brig-sloop 19	Standing figure – ship plan Fl (French)	NMM ZAZ4348
Atholl	1820-1863	Sixth Rate 28	Female bust – Hellyer design 1844 – £7.10.0	TNA ADM 87/14
Atlas	1782-1821	Second Rate 90	Male bust – Hellyer design 1806 – £25	TNA ADM 106/1884
			Full-length figure – ship plan	NMM ZAZ0328
	1860-1904	Screw Second Rate 91	Male bust – Hellyer design 1859 – £40	TNA ADM 87/71
Audacious	1785-1815	Third Rate 74	Male bust – Hellyer design 1806 – £21	TNA ADM 106/1884
Augusta	1736-1765	Fourth Rate 60	Full-length crowned lion with Chinese dragon in trailboard – ship plan	NMM ZAZ1761
Aurora	1814-1851	Fifth Rate 38	Female standing fig. – Grayfoot & Overton des. 1820 – £10	TNA ADM 106/1795
	Uncertain	?	Female bust – last recorded Devonport *c*1936	Believe lost *c*1945
	1861-1881	Wood screw frigate	Carved by Hellyer of Cosham 1855 – £24.10.0	TNA ADM 88/11 & 12
			Female bust – surviving	Plymouth NB Museum
Avon	1805-1814	Brig-sloop 18	Female bust – Hellyer design 1813 – £3	TNA ADM 106/1887
Babet	1794-1801	Sixth Rate 20	Uncrowned lion – ship plan	NMM ZAZ 3900
Banshee	1847-1864	Paddle packet	Female 3/4-length bust – Hellyer design 1856 – £7	TNA ADM 87/62
Barfleur	1716-1764	Second Rate 90	Male full-length – Navy Board model *c*1740	NMM – SLR0453
	1768-1819	Second Rate 98	Full-length uncrowned lion – gilt – Navy Board model	Science Museum Pictorial
	1892-1910	Battleship	Lion couchant & royal arms – ship plan	NMM NPA6456
			Lion couchant & royal arms – surviving	HMS *Nelson* Portsmouth
Barge (Royal)			Full-length dolphin – ship plan	NMM ZAZ7158 & 9
Barracouta	1820-1836	Brig-sloop 10	Shield & foliage – Grayfoot & Overton design 1819 – £4	TNA ADM 106/1795
	1851-1881	Wood paddle sloop	Female 3/4-length bust – Hellyer design 1849	TNA ADM 87/26
Barrosa	1860-1877	Wood screw corvette	Female bust – Hellyer design 1859 – £20	TNA ADM 87/72
Basilisk	1848-1882	Wood paddle sloop	Carved by Hellyer of Rotherhithe 1847	TNA ADM 88/7
			Female bust – surviving	Plymouth NB Museum
Beagle	1820-1846	Brig-sloop 10	Fore-part of dog – Grayfoot & Overton design 1819 – £4.4.0	TNA ADM 106/1795
Beaver (Prize)	1778-1780	Sloop 18	Full-length male in kilt – ship plan	NMM ZAZ4207
Bedford	1775-1817	Third Rate 74	Full-length warrior – ship plan	NMM ZAZ1304
Bee	1842-1874	Wood s. & pad vessel	Female bust – Hellyer design 1841 – £4.10.0	TNA ADM 87/11
Belleisle	1761-1819	Third Rate 64	Full-length uncrowned lion – ship plan 1761	NMM ZAZ1444
Belle Poule	1780-1801	Fifth Rate 36	Full-length uncrowned lion – ship plan – (French)	NMM ZAZ3117
	1806-1818	Fifth Rate 38	Female demi-head with chicken in trailboard – design for the head – ship plan – (French)	NMM ZAZ6878

SHIP	DATES	SHIP TYPE	FIGUREHEAD/ORIGIN/DATE/COST	LOCATION/REF.
Bellerophon	1786-1824	Third Rate 74	Helmeted head only surviving	NMRN Portsmouth
	1824-1892	Third Rate 80	Bust of a warrior – surviving	NMRN Portsmouth
	1865-1904	Battleship	Bow decoration – bust in a cartouche – Dickerson design	Dickerson Archive
Bellona	1760-1814	Third Rate 74	Full-length female warrior – Georgian ship model	NMM SLR0338
			Full-length female warrior – painted – skeleton model	NMM SLR0503
Belvidera	1809-1906	Fifth Rate 36	Female standing figure – Hellyer design 1817 – £15	TNA ADM 106/1889
			Female bust – Hellyer design 1817 – £6 (approved)	TNA ADM 106/1889
	1860-1864	Wood screw frigate	Female 3/4-length bust – Hellyer design 1860 – £24.10.0	TNA ADM 87/76
Belzebub	1842	Wood paddle frigate	Male bust – Hellyer design 1842 – £8.10.0	TNA ADM 87/12
Benbow	1813-1892	Third Rate 72	Male bust – surviving	Portsmouth NB Prop Trust
Berwick	1743-1760	Third Rate 70	Full-length lion – gilt – Navy Board model 1747	Science Museum Pictorial
	1775-1805	Third Rate 74	Full-length warrior – ship plan	NMM ZAZ0825
	1809-1821	Third Rate 74	Former Duke – lost in 'The Great Fire', Devonport 1840	See Chapter 3.I
Bittern	1796-1833	Sloop 18	Female full-length – Bucklers Hard designer	Beaulieu BH/II/PD5 61
	1840-1860	Brig 12	Standing bird – Hellyer design 1839 (not approved)	TNA ADM 87/9
Black Eagle	1843-1876	Admiralty yacht	Carved by Hellyer of Portsmouth 1845	TNA ADM 91/11
			Standing eagle – surviving	NMRN Portsmouth
Black Prince	1861-1923	Armoured frigate	Carved by Kay & Reid, Glasgow 1860	*Ship Carvers* – P Thomas
			3/4-length Prince of Wales – last seen Devonport c1900	Lost c1905
Blanche	1819-1865	Fifth Rate 46	Female standing figure – unnamed carver 1818 – £20	TNA ADM 106/1824
			Female bust – unnamed carver 1818 – £6 (approved)	TNA ADM 106/1824
Blazer	1834-1853	Wood paddle sloop	Carved by Robert Hall of Rotherhithe 1834 – £6.10.0	TNA ADM 88/1
			Sunburst – surviving	NMRN Portsmouth
Blenheim	1813-1865	Third Rate 74	Male bust – surviving	NMM FHD0064
Blonde	1805-1811	Fifth Rate 38	Male bust – unnamed carver 1806 – £6	TNA ADM 106/1820
Bloodhound	1845-1866	Iron paddle vessel	Full-length dog – Hellyer design 1854 – £6.10.0	TNA ADM 87/50
Boadicea	1875-1905	Iron screw corvette	Female 3/4-length bust – photograph	IWM photo Q 38338
Bolton	1709-1817	Yacht 6	Double equestrian with riders – Navy Board model	NMM SLR0395
Bonaventure	1683-1699	50 gun ship	Full-length crowned lion – Navy Board model	NMM SLR0374
Bonetta	1797-1801	Brig-sloop 18	Standing warrior with sword & shield – ship plan	NMM ZAZ4528
Boomerang	1890-1905	Torpedo gunboat	3/4-length aboriginal male in scroll – surviving	Melbourne, Australia
Boreas	1774-1802	Sixth Rate 28	Full-length male with spear – ship plan	NMM ZAZ3248
Boscawen	1844-1874	Third Rate 70	Male bust – ship plan	NMM ZAZ0930
Bourdelais	1799-1804	Sixth Rate 24	Male standing figure – ship plan (French)	NMM ZAZ3724
Boyne	1692-1763	Second Rate 80	Crowned lion – gilt – Navy Board model	NMM SLR0006
	1790-1795	Second Rate 98	King William III on horseback – ship model 1790	Science Museum 1916-46
	1810-1834	Second Rate 98	Bust of King William III – Hellyer design 1834 – £30	TNA ADM 87/4
Braak	1799-1802	Sixth Rate 24	Female standing figure – ship plan	NMM ZAZ3632
Brazen	1799-1800	Sloop 18	Standing warrior – ship plan	NMM ZAZ4034
Brilliant	1779-1811	Sixth Rate 28	Female full-length + dolphin in trailb'ds – Henry Adams design	Buckler's Hard Mar. Mus.
	1843-1889	Fifth Rate 22	Female bust – ship plan dated 1846	NMM ZAZ3755
Brisk	1819-1843	Brig-sloop 10	Standing bird – unnamed carver 1818 – not approved	TNA ADM 106/1824
	1886-1906	Torpedo cruiser	Female 3/4-length – Kay & Reid design 1886	NMM NPA7535

SHIP	DATES	SHIP TYPE	FIGUREHEAD/ORIGIN/DATE/COST	LOCATION/REF.
Bristol	1775-1810	Fourth Rate 50	Male full-length – ship plan	NMM ZAZ1749
			Full-length George III with royal arms –	
			Georgian ship model 1774	Art Gallery of Ontario
	1861-1883	Wood screw frigate	Female 3/4-length bust – Hellyer design 1860 – £27.10.0	TNA ADM 87/74
			Female 3/4-length bust (white) – ship model	Science Museum 1931-660
			Female head and neck – surviving	NMM FHD0066
Britannia	1682-1715	First Rate 100	Equestrian figure trampling on rivals – gilt – Navy Board model	USNA Museum Annapolis
	1719-1749	First Rate 100	Mounted male with union flag – painted on block model	NMM SLR0410
			Group figurehead – unnamed designer	Dickerson Archive
			Double sea-lions, supporters, etc – Georgian ship model	NMM SLR0223
	1820-1869	First Rate 100	Standing figure of Britannia – surviving	BRNC Dartmouth †
Bust of Britannia			Bust with helmet – last seen BRNC Dartmouth c1969	Believe lost c1970
Britomart	1847-1863	Brig 8	Female 3/4-length bust – Hellyer design 1846 – £16	TNA ADM 87/16
			Female 3/4-length bust – surviving	Historic D'yard Chatham
Briton	1812-1860	Fifth Rate 38	Female bust – Last seen Upnor Armament Depot	Believe lost 1950s
Brune	1761-1792	Fifth Rate 32	Male full-length – ship plan (French)	NMM ZAZ2933
	1808-1838	Fifth Rate 38	Female full-length – ship plan	NMM ZAZ2934
Brunswick	1855-1867	Screw Third Rate 80	Male demi-head – Hellyer design 1850 – £20	TNA ADM 87/48
			Male bust – Hellyer design 1850 – £14	TNA ADM 87/48
Bulldog	1845-1865	Wood paddle sloop	Full length dog and shield – Hellyer design 1844 – £9	TNA ADM 87/14
			Full length dog and shield – surviving	NMM FHD0068
Bulwark	1807-1826	Third Rate 74	3/4-length figure of Britannia – Hellyer design 1806 – £32	TNA ADM 106/1884
			Bust of Britannia – Hellyer design 1806 – £21 – approved	TNA ADM 106/1884
	1859-1873	Screw Second Rate 81	Bust of Britannia – Hellyer design 1860 – £45	TNA ADM 87/76
			Bust of Britannia – surviving	Historic D'yard Chatham
Bustard	1818-1829	Brig-sloop 10	Standing bird – unnamed carver 1818 – not approved	TNA ADM 106/1824
Buzzard	1849-1883	Wood paddle sloop	Standing bird – Hellyer design 1848 – £9.10.0	TNA ADM 87/19
			Replacement figurehead – Dickerson 1857 – £6	TNA ADM 88/13
			Female 3/4-length bust – Dickerson design 1862	Dickerson Archive
Cadmus	1856-1879	Wood screw corvette	Carved by Hellyer of Blackwall 1855 – £10	TNA ADM 88/11 & 12
			Male bust – surviving	Plymouth NB Museum ‡
	1903-1921	Sloop	Male demi-head – last seen Hong Kong	Believe lost c1959
Caesar	1793-1821	Third Rate 80	Male full-length – Dickerson design – undated	Dickerson Archive
	1853-1870	Screw Second Rate	Male bust – Dickerson design 1851	Dickerson Archive
Calcutta	1831-1908	Second Rate 84	Male 3/4-length bust – surviving privately owned	Thetford, Norfolk ‡
Caledonia	1808-1856	First Rate 120	Crowned male bust – ship plan	NMM ZAZ0106
			Female bust with a trident in trailboards – sectional ship model	NMM SLR0120
			Female bust with bagpipes – ship model	NMM SLR2723
			Bust with bonnet and thistles – sectional ship model	NMM SLR2908
			Male bust on base edged with leaves – gilt – ship model	Plymouth Mus. & Art Gal.
Calliope	1808-1829	Brig-sloop 10	Female 3/4-length – surviving	NMRN Portsmouth
	1837-1883	Sixth Rate 28	Female bust – Hellyer design 1837 – £6 – approved	TNA ADM 87/7
			Female demi-head – Hellyer design 1837 – £7.10.0	TNA ADM 87/7
			Three female 3/4-length – Robert Hall designs 1837 – £7	TNA ADM 87/7
			Female demi-head – ship plan	NMM ZAZ3215 & 3293
			Female bust – surviving	Plymouth NB Museum
Calypso	1845-1866	Sixth Rate 20	Female bust – surviving	NMRN Portsmouth
			Female bust – Hellyer design 1843 – £8.18.0	TNA ADM 87/13
Cambrian	1797-1828	Fifth Rate 40	Male bust – Hellyer design 1807 – £9	TNA ADM 106/1884
			Bust, painted brown – half block design model	NMM SLR0592
	1841-1892	Fifth Rate 36	Male bust with hat & cape – Dickerson design 1840 – £10	TNA ADM 87/10
			Male bust with coronet – Dickerson design 1840 – £10	TNA ADM 87/10
			Male demi-head with harp – Hellyer design 1840 – £15	TNA ADM 87/10
			Male bust – Hellyer design 1840 – £9	TNA ADM 87/10
	1841-1892	Fifth Rate 36	Female 3/4-length bust, gilt – half block model	NMM SLR0800

SHIP	DATES	SHIP TYPE	FIGUREHEAD/ORIGIN/DATE/COST	LOCATION/REF.
Cambridge	1755-1808	Third Rate 80	Royal bust with figures – Dickerson Design – undated	Dickerson Archive
	1815-1869	Third Rate 80	Seated lion with royal arms – last seen Devonport c1947	Lost c1950
Camelion	1860-1883	Wood screw sloop	Male bust in headdress – Hellyer design 1859 – £10	TNA ADM 87/72
Camilla	1776-1831	Sixth Rate 20	Female full-length – ship plan	NMM ZAZ4009
	1847-1861	Sloop 16	Female bust – Hellyer design 1847 – £6.15.0	TNA ADM 87/17
Camperdown	1825-1882	First Rate 106	Nelson changed to Duncan – Robert Hall work 1834 – £8	TNA ADM 87/3 & 88/1
Canada	1881-1897	Screw corvette	Bow decoration – Dominion of Canada arms – surviving	Mar Mus British Columbia
Canopus	1798-1887	Third Rate 80	Helmeted male bust – ship plan – 1815	NMM ZAZ0584
			Helmeted male bust – ship model – modern replacement	Art Gallery of Ontario
			Carved at Plymouth 1801 – £33	TNA ADM 106/1936
			Helmeted male bust – surviving	NMM FHD0069
Captain	1678-1762	Third Rate 70	Full-length lion – gilt – Navy Board model 1708	Science Museum Pictorial
	1787-1813	Third Rate 74	Union Flag shield with helmet – Dickerson design 1798	Dickerson Archive ‡
Caradoc	1847-1870	Iron paddle gunboat	Turbaned male bust – surviving	NMRN Portsmouth
Carnatic	1823-1914	Third Rate 72	Turbaned male bust – surviving	NMRN Portsmouth
Carolina	1716-1733	Royal Yacht	Full-length crowned lion – gilt – modern ship mod. 1988	Art Gallery of Ontario
Castor	1785-1819	Fifth Rate 32	Helmeted male bust – Dickerson design 1798	Dickerson Archive ‡
Centaur	1759-1782	Third Rate 74	Full-length centaur – ship plan (as taken) – 1760	NMM ZAZ0730
	1797-1819	Third Rate 74	Full-length centaur – Dickerson design 1800	Dickerson Archive
	1845-1864	Wood paddle frigate	Carved at Portsmouth 1842	TNA ADM 91/10
			Full-length centaur – surviving	Plymouth NB Museum
Centurion	1844-1870?	Third Rate 80	Carved by Hellyer of Portsmouth 1843	TNA ADM 87/13
			Bust of a warrior – surviving	Topsham Mus. Devon ‡
	1892-1910	Battleship	Bust of a warrior – surviving	NMRN Portsmouth
			Escutcheon holding mural crown & wreath – ship plan	NMM NPA8370
Cephalus	1807-1830	Brig-sloop 18	Male bust – Hellyer design 1814 – £3	TNA ADM 106/1887
Cerberus	1827-1866	Fifth Rate 46	Fore-part of three-headed dog – Dickerson design 1822	TNA ADM 106/1946
Challenger	1858-1921	Wood screw corvette	Bust of a warrior – Hellyer design 1857 – £10	TNA ADM 87/63
			Bust of a warrior – survivor	S'ton Ocean. Centre
Champion	1824-1867	Sloop 18	Bust of a warrior – Hellyer design 1824 – £4	TNA ADM 106/1889
Chanticleer	1861-1875	Wood screw sloop	Standing cockerel – Hellyer design 1860 – not approved	TNA ADM 87/76
Charles Galley	1676-1729	Fifth Rate 32	Full-length crowned lion – ship plan	NMM ZAZ0483
Charlotte	1710-1761	Royal Yacht 8	Full-length crowned lion – ship plan 1711	NMM NPD0738
			Full-length crowned lion – gilt – modern ship mod. 1988	Art Gallery of Ontario
Charon	1778-1781	Fifth Rate 44	Male full-length with spear – ship plan	NMM ZAZ2114
Charybdis	1859-1884	Wood screw corvette	Female demi-head – A P Elder design 1857 – £20	TNA ADM 87/64
			Female demi-head – last seen Rosyth Dockyard c1969	Believe lost 1970s
Chasseur	1855-1901	Iron floating factory	Uniformed male 3/4-length – surviving	Historic Docky'd Chatham
Chatham	1741-1867	Yacht 6	Full-length crowned lion – Georgian model	NMM SLR0460
	1793-1842	Yacht 6	Female standing figure with sprig of leaves – ship plan	NMM NPD0777
			Standing robed figure & sprig of leaves – ship plan 1826	NMM NPD0772
	1842-1867	Yacht 6	Standing child's figure – Hellyer design 1842	TNA ADM 87/12
Chesapeake	1855-1867	Wood screw frig. 51	Female 3/4-length bust – Hellyer design 1855 – £24	TNA ADM 87/52
			Female 3/4-length bust – restored by Andrew Peters	Blue Town Mus. Sheppey
Chester	1708-1750	Fourth Rate 50	Lion – carved by Crichley of Chatham 1719 – £10	*Ship Carvers* – P Thomas
Childers	1827-1865	Brig-sloop 16	Head and neck of a horse – Hellyer design 1846 – £6.10.0	TNA ADM 87/16

SHIP	DATES	SHIP TYPE	FIGUREHEAD/ORIGIN/DATE/COST	LOCATION/REF.
Cleopatra	1779-1814	Fifth Rate 32	Cleopatra – lost in 'The Great Fire', Devonport 1840	See Chapter 3.I
	1835-1862	Sixth Rate 26	Carved by Robert Hall of Rotherhithe 1834	TNA ADM 87/5
			Female 3/4-length bust – surviving	NMRN Portsmouth
	1878-1922	Screw corvette	Female bust in armour – surviving	Cutty Sark Collection
Clorinde	1803-1817	Fifth Rate 38	Female bust – figurehead design – ship plans – 1808	NMM ZAZ2640
Clown	1856-1871?	Wood screw gunboat	Full-length jester – surviving	NMM FHD0086 †
Collingwood	1841-1867	Third Rate 80	Male uniformed bust – ship plan	NMM ZAZ0508
			Bust in uniform – Dickerson design 1839 – not approved	TNA ADM 87/9
			Bust in uniform – last seen Castles' Yard	Lost 1941 in London Blitz
Bust of Collingwood	Uncertain	?	Bust in uniform – surviving	New Bedf'd Whaling Mus
Colossus	1848-1867	Third Rate 80	Male bust, bearded – Hellyer design 1847 – £36	TNA ADM 87/18
			Male bust – last seen Castles' Yard	Lost 1941 in London Blitz
Columbine	1826-1849	Sloop 18	Female 3/4-length – ship plan	NMM ZAZ4697
	1862-1875	Wood screw sloop	Carved by Hellyer of Portsmouth 1860 – £10	TNA ADM 88/16
			Female 3/4-length bust – surviving	HMS *Sultan*, Gosport
Comet	1742-1749	Bomb 14	Full-length kilted male with shield – ship plan	NMM ZAZ7930
	1783-1800	Fireship	Female full-length – ship plan	NMM ZAZ5581
	1828-1862	Sloop 18	Male bust – Hellyer design 1843 – £6	TNA ADM 87/13
Commerce de Marseilles	1793-1802	First Rate 120	French Arms with crown and wings – ship plan	NMM ZAZ0043
Concorde	1783-1811	Fifth Rate 36	Full-length uncrowned lion – ship plan (French)	NMM ZAZ2509
Condor	1876-1889	Comp screw gunvess	Female 3/4-length figure – surviving	Wellington, New Zealand
Confiance	1808-1810	Sixth Rate 22	Female full-length – ship plan – 1805 (French)	NMM ZAZ3673
Conflict	1846-1863	Wood screw sloop	Carved by Hellyer of Portsmouth 1845 – £7.15.0	TNA ADM 87/15
			Bust of a warrior – surviving	HMS *Caledonia*, Rosyth
Conqueror	1773-1794	Third Rate 74	Full-length warrior – ship plan	NMM ZAZ0694
	1801-1822	Third Rate 74	Bust of Nelson – Dickerson design c1806	Dickerson Archive
			William the Conqueror – lost 'The Great Fire', Devonport, 1840	See Chapter 3.I
	1855-1861	Screw First Rate 101	Carved by Dickerson of Plymouth 1854 – £35	TNA ADM 91/16
			Crowned male – head only surviving	Halifax, Nova Scotia
Constance	1846-1875	Fourth Rate 50	Female bust – Dickerson design 1844 – £15	TNA ADM 87/14 ‡
			Female 3/4-length bust – gilt – ship model	NMM SLR0095
			Carved by Hellyer of Portsmouth 1846 – £24	TNA ADM 87/15
			Female 3/4-length bust – surviving	HMS *Excellent*, Portsm'th ‡
	1880-1899	Screw corvette	Female 3/4-length bust – lost c1956	Cordite factory, Holton Heath
Contest	1874-1889	Comp screw gunboat	Oarsman holding an oar – single sculls in trailboard – ship plan	NMM NPD 0929
Conway (ex-*Nile*)	1876-1856	Training ship	Demi-head of Nelson – surviving	HMS *Nelson*, Portsmouth ‡
			Ship model showing 1937 demi-head of Nelson	NMRN Portsmouth
Cordelia	1856-1870	Wood screw sloop	Female 3/4-length bust – Dickerson design 1855	Dickerson Archive
Cormorant	1781-1786	Brig-sloop 12	Male full-length – ship plan	NMM ZAZ4532
	1842-1853	Wood paddle sloop	Male bust – Hellyer design 1841 – not approved £7.10.0	TNA ADM 87/11
			Standing bird – Hellyer design 1841 £6.10.0	TNA ADM 87/11
	1877-1946	Comp screw sloop	Female 3/4-length with bird beside her – Hellyer design	Private coll'n, Stockholm
			Female 3/4-length with long hair – ship plan – 1878	NMM NPA9335
Cornwallis	1813-1916	Third Rate 74	Busthead carved by Overton & Co 1813 – £21	TNA ADM 106/1794
			Uniformed full-length male – surviving	Missing †
Coronation	1685-1691	Second Rate 90	Full-length crowned lion ridden by cherub – NB model	Kriegstein Collection USA
Cossack	1886-1905	Torpedo cruiser	Male demi-head – Kay & Reid design 1886	NMM NPA9386
Courageux	1761-1796	Third Rate 74	Full-length warrior – ship plan (French)	NMM ZAZ1245

SHIP	DATES	SHIP TYPE	FIGUREHEAD/ORIGIN/DATE/COST	LOCATION/REF.
Creole	1845-1875	Sixth Rate 26	Female bust – last recorded Devonport c1936	Lost in Blitz 1941
Crescent	1810-1854	Fifth Rate 38	Standing figure of Fame – Grayfoot & Overton design 1819	TNA ADM 106/1795
Cressy	1853-1867	Screw Third Rate 80	Male warrior bust – Hellyer design 1848 – £40	TNA ADM 87/23
			Male warrior bust – last seen Castles' Yard	Lost 1941 in London Blitz
Crocodile	1781-1784	Sixth Rate 24	Male full-length with crocodile in trailboard – ship plan	NMM ZAZ3672
Cruizer	1732-1744	Sloop 14	Full-length young merman with coiled tail in t'board – ship plan	NMM ZAZ4721
	1828-1849	Brig-sloop 18	Bust of a sailor – Hellyer design 1844 – £7	TNA ADM 87/14
	1852-1893	Wood screw sloop	Demi-head of a sailor – Hellyer design – not approved	TNA ADM 87/38
			Bust of a sailor – Hellyer design 1851 – £6.10.0	TNA ADM 87/38
			Bust of a sailor – surviving	NMRN Portsmouth
Culloden	1747-1770	Third Rate 74	Full-length crowned lion – ship plan	NMM ZAZ0976
	1776-1781	Third Rate 74	Male full-length in armour – ship plan	NMM ZAZ0978
Cumberland	1739-1742	Fireship 8	Full-length crowned lion – ship plan	NMM CHN0177
	1774-1805	Third Rate 74	Full-length figure of Neptune – ship plan	NMM ZAZ0985
	1807-1870	Third Rate 74	Bust of a warrior – ship plan	NMM ZAZ0991
			Bust in plumed helmet – last recorded Chatham 1948	Believe lost 1950s
	1842-1889	Third Rate 70	Demi-head of Sir James Graham – Hellyer & Browning design 1836 – £21	TNA ADM 87/6
			Busthead – Hellyer & Browning proposal 1836 – £17.17.0	TNA ADM 87/6
			Male bust – Robert Hall design 1836	TNA ADM 87/6
			Male bust – gilt – half block design model	NMM SLR0808
Curacoa	1854-1869	Wood screw frigate	Female bust – Hellyer design 1852	TNA ADM 87/41
Curlew	1854-1865	Wood screw sloop	Standing bird – Hellyer design 1854 – £5.15.0	TNA ADM 87/47
Cygnet	1874-1889	Comp screw gunboat	Female 3/4-length – ship plan	NMM NPD 0915
			Female 3/4-length figure – design by unnamed carver	Admlty Library Ref P1030
Daedalus	1826-1911	Fifth Rate 46	Male bust – photographed on ship's bow – now lost	Bristol Mus. & Art Gallery
Danae	1759-1771	Fifth Rate 38	Male full-length – ship plan (French)	NMM ZAZ2636 & 2637
	1798-1800	Sixth Rate 20	Oval escutcheon – ship plan (French)	NMM ZAZ3748
Daphne	1776-1802	Sixth Rate 20	Female full-length figure – ship plan	NMM ZAZ3996
	1796-1798	Sixth Rate 24	Female demi-head – ship plan	NMM ZAZ3777
	1838-1864	Corvette 18	Carved by Robert Hall of Rotherhithe 1835	TNA ADM 87/5
			Female bust – surviving	NMM FHD0072
	1888-1904	Sloop	Female 3/4-length wearing a tiara – ship plan	NMM NPA9882
Daring	1844-1864	Brig 12	Bust of a sailor – Hellyer design 1843 – £7	TNA ADM 87/13
			Bust of a sailor – surviving	NMM FHD0073
Dart	1847-1863	Brigantine	Female bust – Hellyer design 1846 – £6.10.0	TNA ADM 87/16
Dasher	1837-1885	Wood pad packet	Male bust – Hellyer & Browning design 1837 – £3.10.0	TNA ADM 87/7
Dauntless	1847-1885	Wood screw frigate	Uncrowned lion with escutcheon – Hellyer design 1846	TNA ADM 87/16
Deal Castle	1756-1780	Sixth Rate 20	Roman figure of Mars – carved by Thos Burrough – £7.4.0	*Ship Carvers* – P Thomas
Decade	1798-1811	Fifth Rate 36	Female full-length – ship plan (French)	NMM ZAZ2250
Dedaigneuse	1801-1823	Fifth Rate 36	Female full-length – ship plan (French)	NMM ZAZ2754
Dee	1832-1871	Wood paddle vessel	Crowned male bust – surviving	NMM FHD0074
Defiance	1783-1817	Third Rate 74	Bust of a warrior – Hellyer design 1812 – £21	TNA ADM 106/1886
	1861-1931	Screw Second Rate 81	Bust of a warrior – Hellyer design 1859 – £40	TNA ADM 87/71
			Bust of a warrior – surviving	Plymouth NB Museum
Deptford	1687-1726	Fourth Rate 50	Crowned lion – ship plan 1719	Science Museum B004825
Desiree	1800-1832	Fifth Rate 36	Female bust – Hellyer design 1808 – £6	TNA ADM 106/1885
Determinee	1799-1803	Sixth Rare 24	Male standing figure – ship plan (French)	NMM ZAZ3784

SHIP	DATES	SHIP TYPE	FIGUREHEAD/ORIGIN/DATE/COST	LOCATION/REF.
Devastation	1841-1866	Wood paddle sloop	A dragon's head – Hellyer proposal – not approved	TNA ADM 87/10
			Bust of a warrior – Hellyer design 1840 – £7	TNA ADM 87/10
			Replacement approved 1843 – £8.13.4	TNA ADM 88/6
Devonshire	1812-1862	Third Rate 74	Male bust – lost Sheerness c1950	Navy & Army Illust (1901)
Dexterous	1805-1816	Brig 12	Uniformed male bust – Hellyer design 1814 – £3	TNA ADM 106/1887
Diadem	1856-1875	Wood screw frigate	Female 3/4-length bust – Dickerson design 1860 – £18	Dickerson Archive
Diamond	1708-1722	Fifth Rate 50	Full-length crowned lion with supporters – Navy Board model	Kriegstein Collection USA
	1848-1885	Sixth Rate 28	Female 3/4-length bust – Hellyer design 1847 – £12	TNA ADM 87/17
Diana	1757-1793	Fifth Rate 32	Full-length crowned lion – ship plan	NMM ZAZ3032
	1794-1815	Fifth Rate 38	Female full-length with bow – Navy Board model	NMM SLR0572
			Female full-length with bow – Georgian ship model	NMM SLR0342
			Female full-length with bow – William Anderson sketch	V & A Museum
	1822-1874	Fifth Rate 46	Female bust – design by unnamed carver 1820 – £6	TNA ADM 106/1824
			Female bust – surviving	Historic D'yard, Chatham
Dido	1836-1903	Corvette 18	Female 3/4-length – ship plan	NMM ZAZ4066
			Female 3/4-length bust, gilt – full hull model	NMM SLR0757
Diligence	1756-1779	Sloop 10	Full-length kilted warrior with sword – ship plan	NMM ZAZ5013
Dispatch	1851-1901	Brig-sloop	Demi-figure of Hermes – Hellyer design – not approved £7	TNA ADM 87/17
			Bust of Hermes – Hellyer design 1847 – £6.10.0	TNA ADM 87/17
Dolphin	1731-1755	Sixth Rate 20	Full-length crowned lion – Navy Board model	NMM SLR0226
	1781-1817	Fifth Rate 44	Male full-length – ship plan	NMM ZAZ2206
	1836-1894	Brigantine 3	Female 3/4-length – ship plan	NMM ZAZ5050
			Female 3/4-length bust (white) – ship model 1836	Science Museum 1977-186
Donegal	1798-1845	Third Rate 76	Full-length kilted male warrior – ship plan	NMM ZAZ0643
	1858-1886	Screw First Rate 101	Female 3/4-length bust – Dickerson design 1855	Dickerson Archive
			Uniformed male bust – Dickerson design 1855 – £35	Dickerson Archive
Dorset	1753-1815	Yacht 10	Female full-length – Georgian block model	NMM SLR0493
Dragon	1782-1785	Cutter 10	Full-length winged dragon – ship plan	NMM ZAZ6356
	1798-1842	Third Rate 74	Bust of a warrior – Hellyer design 1807 – £21	TNA ADM 106/1883
	1845-1864	Wood paddle frigate	Standing dragon – Dickerson design 1844 – £7	Dickerson Archive
	1878-1892	Comp screw sloop	Head of a dragon – last recorded St Budeaux Plymouth	Believe lost 1960s
Dreadnought	1801-1857	Second Rate 98	Royal arms with a crouched lion above – ship plan	NMM ZAZ0196
Driver	1797-1834	Sloop 18	Uniformed male bust – Hellyer design 1814 – £4	TNA ADM 106/1887
	1840-1861	Wood paddle sloop	Male bust – Hellyer design 1840 – £6	TNA ADM 87/10
Dublin	1757-1784	Third Rate 74	Full-length bearded male – ship plan	NMM ZAZ1013
Duc de Chartres	1781-1784	Ship-sloop	Male full-length in frock coat – ship plan – (French)	NMM ZAZ3912
Duc d'Estissac	1781-1783	Sloop 18	Formal male full-length in wig – ship plan – 1779 (French)	NMM ZAZ3924
Duke	1777-1843	Second Rate 90	Group figurehead – Royal bust, arms, Neptune and cherubs – ship plan	NMM ZAZ0213
			Group figurehead – bust, arms, Neptunes riding sea horses – gilt – ship model	USNA Museum Annapolis
Duke of Kent (Project)	1809		Standing male brandishing sword – design ship model	NMM SLR0660
Duke of Wellington	1852-1904	Screw First Rate 131	Carved by Hellyer of Blackwall 1852 – £100	TNA ADM 87/42
			Uniformed bust of the duke – last seen Castles' Yard	Lost 1941 in London Blitz
Duncan	1859-1910	Screw First Rate 101	Uniformed bust – Hellyer design 1859 – £54	TNA ADM 87/72
			Uniformed bust of the admiral – surviving	HMS *Caledonia*, Rosyth ‡
Dwarf	1843-1853	Iron screw vessel	Female 3/4-length bust – Hellyer design 1844 – £4.10.0	TNA ADM 87/14
Eagle	1804-1918	Third Rate 74	Male bust – only head and neck surviving	HMS *Eaglet*, Liverpool
Echo	1782-1797	Sloop 16	Full-length uncrowned lion – ship plan	NMM ZAZ3835

SHIP	DATES	SHIP TYPE	FIGUREHEAD/ORIGIN/DATE/COST	LOCATION/REF.
Eclipse	1860-1867	Wood screw sloop	Female 3/4-length figure – surviving	Auckland, New Zealand ‡
Edgar	1779-1814	Third Rate 74	Full-length crowned & robed king – ship plan	NMM ZAZ0891
			King Edgar – lost in 'The Great Fire', Devonport 1840	See Chapter 3.I
	1858-1904	Third Rate 74	Bust of the king – Hellyer design 1855 – £40	TNA ADM 87/56
Edinburgh	1716-1771	Third Rate 70	Full-length crowned lion – gilt – Navy Board model 1721	Art Gallery of Ontario
	1811-1865	Third Rate 74	City arms & supporters – Hellyer des. – not approved £44	TNA ADM 106/1889
			Kilted standing male – Hellyer des. – not approved £36	TNA ADM 106/1889
			Uniformed bust – Hellyer design 1819 – £21	TNA ADM 106/1889
			Uniformed bust with feather bonnet – surviving	Newport News, Virginia
Egmont	1768-1799	Third Rate 74	Full-length cloaked male – ship model 1768	Science Museum 1892-89
			Male standing figure – Navy Board model – 1980	NMM SLR0144
Egyptienne	1801-1817	Fifth Rate 40	Female standing figure with hand-mirror – ship plan – (French)	NMM ZAZ2079
Elephant	1786-1830	Third Rate 74	Male bust – Hellyer design 1814 – not approved £14	TNA ADM 106/1889
Elfin	1849-1901	Paddle yacht	Female standing figure – Hellyer design 1848 – £20	TNA ADM 87/24
			Female bust – Hellyer proposal 1849 – £5	TNA ADM 87/27
			Female bust – surviving	NMRN Portsmouth
Elizabeth	1737-1766	Third Rate 64	3/4-length Queen Elizabeth I – surviving	Sir Max Aitken Museum †
Elk	1847-1863	Brig-sloop 16	Head & neck of an elk – Hellyer design 1847 – £6.10.0	TNA ADM 87/17
Elphinstone	1824-1862	Sloop 18	Male 3/4-length figure – surviving	New Delhi, India
Elvin	1807-1814	Sloop 18	Female 3/4-length – ship plan (Danish)	NMM ZAZ4251
Emerald	1856-1869	Wood screw frigate	Female 3/4-length reaching forward – design model of ship's bow	NMM SLR2189
	1876-1906	Comp screw corvette	Female 3/4-length bust – ship plan	NMM NPB1318
Enchantress	1862-1889	Despatch vessel	Female 3/4-length figure – Dickerson design 1861	Dickerson Archive
Encounter	1873-1888	Wood screw corvette	Male bust – surviving	HMAS *Cerberus*, Australia
Endymion	1779-1790	Fifth Rate 44	Female full-length with harp – ship model – 1779	Science Museum 1934-630
	1797-1864	Fourth Rate 50	Royal arms in oval escutcheon – Hellyer design 1815	TNA ADM 106/1888
	Uncertain	?	Male standing figure – ship plan – 1799	Dickerson Archive
Enterprise	1774-1807	Sixth Rate 28	Male full-length – gilt – Navy Board model 1775	Science Museum Pictorial
	1864-1886	Ironclad sloop	Bust of a warrior – Dickerson design 1863	Dickerson Archive
Epervier	1803-1811	Brig-sloop 16	Standing sparrowhawk – ship plan (French)	NMM ZAZ4305
Erebus	1856-1884	Floating battery	Crowned male bust – surviving	HMS *Sultan*, Gosport
	1856-1884	Floating battery	Male bust – last seen RN Armament Depot, Upnor 1948	Believe lost 1950s
Espiegle	1794-1795	Brig-sloop 14	Oval escutcheon with foliage – ship plan (French)	NMM ZAZ4640
	1900-1923	Sloop	Female 3/4-length figure – surviving	NMRN Portsmouth
Espion	1793-1794	Sloop 16	Full-length uncrowned lion – ship plan	NMM ZAZ4656 & 4658
Espoir	1860-1869	Wood screw gunves.	Female 3/4-length bust – Dickerson design 1859 – £6	Dickerson Archive
Etna	1796-1797	Sixth Rate 20	Standing bird – ship plan (French)	NMM ZAZ4510
Eugenie	1797-1803	Sloop 16	Female standing figure – ship plan	NMM ZAZ4110 & 4111
Euryalus	1853-1867	Wood screw frigate	Male bust – Nehemiah Williams design 1850 – £12	TNA ADM 87/31
			Demi-head – Hellyer proposal £24.10.0 – not approved	TNA ADM 87/40
			Bust of a warrior – Hellyer design 1852 – £18.10	TNA ADM 87/40
			Bust of a warrior – Dickerson design 1854 – £18.10.0	Dickerson Archive
			Bust of a warrior – gilt – ship model	NMM SLR0100
	1877-1897	Iron screw corvette	Royal arms with lion above & warrior supporter – Hellyer design 1877	NMM NPB 1672
Eurydice	1781-1834	Sixth Rate 24	Female full-length – ship plan	NMM ZAZ5885
	1843-1878	Sixth Rate 24	Female 3/4-length with an imp – Hellyer design 1842 – £18	TNA ADM 87/12
			Female 3/4-length with an imp – half block design model	NMM SLR0811
			Female 3/4-length – surviving	NMRN Portsmouth

SHIP	DATES	SHIP TYPE	FIGUREHEAD/ORIGIN/DATE/COST	LOCATION/REF.
Exeter	1697-1763	Fourth Rate 60	Full-length crowned lion – gilt – Navy Board model	Science Mus. 1935-0515
Experiment	1774-1778	Fourth Rate 50	Female full-length with a lyre – ship plan	NMM ZAZ1661
			Female full-length with a lyre – gilt – Navy Board model 1775	Science Museum Pictorial
Fairy	1845-1868	Iron screw yacht	Female 3/4-length holding flowers – ship plan – 1844	NMM NPD0746
			Female bust – small – ship plan	NMM NPD0704
			Royal arms with a crown above – ship plan – 1844	NMM NPD0744 & 0745
			Royal arms with a crown above – ship plan – 1858	NMM NPD0751
			Royal arms with a crown above – ship plan – 1863	NMM NPD0694
			Royal arms with a crown above – ship model	Science Museum 1908-78
			Female 3/4-length bust – surviving	NMRN Portsmouth
Falcon	1820-1834	Brig-sloop 10	Female 3/4-length – surviving	Privately owned Tasmania
	1854-1869	Wood screw sloop	Standing falcon – Dickerson design 1854	Dickerson Archive
Fantome	1839-1864	Brig-sloop 16	Female 3/4-length – Robert Hall design 1839 – £5	TNA ADM 87/9
Favourite	1757-1784	Sloop 14	Female full-length – ship plan	NMM ZAZ4211
	1829-1905	Sloop 18	Female 3/4-length – surviving	NMM FHD0075
Fawn	1856-1884	Wood screw sloop	Standing fawn – Hellyer design 1855 – £7.10.0 – not approved	TNA ADM 87/56
			Female bust – Hellyer design 1855 – £7.10.0	TNA ADM 87/56 & 88/12
Fearless	1837-1875	Wood paddle vessel	Female bust – Hellyer design 1845 – £4.15.0	TNA ADM 87/15
Ferret	1840-1869	Brig 8	Standing ferret – Davies & Dickerson design – not approved	TNA ADM 87/10
			Male bust – Davies & Dickerson design 1840 – not approved	TNA ADM 87/10
			Male bust – Dickerson design 1850	Dickerson Archive
Firebrand	1778-1781	Fireship	Full-length crowned lion – Georgian ship model	NMM SLR0536
	1877-1905	Comp screw gunboat	Female 3/4-length fig – design by unknown carver 1876	Admlty Library Ref P1030
Firefly	1828-1835	Schooner 6	Female 3/4-length – G Faldo design 1832 – £6 – not approved	TNA ADM 87/3
			Female 3/4-length – Robt Hall design 1832 – approved	TNA ADM 87/3
			Female 3/4-length – G Faldo alternative design 1832	TNA ADM 87/3
Firm	1877-1907	Comp screw gunboat	Demi-head of a sailor – design by unknown carver 1876	Admlty Library Ref P1030
Fisgard	1797-1814	Fifth Rate 44	Female full-length – ship plan	NMM ZAZ 2376 & 2411
			Female full-length – gilt – design half-block model	NMM SLR0588
	1819-1879	Fifth Rate 46	Male bust – surviving	HMS *Raleigh*, Torpoint ‡
Fleche	1797-1810	Sloop 18	Female bust – Dickerson design 1804 – £5.5.0	TNA ADM 106/1937
Flora	1844-1891	Fifth Rate 36	Female 3/4-length – Dickerson design 1854 – £14.10.0	Dickerson Archive
			Female 3/4-length bust – surviving	Simonstown, South Africa
Fly	1732-1750	Sloop 12	Male full-length with a club – ship plan	NMM ZAZ4666
	1776-1802	Sloop 14	Female full-length – ship plan	NMM ZAZ4667
Flying Fish	1844-1852	Brig 12	Female 3/4-length – ship plan	NMM ZAZ4957
			Full-length fish – Hellyer design 1843	TNA ADM 87/13
	1855-1866	Despatch vessel	Female 3/4-length bust – Dickerson design 1855 – £6	Dickerson Archive
Forester	1832-1843	Brig-sloop 10	Male bust – surviving	NMM FHD0076
Formidable	1825-1906	Second Rate 84	Bust of a warrior – surviving	Newport News, Virginia
Forte	1858-1905	Screw frigate 51	Carved by Hellyer of Cosham 1857 – £24	TNA ADM 91/20 & 88/13
			Male bust – under restoration	Historic D'yard, Chatham
			Male bust – replica	Marine Parade, Sheerness
Fortune	1778-1780	Sloop 14	Female full-length with a shield – ship plan	NMM ZAZ5078
Forward	1877-1904	Comp screw gunboat	Male 3/4-length – surviving	Halifax, Nova Scotia
Foudroyant	1758-1787	Second rate 80	Male full-length – ship plan (French)	NMM ZAZ0633
			Male full-length with small beard – ship plan	NMM NPD0874
	1758-1787?	Second Rate 80	Standing eagle – Dickerson design – undated	Dickerson Archive
	1798-1897	Second Rate 80	Crowned male bust – surviving	Stored by Mus. Service †

SHIP	DATES	SHIP TYPE	FIGUREHEAD/ORIGIN/DATE/COST	LOCATION/REF.
Fox	1829-1882	Fifth Rate 46	Bust of a huntsman – Last recorded Plymouth	Destroyed 1961
Frederick William	1860-1953	Screw First Rate 110	Uniformed male bust – Hellyer design 1860 – £54	TNA ADM 87/74
			Uniformed demi-head – Hellyer design – £60 – not approved	TNA ADM 87/74
			Uniformed bust – surviving	NMM FHD0077
Fubbs	1682-1781	Royal Yacht	Crowned arms with female supporters and winged putti – Navy Board model	NMM SLR0430
Furieuse	1809-1816	Fifth Rate 38	Female demi-head – Hellyer design 1811 – £6	TNA ADM 106/1886
Furious	1850-1884	Wood paddle frigate	Bust of a warrior – Hellyer design 1849 – £10.12.0	TNA ADM 87/25
Fury	1845-1864	Wood paddle sloop	Female 3/4-length – Hellyer design 1845 – £7.15.0	TNA ADM 87/15
Ganges	1821-1906	Second Rate 84	Crowned male bust – surviving	Shotley, Suffolk
Gannet	1857-1877	Wood screw sloop	Carved by Dickerson of Devonport 1856	TNA ADM 88/11 & 12
			Standing gannet – surviving	NMM FHD0079
	1878-1903	Comp screw sloop	Standing gannet – ship plan 1876	NMM ZAZ 2412
			Standing gannet – ship plan 1876	NMM NPB 2412
			Standing gannet – surviving	Flensburg, Germany
			Standing gannet – replica	Historic D'yard Chatham
Garland	1800-1803	Sixth Rate 22	Standing warrior – ship plan	NMM ZAZ3610
Genoa	1814-1838	Third Rate 78	Crowned male standing figure – ship plan – 1815	NMM ZAZ0898
			Warrior figure – lost in 'The Great Fire', Devonport 1840	See Chapter 3.I
Geyser	1841-1866	Wood paddle sloop	Male bust – Dickerson design 1840 – £5.5.0	TNA ADM 87/10 & 88/4
			Male bust – Hellyer design 1840 – £6.10.0	TNA ADM 87/10 & 88/4
			Scroll-head approved – £5.5.0	TNA ADM 91/9
Gibraltar	1780-1836	Second Rate 80	Full-length crowned lion – ship plan	NMM ZAZ0754
	1860-1889	Screw First Rate 101	Uniformed male bust – Dickerson design 1859 – £35	Dickerson Archive
	1892-1923	First Class cruiser	Bow decoration – Union flag in cartouche	Navy & Army Illust. (1896)
Gier	1799-1803	Brig-sloop 14	Standing soldier with a rifle – ship plan (Dutch)	NMM ZAZ4932
Gladiator	1783-1817	Fifth Rate 44	Full-length warrior – Henry Adams design	Buckler's Hard Mar. Mus.
	1844-1879	Wood paddle frigate	Male bust – Hellyer design 1844 – £8.10.0	TNA ADM 87/14
			Demi-head – Hellyer proposal 1844 – £12.10.0 – not approved	TNA ADM 87/14
			Bust of a warrior – last recorded at Devonport	Destroyed 1945
Glasgow	1814-1829	Fourth Rate 50	Standing kilted soldier – surviving	NMRN Portsmouth
	1861-1884	Wood screw frigate	Male 3/4-length bust – Hellyer design 1860 – £27.10.0	TNA ADM 87/76
			Male bust – surviving	Fall River, Massachusetts
Gleaner	1838-1849	Wood pad. gunvessel	Female 3/4-length bust – surviving	Fort Blockhouse, Gosport†
Glory	1788-1825	Second Rate 90	Standing warrior with plumed helmet – ship plan	NMM ZAZ0221
Gluckstadt	1807-1814	Brig-sloop 18	Bust wearing a beret – ship plan (Danish)	NMM ZAZ4254
			Female bust – Geo Williams proposal 1808 – £3	TNA ADM 106/1821
Goliath	1781-1812	Third Rate 74	Goliath – lost 'The Great Fire', Devonport 1840	See Chapter 3.I
	1842-1875	Second Rate 80	Bust of a warrior – Hellyer design 1841 – £30	TNA ADM 87/11
			Crowned male bust – under restoration	Historic D'yard, Chatham
Gorgon	1837-1864	Wood paddle frigate	Bust of a Gorgon – Hellyer design 1852 – £9.10.0	TNA ADM 87/42
Goshawk	(Renamed)	Brig-sloop 12	Standing hawk – Hellyer design 1844 – £7	TNA ADM 87/14
Grafton	1679-1707	Third Rate 70	Full-length lion – gilt – Navy Board rigged model	USNA Museum Annapolis
Grampus	1782-1794	Fourth Rate 50	Full-length lion – gilt – ship model (1957)	Merseyside Mar. Mus.
	1845-1897	Fourth Rate 50	Crowned bust of Neptune – Hellyer design 1845 – £5.15.0	TNA ADM 87/15
			Crowned bust of Neptune – surviving	NMRN Portsmouth
Grana	1781-1806	Sixth Rate 28	Full-length crowned lion – ship plan (Spanish)	NMM ZAZ3058 & 3059

SHIP	DATES	SHIP TYPE	FIGUREHEAD/ORIGIN/DATE/COST	LOCATION/REF.
Granado	1742-1763	Bomb 12	Full-length Hermes with winged helmet & caduceus – ship plan	NMM ZAZ5628
Grasshopper	1813-1832	Brig-sloop 18	Female bust – Hellyer design 1813 – £3	TNA ADM 106/1887
Grecian	1838-1865	Brig-sloop 16	Female 3/4-length bust – last recorded Devonport c1936	Lost in Blitz 1941
Greyhound	1773-1781	Sixth Rate 28	Female full-length with a greyhound in trailboard – Henry Adams design	Buckler's Hard Mar. Mus.
	1783-1808	Fifth Rate 32	Female bust – unknown designer – £5	TNA ADM 106/1820
	1859-1906	Wood screw sloop	Racing greyhound – Dickerson design 1856	Dickerson Archive
Growler	1841-1854	Wood paddle sloop	Demi-head of a sailor – Hellyer design 1840 – £8 not approved	TNA ADM 87/10 & 88/4
			A dog – Hellyer proposal 1840 – £9	TNA ADM 88/4 & 91/9
Guay Trouin	1780-1783	Sloop 18	Full-length warrior with a sword – ship plan (French)	NMM ZAZ4271
Halifax	1800-1801	Brig 12	Female 3/4-length – ship plan	NMM ZAZ4867 & 4868
Hamadryad	1823-1905	Fifth Rate 46	Carved by Dickerson of Plymouth 1822 – £8	TNA ADM 106/1946
			Female bust – surviving	Pembroke Dock
Hampton Court	1678-1701	Third Rate 70	Full-length crowned lion – gilt – ship model	Wilton House, Wilton
	1744-1774	Third Rate 64	Full length lion – painted on block – design model	NMM SLR0467
Hannibal	1854-1904	Screw Second Rate 91	Demi-head of a warrior – Hellyer design 1852 – £40	TNA ADM 87/42
Harlequin	1836-1889	Brig-sloop	Original carved by Robert Hall 1833	TNA ADM 87/3
			Replacement female bust – Hellyer design 1845	TNA ADM 87-3
			Female bust – surviving	NMM FHD0081
Harrier	1854-1866	Wood screw sloop	Full-length dog – Hellyer design 1852 – £6.10.0	TNA ADM 87/41
Hastings	1819-1885	Third Rate 74	Replacement carved by Hellyer 1855	TNA ADM 88/11 & 12
			Male uniformed bust – surviving	Mar. Museum, Liverpool
Havick	1796-1800	Sloop 16	Standing goose or swan – ship plan (Dutch)	NMM ZAZ3791
Hawke	1820-1865	Third Rate 74	Full-length – Grayfoot & Overton proposal 1818 – £38	TNA ADM 106-1795
			Bust – Grayfoot & Overton proposal 1818 – £21 not approved	TNA ADM 106-1795
			Bust of the admiral – Hellyer design 1847 – £35	TNA ADM 87/18
Hector	1774-1816	Third Rate 74	Full-length warrior with a sword & shield – ship plan	NMM ZAZ1023
			Full-length warrior with sword, etc – painting of Navy Board model	Kriegstein Collection USA
Helder	1809-1817	Fifth Rate 36	Female bust – figurehead design – ship plan – 1808	NMM ZAZ2699
Heldin	1799-1802	Sixth Rate 28	3/4-length Britannia-like figure – ship plan (Dutch)	NMM ZAZ3408
Helena	1843-1921	Brig-sloop 16	Female 3/4-length bust – Hellyer design 1839 – £5.5.0	TNA ADM 87/9
Henrietta	1679-1721	Yacht 8	Full-length lion – gilt – ship model	USNA Museum Annapolis
Henry Grace a Dieu	1514-1547	Galleon 80	Seated lion – ship model	NMM SLR0325
Herald	1824-1862	Sixth Rate 28	Male bust – Hellyer design 1824 – £6	TNA ADM 106/1896
Hercule	1798-1810	Third Rate 74	Full-length Hercules wearing a lion-skin – ship plan (French)	NMM ZAZ0881
			Male full-length – Dickerson design	Dickerson Archive
Hercules	1815-1865	Third Rate 74	Male bust, gilt – half block model	NMM SLR0683
Hero	1858-1871	Screw Second Rate 91	Bust of a warrior – Hellyer design 1857 – £40	TNA ADM 87/64
Heroine	1783-1806	Fifth Rate 32	Full-length female warrior – Henry Adams design	Buckler's Hard Mar. Mus.
	1841-1878	Packet brig 8	3/4-length female warrior bust – Hellyer design 1841 -£6	TNA ADM 87/11
Heron	1847-1859	Brig 16	Standing heron – Hellyer design 1847 – £7	TNA ADM 87/17
Heureux	1799-1806	Sixth Rate 22	Female standing figure – ship plan (French)	NMM ZAZ3781

SHIP	DATES	SHIP TYPE	FIGUREHEAD/ORIGIN/DATE/COST	LOCATION/REF.
Hibernia	1804-1902	First Rate 110	Britannia with harp – Hellyer proposal – £50 – not approved	TNA ADM 87/15
			Male 3/4-length with harp – Hellyer design 1845 – £47	TNA ADM 87/15
			Male 3/4-length with harp – surviving	Vittoriosa, Malta ‡
Highflyer	1851-1871	Wood screw frigate	Bird with spread wings – gilt – ship model 1851	Science Museum 1902-88
Himalaya	1854-1895	Iron screw troopship	Male 3/4-length with a sword – gilt – ship model	Science Museum 1888-241
			Male 3/4-length with turban & sword – surviving	NMM FHD0082
Hindostan	1841-1921	Second Rate 80	Male 3/4-length – W C Gofe design 1841 – £30	TNA ADM 87/11
Hogue	1811-1865	Third Rate 74	Uncrowned crouching lion and royal arms – surviving	NMM FHD0083
Hood	1859-1888	Screw Second Rate 91	Bust of the admiral – Hellyer design 1850 – £20.18.0	TNA ADM 87/48
			Male bust, gilt – half block model	NMM SLR0838
			Bust of the admiral – last seen Castles' Yard	Lost 1941 in London Blitz
Hope	1808-1819	Brig-sloop 10	Female standing fig. with anchor – Hellyer des. – not approved	TNA ADM 106/1886 ‡
	1824-1882	Packet brig 3	Female bust – Dickerson design 1824 – £3	TNA ADM 106/1949
Horatio	1807-1865	Fifth Rate 38	Bust of Lord Nelson – surviving	NMM FHD0084
Hornet	1854-1868	Wood screw sloop	Female 3/4-length figure – Hellyer design – £9 not approved	TNA ADM 87/42
			Female bust – Hellyer proposal 1852 – £6.10.0	TNA ADM 87/42
			Female bust – Hellyer design 1859 – £10	TNA ADM 87/73
Hotspur	1870-1904	Armoured ram	Bow decoration – Cartouche with Percy family arms	Newport News, Virginia
Hound	1846-1887	Brig 8	Head and neck of a hound – Hellyer design 1846 – £5.15.0	TNA ADM 87/16
Howe	1815-1854	First Rate 120	Male bust with supporters – Geo. Williams 1814 – £126	TNA ADM 106/1823
			Male bust – Hellyer proposal 1835 – £30 – not approved	TNA ADM 88/22
			Male bust – Robt. Hall proposal 1835 – £20 – not approved	TNA ADM 88/22
			Beardrd male bust – surviving	Lloyds, Chatham †
	1860-1885	Screw First Rate 110	Bust of the admiral – Hellyer design 1859 – £54	TNA ADM 87/70
			Uniformed bust – gilt – full hull model	NMM SLR0914
			Bust of the admiral – surviving – privately owned	Great Missenden, Bucks.
Hugh Lindsay	1829-1859	Wood paddle sloop	Male bust – surviving	Mumbai, India
Hussar	1807-1833	Fifth Rate 38	Uniformed Hussar – lost in 'The Great Fire', Devonport 1840	See Chapter 3.I
Hyperion	1807-1833	Fifth Rate 32	A sunburst – ship plan	NMM ZAZ3002 & 3003
Icarus	1858-1875	Wood screw sloop	Male bust with wings – Hellyer design 1858 – £9.10.0	TNA ADM 87/67
Illustrious	1789-1795	Third Rate 74	Full length warrior – unnamed carver's design	Bucklers Hard, Hants
	1803-1868	Third Rate 74	Crowned male bust – Hellyer design 1808 – £21	TNA ADM 106/1885
			Crowned male bust – Hellyer design 1816 – £21	TNA ADM 106/1888
			Bust of George III – surviving	NMRN Portsmouth
Imaum	1836-1863	Third Rate 76	Female bust with a large symbol in trailboards – ship plan	NMM ZAZ1095
			Female bust – surviving	Halifax, Nova Scotia
Immortalite	1798-1806	Fifth Rate 42	Female full-length – ship plan (French)	NMM ZAZ2743
	1859-1883	Wood screw frigate	Female demi-head – Hellyer proposal – £23 – not approved	TNA ADM 87/39
			Female bust – Hellyer design 1852 – £18.10.0	TNA ADM 87/39
			Female 3/4-length bust – waterline model	NMM SLR0912
Imperieuse	1793-1803	Fifth Rate 40	French arms and decorations – ship plan (French)	NMM ZAZ2163
	1805-1838	Fifth Rate 38	Female bust with tiara – figurehead design – ship plan	NMM ZAZ2584
	1852-1867	Wood screw frigate	Female bust – Hellyer proposal 1851 – £18 – not approved	TNA ADM 87/38
			Female demi-head – Hellyer design 1851 – £24.10.0	TNA ADM 87/38
			Female demi-head – last seen Castles' Yard	Lost 1941 in London Blitz
Implacable	1805-1949	Third Rate 74	Head & shoulders only of a Gorgon – ship plan	NMM ZAZ1180
			A Gorgon bust – surviving	NMM FHD0085
Impregnable	1810-1888	Second Rate 98	Male bust with castle badge – surviving	Charleston, S Carolina
Inconstant	1783-1817	Fifth Rate 36	Female full-length – ship model 1785	Science Museum 1938-632

SHIP	DATES	SHIP TYPE	FIGUREHEAD/ORIGIN/DATE/COST	LOCATION/REF.
Indefatigable	1848-1914	Fourth Rate 50	Uniformed male bust – white – ship model Carved by Dickerson of Devonport 1846 – £20 Uniformed male bust – surviving	Plymouth Mus. & Art Gal. TNA ADM 87/16 Merseyside Mar. Mus.
Indus	1839-1898	Second Rate 80	Turbaned male bust – last seen 1913 at Devonport	Believe lost pre-1936
Infernal	1843-1844	Wood paddle sloop	Crowned male bust – Hellyer design 1843 – not approved Winged male bust – Hellyer design 1843 – £7.10.0	TNA ADM 87/13 TNA ADM 87/13
Inflexible	1845-1864	Wood paddle sloop	Bust of a sailor – Dickerson design 1844 – £6	Dickerson Archive ‡
Inspector	1782-1802	Sloop 16	Female full-length – ship plan	NMM ZAZ4474
Intrepid	1770-1828	Third Rate 64	Male full-length with a sword – gilt – Navy Board model 1773	Science Museum Pictorial
Invention	1801		Male standing figure – ship plan (French)	NMM ZAZ0482
Investigator	1903-1919	Survey vessel	Female 3/4-length – surviving	Sydney, Australia †
Invincible	1808-1857?	Third Rate 74	Male demi-head – Dickerson design undated	Dickerson Archive
Ipswich	1694-1730 1730-1757	Third Rate 70 Third Rate 70	Full-length crowned lion – ship plan 1712 Full-length crowned lion – Georgian model	NMM HIL0004 NMM SLR0434
Iris	1777-1781 1774-1810 1877-1905	Sixth Rate 28 Fourth Rate 50 Despatch vessel	Male standing figure – ship plan Female full-length – ship plan Winged female 3/4-length – carver's design 1877 Winged female 3/4-length – photographed on the bow	NMM ZAZ2982 NMM ZAZ1831 NMM NPB4659 Imperial War Mus Q39285
"*Ironsides*"	Uncertain	?	Crowned male bust – Nore Command (Sheerness)	Admlty Library Ref Dh 22 ‡†
Irresistible	1859-1894	Screw Sec'nd Rate 80	Crowned male demi-head – Hellyer design 1851 Crowned male demi-head – surviving	TNA ADM 87/39 Historic D'yard Chatham
Isis	1747-1766 1774-1810 1819-1867 Female bust in armour – surviving	Fourth Rate 50 Fourth Rate 50 Fourth Rate 50	French arms, crown, etc – redecoration by Wm Smith 1747 – £13.2.0 Female full-length – ship plan Replacement carved by Hellyer 1852 – £18 HMS *Unicorn*, Dundee	*Ship Carvers* – P Thomas NMM ZAZ1831 TNA ADM87/39
Jalouse	1809-1819	Sloop 18	Female bust – Dickerson design 1809 – £4	TNA ADM 106/1940
James Watt	1853-1875	Screw Second Rate 80	Male bust – Hellyer design 1852 Ship docked at Devonport – photograph 1854	TNA ADM 87/41 & 91/15 Photos of Linnaeus Tripe
Jason	1747-1763 1804-1815 1859-1877	Fifth Rate 44 Fifth Rate 32 Wood screw corvette	Full-length warrior with a sword – carved work detail – (French) Bust of a warrior holding a sheep – carver unnamed – not approved Bust of a warrior – Dickerson design 1858 – £12	NMM ZAZ6877 TNA ADM 106/1791 Dickerson Archive
Java	1815-1862	Fourth Rate 52	Female bust – Hellyer design 1846 – £18 Female 3/4-length bust, gilt – design half block model Original figurehead – lost 'The Great Fire', Devonport 1840	TNA ADM 87/16 NMM SLR0684 See Chapter 3.I
Jersey	1736-1783	Fourth Rate 60	Full-length crowned lion – ship plan Lion – carved by Mattingly of Plymouth – £17.10.0	NMM ZAZ1691 *Ship Carvers* – P Thomas
Juno	1780-1811 1844-1878	Fifth Rate 32 Sixth Rate 26	Full-length figure – ship plan Female bust – Hellyer design 1843 – £8	NMM ZAZ3089 TNA ADM 87/13
Kangaroo	1852-1863	Brig 12	Standing kangaroo – Hellyer design 1852 – £6.10.0	TNA ADM 87/39
Kent	1798-1881	Third Rate 74	Standing kilted warrior – designer unknown 1819 – £35 Standing kilted warrior – last recorded Devonport c1936	Dickerson Archive ‡ Lost in Blitz 1941
King Edward VII	1904	Model brig	Bust of King Edward VII in uniform – surviving	NMM FHD0065 †
Kingfisher	1770-1778 1845-1890	Sloop 14 Brig 12	Full-length warrior with a spear – ship plan Male full-length – gilt – Navy Board model 1775 Female bust – Hellyer design 1844 – £6.15.0 Female 3/4-length – ship plan	NMM ZAZ4652 Science Museum Pictorial TNA ADM 87/14 NMM ZAZ4640
Lacedaemonian	1812-1822	Fifth Rate 38	Bust of a warrior – Hellyer design 1812 – £6	TNA ADM 106/1886 ‡

SHIP	DATES	SHIP TYPE	FIGUREHEAD/ORIGIN/DATE/COST	LOCATION/REF.
Landrail	1860-1869	Wood screw gunves.	Female demi-head – Hellyer design 1859 – £6.15.0	TNA ADM 87/72
Lark	1830-1860	Survey cutter 2	Female 3/4-length – ship plan	NMM ZAZ6334
Laurel	1795-1797	Sixth Rate 22	Uniformed male standing figure – ship plan	NMM ZAZ3659
Leander	1848-1867	Fourth Rate 50	Male bust – Hellyer design 1847 – £24.10.0 Male bust – surviving	TNA ADM 87/17 HMS *Collingwood*, Hants ‡
Leda	1800-1808 1828-1906	Fifth Rate 38 Fifth Rate 46	A standing swan – Williams design ? 1800 – £8 Female bust – surviving	TNA ADM 106/1819 NMM FHD0087
Lee	1860-1875	Wood screw gunves.	Female 3/4-length – last recorded at Chatham 1931	Lost pre-1938
Legere	1796-1801	Sixth Rate 24	Female 3/4-length – ship plan (French)	NMM ZAZ3710
Leocadia	1781-1794	Fifth Rate 36	Full-length crowned lion – ship plan (Spanish)	NMM ZAZ2466
Leopard	1790-1814 1850-1867	Fourth Rate 50 Wood paddle frigate	Female full-length with a leopard in trailboard – ship plan Turbaned male demi-head – Hellyer des. 1849 – not approved Turbaned male bust – Hellyer design 1849 – £13 Turbaned male bust – Dickerson design 1857 – £10	NMM ZAZ1726 TNA ADM 87/27 TNA ADM 87/27 Dickerson Archive
Leviathan	1790-1848	Third Rate 74	Full-length Triton – gilt – ship model Bust in the form of Roman trophies – Dickerson design	Merseyside Mar. Mus. Dickerson Archive
Licorne	1778-1783	Fifth Rate 32	Full-length unicorn – ship plan (as taken) (French)	NMM ZAZ3111
Lion	1738-1765 1777-1837 1847-1905 Uncertain	Fourth Rate Third Rate 64 Second Rate 80 ?	Full-length crowned lion – Navy Board model Full-length uncrowned lion – ship plan Uncrowned lion with arms – Hellyer des. – £36 – not approved Crowned lion with arms – Hellyer design 1846 – £40 Crowned lion with arms – last recorded 1913 Devonport Male bust – last recorded Chatham 1948	Kriegstein Collection USA NMM ZAZ1471 TNA ADM 87/16 TNA ADM 87/16 Lost pre-1936 Believed lost 1950s
Lichfield	1730-1744	Fourth Rate 48	Full-length crowned lion – ship plan	NMM ZAZ1730
Liverpool	1860-1875	Wood screw frigate	Female 3/4-length bust – Dickerson design 1860 – £18	Dickerson Archive
Loire	1798-1818	Fifth Rate 40	Full-length cloaked figure – ship plan (French)	NMM ZAZ2252
London	1840-1857 1858-1884	Second Rate 92 Screw ship	Bust – Chatham proposal 1830 Female bust – surviving Female 3/4-length – Dickerson design 1857 – £35	TNA ADM 91/6 NMM FHD0091 Dickerson Archive
Lord Clyde	1864-1885	Ironclad battleship	Bow decoration – standards and portrait of Lord Clyde	Dickerson Archive
Lowestoffe	1723-1744	Fifth Rate 28	Full-length crowned lion – ship plan	NMM ZAZ3799
Loyal London	1666-1670	96-gun ship	Full-length crowned lion – gilt – ship model (c1952)	Trinity House, London
Lutine	1793-1799	Fifth Rate 36	Full-length uncrowned lion – ship plan (French)	NMM ZAZ3013
Lyme	1748-1760	Sixth Rate 28	Full-length crowned lion – ship plan Full-length uncrowned lion & trailboards – ship plan	NMM ZAZ0351 NMM HIL0161
Lyra	1857-1876	Wood screw sloop	Male bust – Hellyer design 1855 – £5.15.0	TNA ADM 87/56
Macedonian	1810-1812	Fifth Rate 38	Bust of Alexander the Great – surviving	US Naval Acad. Annapolis
Madagascar	1811-1819 1822-1863	Fifth Rate 38 Fifth Rate 46	Male bust – Hellyer design 1812 – £6 Head and neck only – surviving	TNA ADM 106/1886 † NMRN Portsmouth
Madras		Name changed	Turbaned male bust – Hellyer design 1844 – £36	TNA ADM 87/14
Magicienne	1781-1810 1849-1866	Fifth Rate 32 Wood paddle frigate	Full-length uncrowned lion – ship plan (French) Female 3/4-length bust – Hellyer design 1848 – £9.10.0 Female 3/4-length bust – last recorded Devonport 1936	NMM ZAZ3131 TNA ADM 87/19 Lost in Blitz 1941
Magnanime	1748-1775	Third Rate 74	Male full-length – ship plan (French)	NMM ZAZ1469
Majestic	1785-1816 1853-1868	Third Rate 74 Second Rate 80	Seated king with emblems – ship plan 3/4-length Queen Victoria – Hellyer design 1851 – £35	NMM ZAZ0703 TNA ADM 87/36

SHIP	DATES	SHIP TYPE	FIGUREHEAD/ORIGIN/DATE/COST	LOCATION/REF.
Malacca		Name changed	Turbaned male bust – Hellyer design 1844 – £34	TNA ADM 87/14
	1853-1869	Wood screw sloop	Male bust – surviving	NMRN Portsmouth
Mallard	1875-1889	Comp screw gunboat	Standing duck – design by unnamed carver – 1875	Admlty Library Ref P1030
Malta	1800-1840	Second Rate 84	A Maltese knight – lost in 'The Great Fire', Devonport 1840	See Chapter 3.I
Maria	1776	Schooner 6	Female full-length with flowing skirt – ship plan	NMM ALC0005
Mariner	1846-1865	Brig 16	Bust of a sailor – Hellyer design 1845 – £7.10.0	TNA ADM 87/15
	1846-1865?	Brig 16	Male bust – surviving	Historic D'yard Chatham †
Marlborough	1706-1752	Second Rate 96	Mounted equestrian with a shield – Navy Board model 1706	Kriegstein Collection USA
	1855-1904	Screw First Rate 121	Demi-head of the Duke – Hellyer proposal £75 – not approved	TNA ADM 87/50
			Bust of the Duke – Hellyer design 1854 – £50	TNA ADM 87/50
			Male bust (short hair) – ship model	NMM SLR0104
			Bust of the Duke – surviving	Gunwharf Quays, Portsm'th
Marquise de Seignelay	1780-1786	Sloop 14	Crowned escutcheon with foliage – ship plan (French)	NMM ZAZ4536
Mars	1848-1929	Second Rate 80	Bust of a warrior – Hellyer design 1847 – £36	TNA ADM 87/17
			Bust of a warrior – surviving	Missing †
		Uncertain	Bust of a warrior – origin doubtful – surviving	Horniman Museum
Martin	1850-1890	Brig 16	3/4-length female bust – Dickerson design 1864	Dickerson Archive
	1890-1907	Training brig	Female 3/4-length – surviving	HMS *Nelson*, Portsmouth ‡
Mary	1660-1675	Yacht 8	Full-length unicorn – Van de Velde drawing	British Museum
			Full-length unicorn – gilt – ship model by Spence (1952)	Trinity House, London
Mary Galley	1727-1743	Fifth Rate 32	Full-length crowned lion – ship plan – 1744	NMM ZAZ2279
Mary Rose	1536-1545	60-gun ship	Tudor Rose – The Anthony Roll	Pepys 2991
			Tudor rose – surviving	Mary Rose Mus. Portsm'th
Medea	1778-1795	Sixth Rate 28	Female full-length in classical robes – ship plan	NMM HIL0080
Medina	1840-1864	Wood paddle packet	Female 3/4-length bust – Dickerson des. 1839 – not approved	TNA ADM 87/9
			Female bust – Dickerson design 1839 – not approved	TNA ADM 87/9
Medusa	1785-1798	Fourth Rate 50	Female full-length – ship plan	NMM ZAZ7816
		?	Female 3/4-length bust – formerly Burgh Island, Devon	Believe lost *c*1950
Medway	1742-1748	Fourth Rate 60	Male full-length blowing a conch shell – Georgian ship model	NMM SLR0328
Meeanee	1848-1856	Second Rate 80	Turbaned 3/4-length male bust – Hellyer des. 1844 – £36	TNA ADM 87/14
	1857-1906	Screw ship 60	Turbaned 3/4-length male bust – Hellyer des. 1859 – £40	TNA ADM 87/72
Megaera	1837-1843	Wood paddle sloop	Female 3/4-length – Hellyer & Browning des. 1837 – £5	TNA ADM 87/72
	1849-1871	Iron screw frigate	Supplied by Fairbairn to a Hellyer design 1846	TNA ADM 91/12
			Female 3/4-length bust – Dickerson design 1861	Dickerson Archive
			Female 3/4-length bust – surviving	NMM FHD0092
Melampus	1820-1906	Fifth Rate 46	Male bust – Dickerson design	Dickerson Archive
Meleager	1806-1808	Fifth Rate 36	Bust of a warrior – Chatham designer 1806	TNA ADM 106/1820
Melpomene	1794-1815	Fifth Rate 38	Cap of Liberty over an escutcheon with young mermen as supporters – ship plan (French)	NMM ZAZ2011
	1857-1875	Wood screw frigate	Female demi-head – Hellyer proposal – £23 – not approved	TNA ADM 87/39
			Female 3/4-length bust – Hellyer design 1852 – £18.10.0	TNA ADM 87/39
Menelaus	1810-1897	Fifth Rate 38	Bust of a warrior – Dickerson design 1809 – £6	TNA ADM 106/1940
			Bust of a warrior – engraving	Author's collection
Merlin	1780-1795	Sloop 10	Full-length dragon breathing fire – ship plan	NMM ZAZ 4627
	1901-1923	Sloop	Male 3/4-length – last recorded Hong Kong	Believe lost *c*1959
Mermaid	1784-1815	Fifth Rate 32	Full-length mermaid – tail in trailboards – Georgian model	NMM SLR0318
Merope	1808-1815	Brig-sloop 10	Standing owl over escutcheon – Geo. Williams design 1803 – £3	TNA ADM 106/1821
Meteor	1823-1832	Bomb 8	A snake breathing flames – Dickerson design *c*1823 – £4	Dickerson Archive

SHIP	DATES	SHIP TYPE	FIGUREHEAD/ORIGIN/DATE/COST	LOCATION/REF.
Milford	1809-1846	Third Rate 78	Lion couchant over an escutcheon – ship plan 1808	NMM ZAZ1047 & 1056
Minden	1810-1861	Third Rate 74	Bust of a warrior – Dickerson design 1841 – £25 – not approved	TNA ADM 87/11
			Bust of a warrior – Dickerson design 1841 – £25	Dickerson Archive
Minerva	1780-1797	Fifth Rate 38	Female full-length with shield – ship plan	NMM ZAZ7956
			Female full-length – Georgian ship model	NMM SLR0317
			Female full-length – Georgian ship model	USNA Museum Annapolis
	1820-1895	Fifth Rate 46	Female bust in armour – surviving	NMRN Portsmouth
		Uncertain	Female standing figure – Hellyer design 1819 – £21.16.0	TNA ADM 106/1889
		Uncertain	Female standing figure – surviving	Plymouth N B Museum
Minx	1846-1899	Iron screw gunboat	Bust of a warrior – last recorded Devonport *c*1936	Lost *c*1947
Miranda	1851-1869	Wood screw corvette	Female 3/4-length bust – Hellyer design 1848 – £9.10.0	TNA ADM 87/24
Moa	1861-1876	Coal depot, ex-brig	A standing bird – last seen Auckland, New Zealand	Destroyed pre-1942 †
Modeste	1759-1800	Third Rate 64	Female full-length – ship plan (French)	NMM ZAZ1350
	1837-1866	Sloop 18	Female 3/4-length bust, gilt	NMM SLR0762
Mohawk	1886-1905	Torpedo cruiser	3/4-length N American Indian – Kay & Reid design 1885	NMM NPB7203
Monarch	1747-1760	Third Rate 74	Male full-length – ship plan (French)	NMM ZAZ1254
			Carved work detail – ship plan (French)	NMM ZAZ1255
Monarco	1780-1791	Third Rate 68	Full-length crowned lion – ship plan (Spanish)	NMM ZAZ1324
Monkey	1837-1887	Wood paddle vessel	Male figure – last recorded Pembroke Dockyard 1911	Lost but date unknown
Monsieur	1780-1783	Fifth Rate 36	Full-length crowned lion – ship plan	NMM ALC0009
Montagu	1779-1818	Third Rate 74	Full-length uncrowned lion – ship plan	NMM ZAZ1057
Montague	1660-1749	52-gun ship	Full-length crowned lion – ship plan – 1716	NMM ZAZ1617
Mordaunt	1683-1693	Fourth Rate 48	Crowned lion with putti – gilt – Navy Board model	NMM SLR0004
Morgiana	1800-1811	Brig-sloop 16	Standing figure with sword – ship plan	NMM ZAZ4369
Morne Fortunee	1804-1809	Schooner 12	3/4-length figure, coated – ship plan – 1803 (French)	NMM ZAZ4921
Muros	1806-1808	Sixth Rate 22	Male standing figure – ship plan	NMM ZAZ3647
Musquito	1851-1862	Brig 16	Male bust – Hellyer design 1849	TNA ADM 87/26
Mutine	1825-1841	Brig-sloop 6	Female bust – Dickerson design 1824 – £3	TNA ADM 106/1949
	1859-1870	Wood screw sloop	Male bust – Hellyer design 1858 – £12	TNA ADM 87/68
Myrmidon	1867-1889	Wood screw gunves.	Male bust – Hellyer design 1860 – £10	TNA ADM 87/77
Naiad	1797-1866	Fifth Rate 38	Female bust – Portsmouth design 1814 – £6	TNA ADM 106/1887
Namur	1746-1749	Third Rate 74	Full-length crowned lion – Georgian model	Kriegstein Collection USA
Nankin	1850-1905	Fourth Rate 50	Bust of naval officer – Hellyer design 1849 – £24	TNA ADM 87/25
			Identified as Adml Sir William Parker	TNA ADM 91/13
			Uniformed male bust, gilt – design half block model	NMM SLR0840
			Uniformed male bust, gilt – full hull model	NMM SLR0841
Narcissus	Canc. 1857	Fourth Rate 50	Male bust – Dickerson design 1852 [vide *Perseverance*]	Dickerson Archive
Naseby	1655-1660	80-gun ship	Cromwell mounted, etc – gilt – Navy Board model 1943	NMM SLR0001
Nassau	1699-1706	Third Rate 80	Full-length crowned lion – gilt – Navy Board model	Art Gallery of Ontario
	1707-1740	Third Rate 70	Lion – carved by Crichley of Chatham 1719 – £14	*Ship Carvers* – P Thomas
	1866-1880	Wood screw gunves.	Female 3/4-length bust – Dickerson design 1860 – £6.10.0	Dickerson Archive
Nelson	1814-1859	First Rate 120	Bust of Nelson with supporters – ship model	NMM SLR0680
			Bust of Nelson with supporters – prints & drawings	NMM PAI7973
			Bust of Nelson – ship model – made 1836	Merseyside Mar. Mus.
			Bust of Nelson – lost in 'The Great Fire', Devonport 1840	See Chapter 3.I
	1860-1928	Screw ship	Demi-head of Nelson – Hellyer design 1859 – £54	TNA ADM 87/73
			Demi-head of Nelson – surviving	ANMM Sydney, Australia

SHIP	DATES	SHIP TYPE	FIGUREHEAD/ORIGIN/DATE/COST	LOCATION/REF.
Neptune	1683-1750	Second Rate 90	Full-length crowned lion – gilt – Navy Board model	Merseyside Mar. Mus.
	1757-1816	Second Rate 90	Neptune riding a sea-horse and others – ship plan 1750	NMM HIL0081
Nereide	1797-1816	Fifth Rate 36	Cap of Liberty over escutcheon – ship plan (French)	NMM ZAZ2272
			Crown over escutcheon – ship plan (French)	NMM ZAZ2273
Newark	1747-1787	Second Rate 80	Full-length crowned lion painted on block – block model	NMM SLR0477
Niger	1846-1869	Wood screw sloop	Male bust – Hellyer design 1846 – £9.10.0	TNA ADM 87/16
Nightingale	1702-1707	Sixth Rate 24	Full-length crowned lion – gilt – Navy Board model	Art Gallery of Ontario
Nile	1839-1876	Second Rate 92	Bust of Nelson – Dickerson design 1851 – £35	Dickerson Archive
Nimble	1860-1906	Wood screw gunves.	Female 3/4-length – Hellyer design 1859 – £6.15.0	TNA ADM 87/73
Nisus	1810-1822	Fifth Rate 38	Crowned male bust – Dickerson design 1809 – £6	TNA ADM 106/1940
Norfolk	1693-1755	Third Rate 80	Full-length crowned lion – ship plan – 1728	NMM ZAZ0543
North Star	1824-1860	Sixth Rate 28	Full-length bear with stars – Greyfoot & Overton 1821 – not approved	TNA ADM 106/1795
	Canc. 1865	Wood screw corvette	Female 3/4-length bust – surviving – cancelled	Science Museum
Northumberland	1794-1795	Third Rate 78	Full-length crowned lion – ship plan (French)	NMM ZAZ1145
Nyaden	1807-1812	Fifth Rate 36	Goose on a plinth – ship plan (Danish)	NMM ZAZ3048
Nymph	1778-1783	Sloop 14	Female full-length – ship plan	NMM ZAZ4686
Nymphe	1888-1920	Comp screw sloop	Female 3/4-length – surviving	Gillingham, Kent
Nymphen	1807-1816	Fifth Rate 36	Female bust – Chatham design 1808 – £8 – not approved	TNA ADM 106/1821
Ocean	1761-1793	Second Rate 90	Bust of Neptune – lost in 'The Great Fire', Devonport 1840	See Chapter 3.1
	1805-1875	Second Rate 98	Crowned bust of King Neptune – lost *c*1967	Queenborough, Kent
Octavia	1849-1876	Fourth Rate 50	Female 3/4-length bust – Hellyer design 1847	TNA ADM 87/17
			Female 3/4-length bust – surviving	RNAS Yeovilton, Somerset
Odin	1846-1885	Wood paddle frigate	Crowned male bust – Hellyer design 1846 – £10	TNA ADM 87/16
Oiseau	1779-1783	Fifth Rate 32	Standing bird – ship plan (French)	NMM ZAZ3025
	1793-1816	Fifth Rate 36	Full-length uncrowned lion – ship plan	NMM ZAZ2475
Opal	1875-1892	Comp Screw Corvette	Female 3/4-length wearing a tiara – ship plan	NMM NPB8151
Opossum	1808-1819	Brig-sloop 10	Bearded male face only – ship plan	NMM ZAZ5156
Orestes	1824-1852	Sloop 18	Helmeted male bust – surviving	NMRN Portsmouth
	1860-1866	Wood screw corvette	Bust of a warrior – Hellyer design 1860 – £20	TNA ADM 87/74
Orion	1854-1867	Screw Second Rate 80	Male bust – Nehemiah Williams design 1850 – £14.8.0	TNA ADM 87/31
			Male bust – Hellyer design 1854 – £40 – not approved	TNA ADM 87/48
			Male demi-head – Hellyer design – £40	TNA ADM 87/48
			Male demi-head – last recorded 1941 in Whitehall	Lost but date unknown
Orlando	1858-1871	Wood screw frigate	3/4-length bust of a warrior – Dickerson design 1856 – £18	Dickerson Archive
			Bust of a warrior – surviving	Mystic, Connecticut, USA
Orpheus	1860-1863	Wood screw corvette	Male bust with lyre in trailboard – Hellyer design 1860 – £20	TNA ADM 87/74
			Helmeted male head – last recorded in Auckland 1911	Missing †
Osborne	1870-1908	Wood paddle yacht	Royal arms with crown above – Hellyer design	NMM NPD0859
			Royal arms with crown above – surviving	BRNC Dartmouth
Osprey	1844-1846	Brig 12	Standing osprey – Hellyer design 1843 – £6.15.0	TNA ADM 87/13
	1876-1890	Comp screw sloop	Male demi-head with glengarry & rifle – osprey holding fish in trailboards – ship plan	NMM NPB8393
Ostrich	1777-1782	Sloop 14	Full-length warrior – ship plan	NMM ZAZ4792
Pallas	1865-1886	Armoured corvette	Athene – 3/4-length in armour – surviving	Newport News, Virginia

SHIP	DATES	SHIP TYPE	FIGUREHEAD/ORIGIN/DATE/COST	LOCATION/REF.
Pandora	1833-1862	Packet brig 3	Female 3/4-length – ship plan	NMM ZAZ5083
			Female 3/4-length bust – ship model	NMM SLR0744
	1861-1875	Wood screw gunves.	Female 3/4-length – Hellyer design 1859 – £6.15.0	TNA ADM 87/73
Pantaloon	1831-1852	Brig 10	Standing figure cf 'Mr Punch' – ship plan	NMM ZAZ5112 & 5113
Pearl	1762-1825	Fifth Rate 32	Full-length crowned lion – ship plan	NMM HIL0066
	1828-1851	Sloop 20	Female demi-head – ship plan	NMM ZAZ4077
			Female demi-head – surviving	HMAS *Cerberus*, Australia
	1855-1884	Wood screw corvette	Female bust – Hellyer design 1854 – £10	TNA ADM 87/50
			Female demi-head – Hellyer proposal – £12 – not approved	TNA ADM 87/50
Pegasus	1776-1777	Sloop 14	Full-length winged horse – ship plan	NMM ZAZ4782
Pelican	1877-1901	Comp screw sloop	Female 3/4-length – design by unknown carver – 1875	Admlty Library Ref P1030
Pelorus	1857-1869	Wood screw corvette	Bust of a warrior – last recorded Devonport c1936	Lost in Blitz 1941
Penelope	1843-1864	Paddle frigate	Carved by Hellyer of Portsmouth 1843 – £18	TNA ADM 91/10 & 88/5
			Female demi-head – surviving	NMM FHD0095
	1867-1912	Armoured corvette	An escutcheon holding a female bust – ship plan	NMM NPB8787
Penguin	1795-1809	Sloop 16	Male full-length with club on shoulder – ship plan	NMM ZAZ4381
	1876-1924	Compos screw sloop	Female 3/4-length – surviving	HMAS *Penguin*, Sydney ‡
Perdrix	1795-1799	Sixth Rate 22	A bower over a partridge's nest – ship plan 1799 (French)	NMM ZAZ3617
Perlin	1807-1846	Fifth Rate 38	A standing bird – ship plan (Danish)	NMM ZAZ2695
Perseus	1861-1904	Wood screw sloop	Bust of a warrior – Dickerson design 1860 – £6.10.0	Dickerson Archive
Perseverance	1781-1823	Fifth Rate 36	Female bust – gilt – Georgian model	USNA Museum Annapolis
	1854-1860	Iron Screw Troopship	Male bust carved for *Narcissus* 1852	TNA ADM 88/15
Peterel	1860-1901	Wood screw sloop	Female 3/4-length bust – Dickerson design 1860 – £6.10.0	Dickerson Archive
			Female 3/4-length bust – surviving	Hist. D'yard, Portsmouth
Phaeton	1848-1875	Fourth Rate 50	Male bust – Hellyer design 1847 – £24	TNA ADM 87/17
			Head only survived – last seen Chatham 1957	Missing
Phoebe	1795-1841	Fifth Rate 36	Female bust – gilt – ship model	NMM SLR0585
Phoenix	1783-1816	Fifth Rate 36	Phoenix rising from flames – Hellyer design 1803	TNA ADM 106/1883
	1832-1864	Wood paddle sloop	Phoenix rising from flames – Hellyer design 1852 – £8	TNA ADM 87/41
Piedmontaise	1815-1815	Fifth Rate 38	Full-length warrior with spear – ship plan	NMM ZAZ7776
Pigmy	1837-1879	Wood paddle packet	Bow decoration – Union flag in rope border – surviving	NMRN Portsmouth
Pilot	1838-1862	Brig-sloop 16	Male demi-head – Dickerson design 1836 – £5.5.0	TNA ADM 87/6
	1879-1907	Training brig 8	Uniformed male demi-head – surviving	Vancouver Maritime Mus.
Pioneer	1856-1865	Wood screw gunves.	Male bust – Dickerson design 1855 – £6	Dickerson Archive
Pique	1800-1819	Fifth Rate 36	Demi-head of a warrior with a shield – ship plan	NMM ZAZ2467
	1834-1910	Fifth Rate 36	Female 3/4-length – ship plan	NMM ZAZ2616
			Female 3/4-length – gilt – ship model	NMM SLR0090
Pitt	1816-1877	Third Rate 74	Male bust – Hellyer design 1815 – £21 – not approved	TNA ADM 106/1888
Plumper	1848-1865	Wood screw sloop	Escutcheon & a naval crown – Hellyer design 1847 – £5.15.0	TNA ADM 87/18
Plymouth	1755-1793	Yacht 6	Full-length Hermes with caduceus – ship plan – c1754	NMM NPD 0741 & 0742
			Full-length fat Hermes with caduceus – ship plan – 1754	NMM HIL0224
			Full-length Hermes with winged helmet & caduceus – Georgian ship model	NMM SLR0494
	1796-1830	Yacht 8	Female standing figure – Dickerson design 1797 – £11	Dickerson Archive ‡
Poictiers	1809-1857	Third Rate 74	Crowned male bust – last on show at Sheerness	Lost 2006 ‡
			Replica by Andrew Peters of Maritima Woodcarving	Blue Town Mus. Sheppey

SHIP	DATES	SHIP TYPE	FIGUREHEAD/ORIGIN/DATE/COST	LOCATION/REF.
Polyphemus	1782-1827	Third Rate 64	Male full-length (a Cyclops) – ship plan	NMM ZAZ1496
			Male head only (a Cyclops) – surviving	NMM FHD0096
	1840-1856	Wood paddle sloop	Male bust – Hellyer & Browning design 1839 – not approved	TNA ADM 87/9
			Sketch of a Cyclops' head	TNA ADM 87/9
Pomona	1761-1776	Sloop 18	Full-length uncrowned lion – ship plan	NMM ZAZ4222
Pomone	1774-1802	Fifth Rate 44	Full-length uncrowned lion – ship plan – 1794 (French)	NMM ZAZ2277
	1811-1816	Fifth Rate 38	Standing figure – ship plan – 1810 (French)	NMM ZAZ2586
Pompee	1793-1817	Third Rate 80	Crown over French escutcheon – ship plan (French)	NMM ZAZ1161
Porcupine	1844-1883	Wood paddle vessel	Female bust – Hellyer design 1844 – £6.10.0	TNA ADM 87/14
Port Antonio	1779-1784	Brig 12	Full-length figure in tunic – ship plan	NMM ZAZ4986 & 4987
Portland	1770-1817	Fourth Rate 50	Female full-length – gilt – Navy Board model 1773-5	Science Museum Pictorial
Porto	1780-1782	Sloop 16	Male full-length – ship plan	NMM ZAZ4537
Portsmouth	1742-1869	Yacht 6	Male standing figure – Hellyer design 1815 – £20	TNA ADM 106/1888
	1747-1767	Transport	Standing cockerel – ship plan	NMM ZAZ5407
Poulette	1799-1814	Sixth Rate 20	Female bust – Dickerson design 1803 – £5.5.0	TNA ADM 106/1936
President	1806-1815	Fifth Rate 38	Female bust – Dickerson design 1810 – £6 – not approved	TNA ADM 106/1940
			Male bust – ordered by Surveyor of the Navy 1810	TNA ADM 106/1940
	1829-1903	Fourth Rate 52	Male bust – surviving	Fishmongers Hall, Lond. ‡
Preston	1742-1749	Fourth Rate 48	Full-l'gth uncrowned lion painted on block – block model	NMM SLR0464
Primrose	1810-1832	Brig-sloop 18	Bird on an escutcheon – ship plan	NMM ZAZ4552
Prince	1670-1692	First Rate 100	Male figure on horseback – gilt – Navy Board model	Science Museum 1895-56
Prince Albert	1864-1899	Iron screw turret ship	Bow decoration – bust in a cartouche – lost 1960s	See Chapter 16
Prince Consort	1862-1882	Ironclad frigate	Bow decoration – bust in a cartouche – Dickerson design	Dickerson Archive
Prince Edward	1781-1802	Third Rate 62	Full-length crowned lion – ship plan	NMM ZAZ1644
Prince Frederick	1715-1784	Third Rate 70	Full-length crowned lion – ship plan – 1714	NMM ZAZ7841
			Full-length crowned lion – gilt – Navy Board model	USNA Museum Annapolis
	1796-1817	Third Rate 64	Male full-length with top hat – ship plan	NMM ZAZ1522
Prince of Wales	1794-1822	Second Rate 90	Bust of the prince – Hellyer design 1809 – £35	TNA ADM 106/1821
	1860-1869	Screw First Rate 121	Demi-head of the prince – Hellyer des. 1853 – £70 not approved	TNA ADM 87/42
			Carved by Hellyer of Portsmouth 1859 – £65	TNA ADM 91/21 & 22
			Bust of the prince – surviving	Scottish Mar. Mus. Irvine
Prince Regent	1823-1873	First Rate 120	Bust of the prince – Hellyer design 1847 – £40	TNA ADM 87/17
Prince Royal	1610-1666	64-gun ship	Mounted horse before crowned helmet – Vroom painting	Franz Hals Mus. Haarlem
			Mounted horse – ship model by Spence (1953)	Trinity House, London
Princess	1740-1784	Third Rate 70	Female full-length – ship plan – 1731 (Spanish)	NMM ZAZ1166
Princess Alice	1844-1878	Iron paddle packet	Carved by Hellyer of Portsmouth 1844	TNA ADM 91/11
			Female bust – surviving	NMRN Portsmouth
Princess Caroline	1807-1815	Third Rate 74	Female head and neck only – surviving	Stockholm
Princess Charlotte	1799-1812	Fifth Rate 38	Female bust under canopy – ship plan	NMM ZAZ 2085
	1825-1875	First Rate 104	Female bust – last seen 1933 ashore in Hong Kong	Lost c1941
Princess Louisa	1728-1736	Fifth Rate 42	Full length crowned lion – ship model	Arlington Court, Devon
Princess of Orange	1799-1822	Third Rate 74	Standing warrior with shield & spear – ship plan (Dutch)	NMM ZAZ1144
Princess Royal	1773-1807	Second Rate 90	Seated princess with others – ship plan	NMM ZAZ0347
			Seated princess with female supporter (stbd) & Neptune (port) – Georgian ship model	USNA Museum Annapolis
	1853-1872	Screw Second Rate 91	Female 3/4-length – Hellyer design 1852 – £35	TNA ADM 87/42
			Female 3/4-length – last seen Castles' Yard	Lost 1941 in London Blitz

SHIP	DATES	SHIP TYPE	FIGUREHEAD/ORIGIN/DATE/COST	LOCATION/REF.
Prometheus	1839-1863	Wood paddle sloop	Male bust – Hellyer & Browning design 1839 – £7.10.0	TNA ADM 87/9
Prompte	1793-1813	Sixth Rate 20	Full-length uncrowned lion – ship plan (French)	NMM ZAZ3800
Proserpine	1798-1806	Fifth Rate 36	Female full-length – ship plan – 1796 (French)	NMM ZAZ2258
Prothee	1780-1815	Third Rate 64	Female full-length – ship plan	NMM ZAZ1339
Psyche	1805-1812	Fifth Rate 36	Female 3/4-length bust, gilt – design half block model	NMM SLR0604
	1862-1870	Paddle despatch ves.	Female 3/4-length bust – Dickerson design 1861	Dickerson Archive
Pylades	1854-1875	Wood screw corvette	Bust of a warrior – Hellyer design 1854 – £10	TNA ADM 87/49
	1884-1906	Comp screw corvette	Bust of a warrior – surviving	HMAS *Cerberus*, Australia
Queen	1839-1871	First Rate 110	3/4-length bust of Queen Victoria – Hellyer design 1858 – £44	TNA ADM 87/69
			3/4-length Queen Victoria – gilt – design ship model	NMM SLR0778
			3/4-length Queen Victoria – builder's model of the bow	NMM SLR2195
Queen Charlotte	1790-1800	First Rate 100	Standing Queen with orb & sceptre with canopy & supporters	
			starboard figurehead study – ship plans	NMM ZAZ0166
			Ditto from port side	NMM ZAZ0167
			Standing figure of Queen Charlotte – carver's design	Trinity House, Hull
			Standing figure of Queen Charlotte – figurehead model	Historic D'yard, Chatham
	1810-1859	First Rate 104	Replacement carved by Hellyer of Portsmouth 1822 -£35	TNA ADM 106/1891 †
			Bust of Queen Charlotte – surviving	HMS *Excellent*, Portsmouth ‡
Queenborough	1718-1777	Yacht 4	Crowned lion – Georgian ship model	NMM SLR0221
Racehorse	1806-1822	Brig-sloop 18	Head & neck of a horse – Hellyer design 1816 – £3	TNA ADM 106/1888
	1830-1901	Sloop 18	Male bust – a jockey – Dickerson design 1853 –	Dickerson Archive
Racer	1833-1852	Brig-sloop 16	Male bust – a jockey – Hellyer design 1832 – £4.10.0	TNA ADM 87/3
			Female bust – Hellyer design 1832 – £4.10.0	TNA ADM 87/3
			Head & neck of a horse – Hellyer dasign 1832 – £4.10.0	TNA ADM 87/3
			Male bust – a jockey – Dickerson design 1848 – £5.5.0	Dickerson Archive
Racoon	1857-1877	Wood screw corvette	Female 3/4-length bust – Hellyer design 1856 – £10	TNA ADM 87/62
	1887-1905	Torpedo cruiser	Male 3/4-length – racoon in trailboards – Devonport design 1886	NMM NPB9623
			Female demi-head – ship photograph 1898	IWM FL 17841
Railleur	1797-1800	Sloop 20	Male standing figure in tailcoat & breeches – ship plan	NMM HIL0003
Rainbow	1823-1838	Sixth Rate 28	Female 3/4-length bust – design half block model	NMM SLR0706
Raisonnable	1758-1762	Third Rate 64	Full-length crowned lion – ship plan (French)	NMM ZAZ1340
Raleigh	1778-1783	Fifth Rate 32	Male full-length – ship plan (American)	NMM ZAZ3127
	1806-1841	Brig-sloop 18	Male standing figure – Dickerson design – £7 – not approved	TNA ADM 106/1943
			Male bust – Dickerson design 1817 – £3	TNA ADM 106/1943
	1845-1857	Fourth Rate 50	Male bust – Hellyer design 1844 – £24	TNA ADM 87/14
	1873-1905	Iron screw frigate	Bow decoration – winged cherub – Chatham design 1872	NMM NPB9660
			Bust of Sir Walter Raleigh – Chatham design 1873	NMM NPB9659
			Bust of Sir Walter Raleigh – Chatham ship plan 1874	NMM NPB9679
			Bust of Sir Walter Raleigh – surviving	HMS *Raleigh*, Torpoint
			Bust of Sir Walter – replica in fibreglass – surviving	HMS *Raleigh*, Torpoint
			Bust of Sir Walter Raleigh – Devonport ship plan 1885	NMM NPB 9670
			Bust of Sir Walter Raleigh – last seen Sheffield 1951	Lost 1970s
Ramillies	1785-1850	Third Rate 74	Duke of Marlborough on horseback – ship plan	NMM ZAZ1243
Rapid	1860-1881	Wood screw sloop	Female 3/4-length bust – Hellyer design 1860 – £10	TNA ADM 87/74
Rattler	1843-1856	Wood screw sloop	Bust of a sailor – Hellyer design 1842 – £7.15.0	TNA ADM 87/12
	1862-1868	Wood screw sloop	Bust of a sailor – Hellyer design 1860 – £12	TNA ADM 87/77
	1886-1919	Compos screw gunb't	A full-length snake – ship photograph	IWM RP 1400
Rattlesnake	1822-1860	Sixth Rate 28	Male bust in headdress – Hellyer design 1846 – £7.15.0	TNA ADM 87/16
			Male bust in headdress – surviving	DERA Farnborough
			Male bust in headdress – replica in concrete	Plymouth NB Museum
	1861-1882	Wood screw corvette	Male bust in headdress – Hellyer design 1860 – £27.10.0	TNA ADM 87/76
			Male bust in headdress – last recorded Devonport *c*1936	Lost in Blitz 1941

SHIP	DATES	SHIP TYPE	FIGUREHEAD/ORIGIN/DATE/COST	LOCATION/REF.
Raven	1799-1804	Brig-sloop 18	Male standing figure – ship plan	NMM ZAZ4524
Recruit	1846-1849	Iron brig 12	Male bust – ship plan	NMM ZAZ4824
Redoutable	1815-1841	Third Rate 74	Bust of a warrior – last recorded at Chatham 1948	Destroyed 1948
Redwing	1806-1827	Brig-sloop 18	A standing bird – Greyfoot & Overton design 1817 – £4	TNA ADM 106/1795
Renard	1797-1805	Sloop 18	Male standing figure – ship plan (French)	NMM ZAZ3904 & 3905
Renown	1857-1870	Screw Second Rate 91	Male bust – Hellyer design 1855 – £40	TNA ADM 87/55
Repulse	1759-1776	Fifth Rate 32	Standing figure with sword – ship plan	NMM ZAZ3119
	1855	Screw Second Rate 91	Bust of a warrior – Hellyer design 1855 – £40	TNA ADM 87/52
Research	1863-1884	Ironclad screw sloop	Bow decoration – Queen's head in cartouche – design Carved by Cornelius Luck of London 1861 – £22.18.0	Dickerson Archive *Ship Carvers* – P Thomas
	1939	Survey vessel	Bow decoration – St George's Cross – design	Philip & Son, Dartmouth
Resistance	1805-1858	Fifth Rate 38	Male demi-head with club – last seen Chatham 1938	Lost but date unknown
	1861-1898	Armoured frigate	Male bust – surviving	Scottish Mar. Mus. Irvine
Resolute	1850-1879	Discovery vessel	Head only of a polar bear – surviving	NMM FHD0117
Retribution	1844-1864	Wood paddle frigate	Female demi-head – Hellyer design £11.10.0 – not approved	TNA ADM 87/14
			Female 3/4-length bust – Hellyer design 1844 – £9	TNA ADM 87/14
			Female bust – gilt – design half-block model	NMM SLR0817
Reunion	1793-1796	Fifth Rate 36	Wings above a badge – ship plan (French)	NMM ZAZ2847
Revolutionaire	1794-1822	Fifth Rate 38	Helmet, armour, flags, etc – ship plan (French)	NMM ZAZ2519
Reynard	1821-1857	Brig-sloop 10	Full-length fox – Dickerson design 1820	Dickerson Archive
	1848-1851	Wood screw sloop	Bust of a huntsman – Hellyer design 1847 – £5.15.0	TNA ADM 87/18
Rhadamanthus	1832-1864	Wood paddle sloop	Male bust with spiked crown – ship model	NMM SLR0741
Rhin	1806-1884	Fifth Rate 38	Female bust – ship plan (French)	NMM ZAZ 2694
Rifleman	1846-1869	Wood screw gunves.	Standing uniformed male – Hellyer design 1845 – £7.10.0	TNA ADM 87/15
Rinaldo	1860-1884	Wood screw sloop	Bust of a warrior – Hellyer design 1859 – £12	TNA ADM 87/72
			Replacement by Hellyer 1860 – £7.8.0	TNA ADM 88/16
			Male demi-head wearing hat – surviving	Plymouth NB Museum
Ringdove	1806-1829	Brig-sloop 18	Male bust – Hellyer design 1818 – £3 – not approved	TNA ADM 106/1889
	1833-1850	Brig-sloop 16	Female standing figure – Dickerson design 1832 – £9	TNA ADM 87/3
			Standing bird – Dickerson design 1832 – £6	TNA ADM 87/3
Rochfort	1814-1826	Second Rate 80	Bust of a warrior – ship plan	NMM ZAZ0711
Rodney	1860-1884	Screw ship	Bust of the admiral – Hellyer design 1859 – £45	TNA ADM 87/71
	1884-1909	Battleship	Bust of the admiral – surviving	Historic D'yard, Chatham
Roebuck	1774-1811	Fifth Rate 44	Female full-length with spear – ship plan	NMM ZAZ2244
Rolla	1808-1822	Brig-sloop 10	Escutcheon with decorated trailboard – ship plan	NMM ZAZ5134
			Original carved at Plymouth 1829 – £3	TNA ADM 106/1960
			Replacement fitted from brig in Ordinary 1843	TNA ADM 91/11
	1829-1868	Brig-sloop 10	Male bust – surviving	NMRN Portsmouth
Rosamond	1846-1865	Wood paddle sloop	Female 3/4-length bust – Hellyer design 1846 – £7.15.0	TNA ADM 87/16
Rosario	1800-1809	Sixth Rate 20	Female full-length with spear – ship plan	NMM ZAZ4072
	1860-1884	Wood screw sloop	Male bust – Hellyer design 1860 – £10	TNA ADM 87/74
Rose	1709-1712	Sixth Rate 20	Full-length crowned lion – Navy Board model	NMM SLR0393
Rotterdam	1781-1799	Fourth Rate 60	Full-length crowned lion – ship plan (Dutch)	NMM ZAZ1798
Rover	1832-1845	Sloop 18	Male bust – gilt – ship model	NMM SLR0740
	1853-1862	Brig 16	Male bust – Dickerson design 1851	Dickerson Archive

SHIP	DATES	SHIP TYPE	FIGUREHEAD/ORIGIN/DATE/COST	LOCATION/REF.
Royal Adelaide	1828-1905	First Rate 104	Female standing figure – gilt – Georgian ship model	USNA Museum Annapolis
			Standing figure of the queen – last seen Chatham 1948	Destroyed 1949
	1833-1877	Yacht	Female 3/4-length with trident & leaves – ship plan	NMM NPD0620
			Carved by Robert Hall of Rotherhithe 1833	TNA ADM 88/1
			Female 3/4-length – surviving	NMRN Portsmouth
Royal Albert	1854-1884	Screw First Rate 121	3/4-length Prince Albert – Hellyer design 1853 – £100	TNA ADM 87/43
			Male demi-head – gilt – ship model	NMM SLR0876
			Bust of Prince Albert with female supporters – ship model	NMM SLR0869
			3/4-length Prince Albert – last seen Portsmouth c1920	Lost but date unknown
Royal Anne	1756?		Double equestrian with female riders – part surviving	Private collection, USA
Royal Charlotte	1824-1832	Yacht 6	3/4-length queen with supporters – gilt – surviving	NMM FHD0097
Royal Frederick	1860		Bust of Frederick, Duke of York – Hellyer des. 1846 – £45	TNA ADM 87/18
			Bust of the duke – last seen HMS *St Vincent* 1940s	Destroyed 1957
Royal George	1756-1782	First Rate 100	Double equestrian with riders – Georgian model 1772	NMM SLR0336
			Double equestrian with riders – gilt – painting of Navy Board model	Science Museum Pictorial
			Double equestrian with riders – gilt – painting of Navy Board model	Kriegstein Collection USA
			Figurehead carved at by Thos Burrough 1756	*Ship Carvers* – P Thomas
	1776	Sloop 20	Female full-length – ship plan – 1777	NMM ZAZ3913
	1817-1905	Yacht	Carved by Grayfoot & Overton 1816	*Ship Carvers* – P Thomas
			Bust of George III with slave supporters – ship plan – 1821	NMM NPD0768
			Bust of the king with supporters, gilt – surviving	NMM FHD0099
	1827-1852	First Rate 120	Head & shoulders of the king – part surviving	NMM FHD0098
	1853-1875	Screw ship 102	Crowned royal bust – Dickerson design 1860 – £35	Dickerson Archive
			Uncrowned royal bust – Dickerson des. 1860 – not approved	Dickerson Archive
Royal James	1671-1672	First Rate 100	Mounted figure in armour – gilt – Navy Board model	Kriegstein Collection USA
	1675-1691	First Rate 100	Full-length crowned lion – Van de Velde drawing	NMM PT 2335
Royal Oak	1713-1741	Third Rate 70	Full-length crowned lion – gilt – Georgian model	Kriegstein Collection USA
	1741-1764	Third Rate 70	Full-length crowned lion – gilt – Navy Board model	NMM SLR0230
	1769-1805	Third Rate 74	Full-length crowned lion – gilt – Navy Board model	Science Museum Pictorial
	1862-1885	Ironclad frigate	Bust of King Charles II – Hellyer design 1860 – £44	TNA ADM 87/76 & 88/16
			Royal arms under a crown – Hellyer design 1860 – £46	TNA ADM 87/76 & 88/16
			Crown over escutcheon with oak tree – Hellyer design 1860	TNA ADM 87/76
			Royal arms under a crown with leaves – Dickerson design	Dickerson Archive
Royal Sovereign	1660-1696	100-gun ship	King Edgar on horseback, etc. – ship plan	NMM ZAZ0047, 48 & 7843
	1701-1768	First Rate 100	Multiple figures – Van de Velde drawing	NMM PAH5023
	1786-1825	First Rate 100	Standing king with royal arms & supporters – Dickerson design	*Plymouth & Devonport* †
			George III – lost in 'The Great Fire', Devonport 1840	See Chapter 3.I
	1804-1849	Yacht	Bust under a canopy – last seen Pembroke Yard 1911	Lost in Dockyard fire 1922
			Bust of Queen Charlotte with canopy and crown over, gilt – ship model	Newport News, USA
	1857-1862	Screw First Rate 121	Bust of Queen Victoria – last seen HMS *St Vincent* 1940s	Destroyed 1946
	1864-1885	Ironclad turret ship	A lion – last recorded HMS *Excellent* 1911	Lost but date unknown
Royal William	1719-1813	First Rate 100	Full-length uncrowned lion – ship plan	NMM ZAZ0143
			Mounted double equestrian – Georgian ship model	NMM SLR0222
			Mounted double equestrian – Navy Board model	NMM SLR0408
			Mounted double equestrian – Georgian ship model	NMM SLR0409
			Mounted double equestrian – gilt – Navy Board model	USNA Museum Annapolis
	1833-1859	First Rate 120	Crowned standing King William IV – surviving	Plymouth NB Museum †
			Crowned standing King William IV – replica in fibreglass	Plymouth NB Museum
	1860-1885	Screw ship 72	Crowned bust of King – Dickerson design 1859 – £35	Dickerson Archive
			Enlarged crown – Dickerson design	Dickerson Archive
Ruby	1776-1821	Third Rate 64	Female full-length – ship plan	NMM ZAZ1473
	1876-1904	Comp screw corvette	Female 3/4-length with tiara – ship plan 1885	NMM NPC0834
Russell	1822-1865	Third Rate 74	Figurehead carved at Deptford 1820 – £21	TNA ADM 91/5
			Bust of the admiral – surviving	NMM FHD0100

SHIP	DATES	SHIP TYPE	FIGUREHEAD/ORIGIN/DATE/COST	LOCATION/REF.
St Albans	1687-1693	Fourth Rate 50	Full-length crowned lion – gilt – Navy Board model	NMM SLR0376
San Damaso	1797-1814	Third Rate 74	Full-length uncrowned lion – ship plan (Spanish)	NMM ZAZ1313
			Full-length uncrowned lion – ship plan	NMM NPD0877
St Fiorenzo	1794-1837		Full-length warrior with shield – ship plan	NMM ZAZ2649
St George	1687-1774	First Rate 96	St George & the dragon – gilt – ship model 1701	USNA Museum Annapolis
			St George on horseback – ship model 1708-14	Merseyside Mar. Mus.
			Figurehead carved by Wm Smith – 1740 rebuild	*Ship Carvers* – P Thomas
	1840-1858	First Rate 120	Standing figure slaying dragon – last recorded Devonport *c*1936	Lost in Blitz 1941
	1859-1883	Screw ship	Bust of a warrior – Dickerson design 1858 – £35	Dickerson Archive
St Jean d'Acre	1853-1875	Screw First Rate 101	Crowned bust in armour – Dickerson design 1852 – £36	Dickerson Archive
San Josef	1797-1849	First Rate 114	Full-length crowned lion – ship plan – 1799	NMM ZAZ0100
			Male bust – ship plan – 1808	NMM ZAZ0101
			Male bust – last seen Deptford Victualling Yard 1900	Lost but date unknown
St Michael	1669-1706	Second Rate 90	Double-headed pelican & figures – Navy Board model	NMM SLR0002
			Pelican & figures – Van de Velde drawing	NMM PAF6608
San Miguel	1782-1791	Third Rate 74	Full-length crowned lion – ship plan (Spanish)	NMM ZAZ1041
St Vincent	1815-1906	First Rate 120	Original figurehead carved at Plymouth 1812 – £35	TNA ADM 106/1941
			Bust of the admiral – Hellyer design 1851 – £35	TNA ADM 87/36
			Bust of the admiral – last seen HMS *Ganges*	Destroyed 1946 †
			Bust of the admiral – replica in concrete – surviving	HMS *Collingwood*
			Bust of the admiral – wooden replica 1993 – surviving	Charleston, S Carolina
Sagesse	1803-1821	Sixth Rate 28	Female standing figure – ship plan (French)	NMM ZAZ3691
Salamander	1544-1559	48-gun ship	A salamander on the beakhead – The Anthony Roll	Brit Library Add MS 22047
Salamis	1863-1883	Paddle despatch vess	A sea monster – surviving	Historic D'yard, Chatham
Saltash	1732-1741	Sloop 14	Young triton blowing shell – ship plan	NMM ZAZ4359
Salvador del Mundo	1797-1815	First Rate 112	Full-length uncrowned lion – ship plan (Spanish)	NMM ZAZ0042
Samarang	1822-1883	Sixth Rate 28	Replacement carved at Portsmouth 1842	TNA ADM 91/10
			Male bust – surviving	Port Office, Gibraltar
Sampson	1844-1864	Wood paddle frigate	Male demi-head – Hellyer proposal – £12.10.0 – not approved	TNA ADM 87/14
			Male bust – Hellyer design 1844 – £8.10.0	TNA ADM 87/14
Sandwich	1679-1770	Second Rate 90	Crowned lion – Van de Velde drawing	NMM PAF6628
Sans Pareil	1851-1867	Screw Second Rate 81	Female bust – Dickerson design 1849	Dickerson Archive
Sappho	1837-1859	Brig-sloop 16	Female 3/4-length bust – Hellyer design 1847 – £6.10.0	TNA ADM 87/18
Saracen	1831-1862	Brig-sloop 10	Turbaned male bust – surviving	St Peter Port, Guernsey
Sardoine	1761-1768	Sloop 14	Female full-length – ship plan (French)	NMM ZAZ4156 & 4157
Satellite	1855-1879	Wood screw corvette	Female 3/4-length bust – Dickerson design 1854	Dickerson Archive
			Female 3/4-length bust – surviving	HMS *Calliope*, Gateshead
Saturn	1786-1868	Third Rate 74	Bust of a warrior in plumed helmet – ship plan – 1814	NMM ZAZ1618
			Surviving 1911 at Pembroke Dockyard – lost post-1911	Admiralty Catalogue 1911
Scourge	1796-1802	Sloop 22	Female full-length holding hat – ship plan (French)	NMM ZAZ3624
			Female full-length holding child – ship plan	NMM ZAZ4073
	1844-1865	Wood paddle sloop	Demi-head of a warrior – Hellyer design 1842 – not approved	TNA ADM87/12
			Female bust – Hellyer design 1842 – £7.10.0	TNA ADM87/12
Scout	1800-1801	Sloop 18	A sea monster with tail in trailboards – ship plan	NMM ZAZ4024
	1856-1877	Wood screw corvette	Female bust – Hellyer design 1855 – £10	TNA ADM 87/56
			Uniformed male bust – Hellyer design 1855 – not approved	TNA ADM 87/56
			Female bust – lost *c*1960	See Chapter 12

SHIP	DATES	SHIP TYPE	FIGUREHEAD/ORIGIN/DATE/COST	LOCATION/REF.
Scylla	1856-1882	Wood screw corvette	Female 3/4-length bust – Hellyer design 1855 – £10 Female 3/4-length bust – surviving Female 3/4-length bust – replica in concrete – surviving	TNA ADM 87/55 & 88/12 Blue Town Mus. Sheppey Portsmouth D'yard Soc.
Seaflower	1873-1904	Training brig 8	Female 3/4-length – surviving	HMS *Nelson*, Portsmouth
Seagull	1831-1852	Schooner 6	Standing seagull – ship plan Carved by Robert Hall 1834 – £2.10.0	NMM ZAZ6154 TNA ADM 88/2
	1868-1887	Wood screw gunvess	Perched seagull on scroll – surviving	NMM FHD0060
Seahorse	1748-1784	Sixth Rate 24	Full-length near-naked Hermes with winged helmet & heels – ship plan 1747	NMM ZAZ3624
Sealark	1843-1898 1904-1919	Brig 8 Survey Vessel	Female 3/4-length – Hellyer design 1860 – £6.15.0 See *Investigator*	TNA ADM 87/74
Seine	1798-1803	Fifth Rate 38	Full-length figure – ship plan	NMM ZAZ2231
Semiramis	1808-1844	Fifth Rate 36	Crowned female bust – Hellyer design 1815 – £6 Female standing figure – surviving	TNA ADM 106/1888 NMM FHD0101
Serapis	1782-1826	Fifth Rate 44	Seated male with sunburst in trailboard – ship plan	NMM ZAZ2132
Seringapatam	1819-1873	Fifth Rate 46	Bird with rider & umbrella – surviving	NMM FHD0102 †
Serpent	1789-1806 1832-1861	Sloop 16 Brig-sloop 16	Full-length snake-charmer – ship plan Full-length snake – Hellyer design 1841 – £6.10.0 Full-length snake – surviving	NMM ZAZ4289 TNA ADM 87/11 NMM FHD0080
	1887-1890	Torpedo cruiser	3/4-length snake-charmer – left half surviving 3/4-length snake-charmer – right half surviving	NMM FHD0103 Privately owned, Spain
Severn	1856-1876	Fourth Rate 50	Carved by Hellyer at Woolwich 1851 Male bust – bald and bearded – lost *c*1962	TNA ADM 88/9 HMS *Dolphin*
Shamrock	1816-1838	Revenue brig	Bust with large hat – ship plan	NMM ZAZ4362
Shannon	1796-1802 1806-1844	Fifth Rate 32 Fifth Rate 38	Female full-length holding a torch – white – ship model Female bust – Dickerson design 1810 – £6 Female bust – surviving	USNA Museum Annapolis TNA ADM 106/1940 Private collection, USA
	1855-1871	Wood screw frigate	Instructions for Hellyer design of Sir Philip Broke 1855	TNA ADM 88/12 & 91/18
Shearwater	1808-1832 1861-1877	Brig-sloop 10 Wood screw sloop	Male bust – carved by George Williams 1808 – £3 Female 3/4-length bust – Dickerson design 1860 – £6.10.0	*Ship Carvers* – P Thomas Dickerson Archive
Sheerness	1787-1805	Fifth Rate 44	Male full-length – ship plan	Buckler's Hard, Hants.
Sheldrake	1825-1855	Brig-sloop 10	A standing duck – Dickerson design 1824 – £4	Dickerson Archive
Sidon	1846-1864	Wood paddle frigate	Turbaned male bust – Hellyer design 1846 – £10	TNA ADM 87/16
Siren	1773-1777 1841-1868	Sixth Rate 28 Brig-sloop 16	Female full-length with lute – ship plan Full-length mermaid – Hellyer design 1840 – not approved Mermaid bust – Hellyer proposal 1840 – £7.4.0	NMM ZAZ3399 TNA ADM 87/10 TNA ADM 87/10
Sophie	1798-1809	Sloop 18	Full-length semi-clad figure – ship plan	NMM ZAZ4012
Southampton	1757-1812 1820-1912	Fifth Rate 32 Fourth Rate 60	Female 3/4-length bust – Hellyer design 1810 – £6 Female bust – last recorded at Hughes Bolckow, Blyth	TNA ADM 106/1885 ‡ Believed lost, no date
Sovereign of the Seas	1637-1660 1637-1660	100-gun ship 100-gun ship	King Edgar on horseback, etc. – ship plan 19th century King Edgar on horseback – ship model *c*1830	NMM ZAZ7843 NMM SLR0356
Spartan	1841-1862	Sixth Rate 26	Female 3/4-length bust – Dickerson des. 1840 – not approved Demi-head of a warrior – Hellyer design 1840 – £7.15.0	TNA ADM 87/10 TNA ADM 87/10
Spartiate	1798-1857	Third Rate 74	Full-length warrior with sword & shield – ship plan (Fr) Bust of a warrior – Grayfoot & Overton design 1815 – £21	NMM ZAZ0724 TNA ADM 106/1794
Spencer	1800-1822	Third Rate 74	Coronet over oval escutcheon with family arms – launching plan	NMM ZAZ6943

SHIP	DATES	SHIP TYPE	FIGUREHEAD/ORIGIN/DATE/COST	LOCATION/REF.
Sphinx	1775-1811	Sixth Rate 20	Full-length sphinx – ship plan	NMM ZAZ3919
			Full-length sphinx – gilt – Navy Board model 1775	Science Museum Pictorial
	1846-1881	Wood paddle sloop	Turbaned male bust – Hellyer design 1845 – £9	TNA ADM 87/15
			A sphinx – Hellyer proposal 1845 – £8.10.0 – not approved	TNA ADM 87/15
			Turbaned male bust – surviving	Plymouth NB Museum
Spiteful	1842-1883	Wood paddle sloop	Female 3/4-length bust – Hellyer design 1841	TNA ADM 87/11
Spitfire	1845-1888	Wood pad. gunvessel	Forepart of a winged dragon – Hellyer des 1844 – £8.10.0	TNA ADM 87/14
Sprightly	1837-1889	Wood paddle packet	Female 3/4-length bust – Hellyer design 1849 – £4.15.0	TNA ADM 87/27
Spy	1841-1862	Brigantine	Male 3/4-length – Hellyer design 1840 – not approved	TNA ADM 87/10
			Male bust – Hellyer proposal 1840 – £6.12.0	TNA ADM 87/10 & 91/9
Squirrel	1853-1879	Brig-sloop 12	Female 3/4-length – Dickerson design 1851	Dickerson Archive
			Female 3/4-length – last recorded St Budeaux c1958	Lost but date unknown
Stag	1830-1866	Fifth Rate 46	Head & neck of a stag – last recorded St Budeaux c1958	Lost but date unknown
Star	1835-1863	Packet brig 8	Original figurehead carved by Robert Hall 1834	TNA ADM 88/2
			Female bust replacement – Hellyer design 1852	TNA ADM 87/41
			Female 3/4-length bust – surviving	Historic D'yard, Chatham
		Uncertain	Female bust – ex-Chatham 1911, 1938 & 1948 – surviving	NMM FHD0114
Stirling Castle	1775-1780	Third Rate 64	Full-length warrior – ship plan	NMM ZAZ1352
	1811-1839	Third Rate 74	Highlander – lost in 'The Great Fire', Devonport 1840	See Chapter 3.I
Styx	1841-1866	Wood paddle sloop	Female 3/4-length bust – Hellyer design 1840 – not approved	TNA ADM 87/10
			The Devil required – £6.10.0 allowed	TNA ADM 87/10
			Male bust – last recorded Devonport c1936	Lost in Blitz 1941
Sultan	1775-1805	Third Rate 74	Grand Turk – lost in 'The Great Fire', Devonport 1840	See Chapter 3.I
Superb	1710-1732	Third Rate 64	Full-length seahorse – ship plan	NMM ZAZ1811
	1760-1783	Third Rate 64	Male full-length, robed and painted – design model	NMM SLR0506
	1842-1869	Second Rate 80	Bust of Queen Victoria – Hellyer design 1842 – £35	TNA ADM 87/12
Supply	1759-1792	Armed tender 8	Scroll-head – ship plan 1786	NMM 4066 & 4066A †
	1854-1879	Iron screw storeship	Female demi-head – surviving	NMRN Portsmouth
Surprise	1774-1783	Sixth Rate 28	Female full-length – ship plan	NMM ZAZ3287
	1796-1802	Sixth Rate 24	Demi-head of a warrior with club – ship plan	NMM ZAZ3067
	1812-1837	Fifth Rate 38	Female demi-head – last recorded Devonport c1936	Lost in Blitz 1941
Sussex	1693-1694	Third Rate 80	Full-length crowned lion – gilt – Navy Board Model	USNA Museum Annapolis
Sutlej	1855-1869	Fourth Rate 50	Turbaned male bust – Hellyer design 1849 – £24.10.0	TNA ADM 87/27
Swallow	1837-1848	Wood paddle packet	Female bust – Hellyer design 1845 – £4.15.0	TNA ADM 87/15
	1854-1866	Wood screw sloop	Male bust – Dickerson design 1854	Dickerson Archive
			Female 3/4-length bust – Hellyer design 1860 – £7.10.0	TNA ADM 87/74 †
Swift	1777-1778	Sloop 14	Full length figure of Hermes – ship plan	NMM ZAZ4732
Sybille	1794-1833	Fifth Rate 44	Female full-length – Woolwich design 1816 – £17.10.0	TNA ADM 106/1794
			Female standing figure – Woolwich design 1816 – £16	TNA ADM 106/1794
	1847-1866	Fifth Rate 36	Female bust – Dickerson design 1844 – £10	TNA ADM 87/14 ‡
			Female 3/4-length bust – Hellyer design 1845- £18	TNA ADM 87/16
			Female standing figure – surviving	Plymouth NB Museum
Talavera	1818-1840	Third Rate 74	Standing figure of Duke of Wellington – Grayfoot & Overton proposal 1817 – £34.10.0 – not approved	TNA ADM 106-1795
			Bust of Duke of Wellington – Grayfoot & Overton proposal 1817 – £21	TNA ADM 106-1795
			Figurehead lost at Devonport in 'The Great Fire of 1840'	See Chapter 3.I
Tamar	1863-1941	Iron screw troopship	Male 3/4-length – surviving	Plymouth NB Museum
			Female 3/4-length – lost when ship scuttled Hong Kong	Lost 1941
Tartar	1734-1755	Sixth Rate 20	Full-length turbaned male – Navy Board Model	NMM SLR0228
	1886-1906	Torpedo cruiser	Male 3/4-length with sword – Kay & Reid design 1886	NMM NPC2804

SHIP	DATES	SHIP TYPE	FIGUREHEAD/ORIGIN/DATE/COST	LOCATION/REF.
Tartarus	1864	Cancelled	Crowned male bust – Dickerson design 1860	Dickerson Archive
Teazer	1846-1862	Wood screw tender	Full-length dragon – Hellyer design 1846 – not approved	TNA ADM 87/16
Temeraire	1759-1784	Third Rate 74	Female full-length – ship plan (French)	NMM ZAZ0652
Termagant	1780-1795	Sixth Rate 26	Female full-length holding flaming torch & sword – ship plan	NMM ZAZ3202 & 3203
	1847-1867	Wood screw frigate	Female 3/4-length bust – Hellyer design 1847 – £10	TNA ADM 87/17
Terpsichore	1847-1866	Sloop 18	Female 3/4-length with lyre – surviving	HMS *President*, London ‡
Terrible	1845-1879	Wood paddle frigate	Male standing figure – Hellyer proposal – £24 not approved	TNA ADM 87/14
			Male demi-head – Hellyer proposal – £17 not approved	TNA ADM 87/14
			Crowned male bust – Hellyer design 1844 – £14	TNA ADM 87/14
Terror	1856-1902	Iron floating battery	Crowned male bust – last recorded Bermuda 1921	Lost but date unknown
Thalia	1869-1920	Wood screw corvette	Female 3/4-length bust – last recorded Devonport 1947	Lost c1947
Thames	1823-1863	Fifth Rate 46	Male head & shoulders – surviving	NMM FHD0107
Theseus	1892-1921	First Class Cruiser	Bow decoration – Greek Cross Fleurie with supporters	IWM FL 19896
Thisbe	1824-1892	Fifth Rate 46	Female bust – last seen Roath Park, Cardiff	Believe lost c1950s
Thunderbolt	1842-1847	Wood paddle sloop	Crowned male bust – Hellyer design 1841 – £7.10.0	TNA ADM 87/11
Thunderer	1831-1869	Second Rate 84	Crowned male bust – Dickerson design 1847	Dickerson Archive
Tiger	1647-1743	32-gun ship	Crowned lion – Van de Velde drawing 1681	NMM VV1219
	1747-1765	Fourth Rate 60	Full-length crowned lion – ship plan	NMM ZAZ1595
	1849-1854	Wood paddle sloop	Full-length tiger – Hellyer design 1848 – £10.15.0	TNA ADM 87/23
Tigress	1808-1814	Gun-brig 12	Bust of a warrior – ship plan	NMM ZAZ4764
Tonnant	1798-1821	Third Rate 80	Male bust with beard – ship plan (French)	NMM ZAZ0640
Topaze	1793-1814	Fifth Rate 38	Hellyer estimate for a bust – 1800 – £7	TNA ADM 106/1882
			French arms with Cap of Liberty above – ship plan – (French)	NMM ZAZ2449
			Female bust – figurehead detail – ship plans – 1800	NMM ZAZ2453
	1814-1851	Fifth Rate 38	Standing angel – ship plan	NMM ZAZ2454
	1858-1884	Wood screw frigate	Female 3/4-length bust – Dickerson design 1856 – £28.10.0	Dickerson Archive
			Female 3/4-length bust – surviving	Plymouth NB Museum
Tourmaline	1875-1904	Comp screw corvette	Female 3/4-length – last recorded Upnor 1948	Lost but date unknown
Tourterelle	1795-1816	Sixth Rate 28	Warrior bust with flags – ship plan (French)	NMM ZAZ3321
Trafalgar	1820-1825	First Rate 106	Standing figure, prob. Nelson – Geo. Williams proposal 1819 – £126 not approved	TNA ADM 106/1824
	1841-1873	First Rate 120	Bust, prob. Nelson – Geo. Williams proposal 1819 – £46	TNA ADM 106/1824
			Standing fig. of Fame – Hellyer & Browning design £42	TNA ADM 87/6
			Demi-head of Nelson – Hellyer & Browning design 1836 £31.10.0	TNA ADM 87/6
			Bust-head with trophies – Hellyer & B'ring proposal – £25	TNA ADM 87/6
			Bust of Nelson – Robt. Hall design 1836 – £55	TNA ADM 87/6
			Replacement – Hellyer estimate 1840 – £45	TNA ADM 87/10
			Bust of Nelson – surviving	NMRN Portsmouth
Trave	1813-1821	Fifth Rate 38	Male standing figure with water jar – ship plan (French)	NMM ZAZ2255
Tremendous	1784-1845	Third Rate 74	Full-length warrior – ship plan	NMM ZAZ1087
			Bust of Hercules – Hellyer design 1845 – £24	TNA ADM 87/15
Tribune	1803-1839	Fifth Rate 36	Male bust – Grayfoot & Overton design 1814 – £10	TNA ADM 106/1794
	1853-1866	Wood screw corvette	Male demi-head – Hellyer design – £24.10.0 – not approved	TNA ADM 87/40
			Male bust – Hellyer design 1852 – £16	TNA ADM 87/40
			Male 3/4-length bust – painted white – builder's model	NMM SLR0862
			Male bust – surviving	NMM FHD0108
Trincomalee	1817-1897	Fifth Rate 46	Original bust carved by Overton & Co 1813 – £6	TNA ADM 106/1794
			Turbaned male bust – Hellyer design 1845 – £12	TNA ADM 87/15
			Turbaned male bust – surviving	Hartlepool

SHIP	DATES	SHIP TYPE	FIGUREHEAD/ORIGIN/DATE/COST	LOCATION/REF.
Triton	1773-1796	Sixth Rate 28	Full-length triton – Henry Adams design	Buckler's Hard Mar. Mus.
			Full-length triton blowing a shell – ship plan	NMM ZAZ3235
	1796-1820?	Fifth Rate 32	Full-length triton – Dickerson design – undated	Dickerson Archive
Triumph	1764-1850	Third Rate 74	Full-length winged Victory – white – ship model	USNA Museum Annapolis
	1862	Renamed	Male bust – Hellyer design 1860 – £45	TNA ADM 87/76 & 88/16
			3/4-length bust of Peace – Hellyer design 1860 – £45	TNA ADM 87/76 & 88/16
Tromp	1796-1815	Fourth Rate 60	Full-length warrior – ship plan (Dutch)	NMM ZAZ1601
Trompeuse	1797-1800	Sloop 18	Standing figure – ship plan	NMM ZAZ4277
Trusty	1782-1815	Fourth Rate 50	Full-length uncrowned lion	NMM ZAZ1715
Turquoise	1876-1892	Comp screw corvette	Female 3/4-length with tiara – ship plan	NMM NPC3956
Tweed	1860	Cancelled 1864	Female 3/4-length – Hellyer design 1859 – £27.10.0	TNA ADM 87/73
Tyne	1826-1862	Sixth Rate 28	Bust of Neptune – Overton & Faldo design 1826 – £9.9.0	TNA ADM 106/1800
Undaunted	1861-1882	Wood screw frigate	Demi-head of a sailor – Hellyer design 1860 – £27.10.0	TNA ADM 87/74
Unicorne	1554-1555	36-gun ship	A unicorn on the beakhead – The Anthony Roll	Brit Lib Add MS 22047 ‡
Unicorn	1824-1968	Fifth Rate 46	Fore-part of a unicorn – replacement – Trevor Ellis 1978	Dundee
Unité	1796-1802	Fifth Rate 38	Arms & foliage – ship plan (French)	NMM ZAZ3181
			Replacement figurehead carved Plymouth 1806 – £9	TNA ADM 106/1938 †
	1803-1858	Fifth Rate 40	Female bust – surviving	HMS *Sultan*, Gosport
Union	1811-1833	Second Rate 98	George III – lost in 'The Great Fire', Devonport 1840	See Chapter 3.I
Uranie	1797-1807	Fifth Rate 38	Escutcheon under a bird – ship plan	NMM ZAZ2498 & 2499
			Bird over union flag badge – Dickerson design 1798	Dickerson Archive
			Cannon & ensigns – Dickerson design 1798 – not approved	Dickerson Archive
Urgent	1855-1903	Iron screw troopship	Female 3/4-length – last seen Halifax, Nova Scotia	Lost c1968
Vainqueur	Fl 1750	Fourth Rate 60	Full-length warrior with scimitar & shield – ship model	NMM SLR0487
Valorous	1851-1891	Wood paddle frigate	Bust of a warrior – Hellyer design 1848 – £9.10.0	TNA ADM 87/19
Vanguard	1835-1867	Third Rate 78	Male bust – gilt – ship model	NMM SLR0750
			Unspecified – Robert Hall proposal 1833 – £30	TNA ADM 87/3 & 88/1
			Unspecified – Dickerson proposal 1833 – £21 not approved	TNA ADM 88/1
			3/4-length of Nelson – lost in Chatham Dockyard fire	Lost 1996
			Large scale ship model made for training purposes	NMRN Portsmouth
Vengeance	1824-1897	Second Rate 84	Crowned male bust – Surveyor of the Navy design	Dickerson Archive
			Crowned male bust – lost 1993	Bourne End
			Crowned male bust – replica – Andrew Peters – 1997	Upper Thames
				Sailing Club
Vernon	1832-1886	Fourth Rate 50	Bust of the admiral – Hellyer design 1849	TNA ADM 87/27
			The arms of Lord Vernon – Hellyer des. 1849 – not approved	TNA ADM 87/27
			Male bust, gilt – ship model	NMM SLR0738
			Male bust, gilt – design half-block model	NMM SLR0739
			Bust of the admiral – surviving	Gunwharf Quays, Portsm'th
Vestal	1777-1777	Sixth Rate 20	Female full-length – ship plan	NMM ZAZ3979
	1779-1803	Sixth Rate 28	Female full-length with hanging cauldron – ship plan	NMM NPD0872
	1809	Brig 10	Female bust – surviving	Mumbai. India
Vesuvius	1839-1865	Wood paddle sloop	Demi-head of a warrior – Hellyer & Browning design 1839 – £6 – not approved	TNA ADM 87/9
			Crowned male demi-head – Hellyer & Browning design 1839 – £6 – not approved	TNA ADM 87/9
			Crowned male bust – Hellyer & Browning design 1839 – £5	TNA ADM 87/9
			Female 3/4-length bust – Hellyer design 1852 – £7.10.0	TNA ADM 87/41
			Female 3/4-length bust – Hellyer design 1860 – £10	TNA ADM 87/77
Victor Emanuel	1855-1899	Second Rate 91	To represent the King of Sardinia – Hellyer to carve 1856	TNA ADM 91/18 †

SHIP	DATES	SHIP TYPE	FIGUREHEAD/ORIGIN/DATE/COST	LOCATION/REF.
Victoria	1859-1893	Screw First Rate 121	3/4-length Queen Victoria – Hellyer design 1859 – £70	TNA ADM 87/71
			3/4-length Q. Victoria, gilt – design half-block model	NMM SLR0905
Victoria and Albert	1843-1854	Wood paddle yacht	Royal arms – ship plan	NMM NPD0832
			Carved by Hellyer of Portsmouth 1843 – £25	TNA ADM 87/13
			Twin royal arms in cartouche – surviving	HM Naval Base Portsmouth
			Crown over twin royal arms – Hellyer design 1856 – £45	TNA ADM 87/50
	1855-1904	Wood paddle yacht	Crown over twin royal arms in cartouche – surviving	NMRN Portsmouth
	1899-1954	Steam yacht	Crown over royal arms – ship plan – 1898	NMM NPD 0861
			Royal arms in cartouche – surviving	HMS *Nelson*, Portsmouth
Victorious	1808-1862	Third Rate 74	Bust of Nelson – Hellyer design 1814 – £21	TNA ADM 106/1887
Victory	1737-1744	First Rate 100	Crown over twin mounted 'sea-horses' – ship plan	NMM ZAZ0145
			Crown over royal arms with figures – Georgian ship model 1740	NMM SLR0449
			Crown over royal arms with figures – Navy Board model 1744	Science Museum Pictorial
			Crown over royal arms with figures – Navy Board model	Cawdor Castle, Nairn
			Figurehead carved by Wm Smith of Portsmouth 1737	*Ship Carvers* – P Thomas
	1765-1800	First Rate 100	Bust of King George with supporters, etc – ship plan	NMM ZAZ0120
			Bust of George III with figures – carver's model	NMM SLR2530
			Bust of George III with figures – Georgian ship model	NMM SLR0512
			Royal arms with cherub supporters – block model	NMM SLR0513
	1800-date		Crown over royal arms with supporters – surviving	HM Naval Base Portsmouth
Vigilant	1745-1759	Fourth Rate 58	Naked full-length Hermes with his caduceus – ship plan – carved work detail (French)	NMM ZAZ6874
	1774-1816	Third Rate 64	Female full-length with baton – ship plan	NMM ZAZ1413 *Vigilant*
			Full-length male in armour – Henry Adams design	Beaulieu
Virago	1842-1876	Wood paddle sloop	Carved by Hellyer of Portsmouth 1842 – £7.10.0	TNA ADM 87/12
			Female 3/4-length bust – surviving	Auckland, New Zealand
	1842-1876?		Female standing figure – surviving	Historic D'yard, Chatham
Virginie	1796-1827	Fifth Rate 38	Female full-length – ship plan (French)	NMM ZAZ2317
Vivid	1848-1894	Wood paddle packet	Female 3/4-length – Hellyer design 1847 – £7.15.0	TNA ADM 87/18
Vixen	1841-1862	Wood paddle sloop	Female 3/4-length bust – Dickerson design 1840	TNA ADM 87/10
			Unspec. – Hellyer proposal 1840 – £5.15.0	TNA ADM 91/9
			Unspec. – Hellyer & Browning proposal 1841 – £10.3.0	TNA ADM 91/9
Volage	1798-1804	Sixth Rate 22	Female 3/4-length bust – ship plan (French)	NMM ZAZ3638
Voltigeur	1798-1802	Sloop 18	A saddled animal – ship plan	NMM ZAZ4018 & 4019
Vryheid	1797-1811	Third Rate 72	Lion and circular badge – last known whereabouts	Dundee
Vulcan	1849-1867	Iron screw frigate	Male demi-head with hammer – half block design model	NMM SLR0837
Vulture	1843-1866	Wood paddle frigate	Standing vulture – Hellyer design 1842 – £9	TNA ADM 87/12
Wanderer	1835-1850	Brig-sloop 16	Female bust – ship plan	NMM ZAZ4376
	1855-1866	Wood screw gunves.	Female bust – surviving	NMRN Portsmouth
Warrior	1781-1857	Third Rate 74	Full-length warrior with sword – ship plan	NMM ZAZ1325
			Full-length kilted warrior – ship model 1781	Science Museum 1938-620
			Male head and neck only – surviving	NMRN Portsmouth
	1860-1904	Iron armoured ship	Original figurehead carved by Hellyer 1860	*Ship Carvers* – P Thomas
			Replacement carved by Hellyer 1872	*Ship Carvers* – P Thomas
			3/4-length warrior – ship model	Science Museum 1913-370
			3/4-length warrior – last seen HMS *Warrior* Northwood	Destroyed 1963
			3/4-length warrior – replica – Jack Whitehead & Norman Gaches 1985	HM Naval Base Portsmouth
Bust of a warrior	?		Bust of a warrior with flags – last recorded Devonport c1936	Lost in Blitz 1941
Warspite	1840-1876	Fourth Rate 76	Male helmeted head & shoulders – ship plan	NMM ZAZ1871
Warwick	1733-1756	Fourth Rate 60	Lion – carved by Mattingly of Plymouth – £17.10.0	*Ship Carvers* – P Thomas

SHIP	DATES	SHIP TYPE	FIGUREHEAD/ORIGIN/DATE/COST	LOCATION/REF.
Wasp	1801-1811	Sloop 14	Standing female – ship plan	NMM ZAZ4267
	1822-1829	Survey ship	Female 3/4-length bust – surviving – sold Christie's 2003	Private collection, Norway
	1850-1869	Wood screw sloop	Female 3/4-length bust – Hellyer design 1848 – £8.15.0	TNA ADM 87/23
Waterloo	1818-1824	Third Rate 80	Standing figure of Duke of Wellington – Hellyer proposal 1818 – £35	TNA ADM 106/1889
	1833-1862	First Rate 120	Bust of the Duke of Wellington – surviving	New York, USA
Watt	1844	Renamed pre-launch	Bust of James Watt – Hellyer design 1842 – £20	TNA ADM 87/12
Wellesley	1815-1868	Third Rate 74	Bust carved by Overton & Co 1813 – £21	TNA ADM 106/1794
			Replacement carved by Dickerson 1842 – £25	TNA ADM 87/12
			Bust of Marquis Wellesley – surviving	Historic D'yard, Chatham
Wellington	1816-1862	Third Rate 74	Bust of the Duke of Wellington – surviving	Plymouth NB Museum
Weymouth	1736-1745	Fourth Rate 60	Full-length crowned lion	NMM ZAZ1787
Wild Swan	1876-1904	Comp screw sloop	Female 3/4-length – last seen ashore Rosyth	Believe lost c1930
Winchelsea	1764-1814	Fifth Rate 32	Full-length figure – Georgian ship model	NMM SLR0316
Windsor Castle	1814-1839	Third Rate 74	Standing crowned king – ship plan – as cut down 1816	NMM ZAZ0354
			Crowned Edward III – lost in 'The Great Fire', Devonport 1840	See Chapter 3.I
	1852	Screw First Rate 131	Crowned lion with escutcheon and castle	Mariner's Mirror 61 1975)†
	1858-1869	First Rate 116	3/4-length Queen Victoria – Hellyer design 1848 – £52	TNA ADM 87/25
			Carved by Hellyer of Blackwall 1854 – £45	TNA ADM 88/10
			3/4-length Queen Victoria – surviving	Plymouth NB Museum ‡
			3/4-length Queen Victoria – replica in fibreglass	Plymouth NB Museum
Wizard	1860-1879	Wood screw gunboat	Male bust – Dickerson design 1860	Dickerson Archive
Wolverine	1863-1923	Wood screw corvette	3/4-length male bust – Hellyer design 1860 – £20	TNA ADM 87/76
			3/4-length male bust – Last seen Auckland New Zealand	Destroyed pre-1942 †
Woodlark	1808-1818	Brig-sloop 16	Female bust – carved by George Williams 1808 – £3	*Ship Carvers* – P Thomas
Worcester	1843-1885	Fourth Rate 52	Male bust – ship plan	NMM NPC7194
Wye	1855-1866	Iron screw storeship	Scroll & elaborate trailboards – Hellyer design 1860	TNA ADM 87/77 †
Zealous	1864-1886	Ironclad	Male demi-head brandishing sword – Hellyer des. 1859 £45 – not approved	TNA ADM 87/73
			Male demi-head with sword – Hellyer design £45 – not approved	TNA ADM 87/73
			Male bust – Hellyer design 1859 – £40	TNA ADM 87/73
			Female bust – Hellyer design 1859 – £40 not approved	TNA ADM 87/73
			Bow decoration – Dickerson design 1863	Dickerson Archive
Zebra	1777-1778	Sloop 14	Full-length horse (no zebra stripes) – ship plan	NMM ZAZ4812
	1780-1812	Sloop 18	Male standing figure in tall peak cap – ship plan	NMM ZAZ4819
	1848-1862	Brig-sloop 16	Head & neck of a zebra – Hellyer design 1844 – not approved	TNA ADM 87/14
			Female bust – Hellyer design 1844	TNA ADM 87/14
	1860-1873	Wood screw sloop	Head & neck of a zebra – Hellyer design 1859 – not approved	TNA ADM 87/72
			Head & neck of a zebra 2 – Hellyer design – not approved	TNA ADM 87/72
			Head & neck of a zebra 3 – Hellyer design – not approved	TNA ADM 87/72
			Fore-part of a zebra – Hellyer design 1859 – £10	TNA ADM 87/72
Zephyr	1809-1818	Brig-sloop 16	Female bust with wings – Hellyer design 1809 – £3	TNA ADM 106-1885 ‡
Unidentified	c1720		Full-length crowned lion with cross of St George – surviving	NMM FHD0088
	?		Bust of a warrior in armour & helmet – surviving	NMM FHD0061 †

NOTES †

Adventure	Although this head has been associated with the 1857 *Adventure*, her origin is doubtful.
Amazon	Plans being developed to move her to the safe environment of the National Museum of the Royal Navy , Portsmouth.
Arethusa 1817	Last seen outside the offices of Hughes Bolckow, shipbreakers, Blyth c1980.
Arethusa 1849	Owned by the Arethusa Venture Centre, she is under restoration by Andrew Peters of Maritime Woodcarving.
Arrogant	Shown in *Nelson's Navy* by Brian Lavery (Conway, 1990).
Clown	Listed in 1911 Admiralty Catalogue as *Jester* but thought there to be from the 1857 *Clown*.
Cornwallis	Last seen when offered for sale by Christie's of South Kensington May 1995. Did not sell.
Elizabeth	This figurehead is reputed to have been carved for the 1737 rebuild of the ship at Chatham.
Foudroyant	The figurehead is in store with the Museum Service pending repairs to Caldicot Castle.
Gleaner	Photographed and named as *Gleaner* when at HMS *Ganges* in 1949.
Howe	Mounted on wall of Medway Council building, Dock Road, Chatham – on loan from Lloyds of London.
Investigator	Formerly at Garden Island, Sydney the figurehead is in long-term conservation at Spectacle Island.
"*Ironsides*"	The Nore Command report on figureheads c1948 contains a photograph of a bust-head, bearded and crowned, named on its pedestal "Ironsides". No such ship appears in the Royal Navy's listings.
King Edward VII	A model brig, based on a 42ft naval cutter, for use by the king's grandchildren on Virginia Water, Surrey.
Mariner	The 1938 Chatham record shows him 'Unidentified'. That of 1948 records him 'Believed to be *Mariner*'.
Mars	Photographed at Ward's shipbreaking yard but last seen New York c1950.
Queen Charlotte	Her head had been carried away and Portsmouth had checked that there were no suitable replacements.
Repulse	The figurehead was later fitted to HMS *Defiance*.
Moa	One of the figureheads described in *Clover's Folly – The Figurehead Collection of HMNZ Naval Base, Auckland* (Peter Dennerly, 2003).
Orpheus	The bearded and helmeted head is associated with the wreck of HMS *Orpheus* in 1863 but is nothing like the Hellyer design.
Royal Sovereign	Dickerson design published in *Plymouth and Devonport: in Times of War and Peace* (H F Whitfield, 1900).
St Vincent	When the original figurehead was used as a mould for copies to be cast, it disintegrated.
Supply	Although scroll and fiddle heads are not generally included, an exception is made here as she was one of the First Fleet, arriving in Australia in 1788.
Swallow	A replacement, her original having been carried away by a vessel fouling her.
Unité	To replace a rotten one – presumably that fitted when captured as *Imperieuse* in 1793.
Victor Emmanuel	Last known whereabouts – ashore in Hong Kong 1911.
Windsor Castle	The Duke of Wellington died on the day she was launched in 1852. Her name changed to HMS *Duke of Wellington*.
Wolverine	One of the figureheads described in *Clover's Folly – The Figurehead Collection of HMNZ Naval Base, Auckland* (Peter Dennerly, 2003).
Wye	A replacement, her original having been carried away in a collision. £20 rejected; £10 accepted.
Unidentified	At one time attributed to the 1781 *Anson* but this doubted because of its small size – only 3ft.

BIBLIOGRAPHY AND SOURCES

Primary Sources

Bermuda, *Figureheads of H M Dockyard, Bermuda 1948*. An album containing five figurehead photographs with descriptions. Admiralty Library Ref Dh 21.

Chatham, *Figureheads in Dockyard, Royal Naval Barracks and Royal Naval Hospital, Chatham*. Stamped 1938. An album on linen pages containing fifty-two figurehead photographs with descriptions. Admiralty Library Ref Dh 23.

Chatham, *Figureheads at Chatham – 31.12.48. Part I: HM Dockyard. Part II: RN Barracks, St Marys, Collingwood, RN Hospital & RN Armament Depot Upnor*. An album on linen pages containing forty-seven figurehead photographs with descriptions. Chatham MCD No 13234.

Crang, E R, *Ships' Figureheads – Part I (Royal Navy)*. An album of photographs of every figurehead known to the author including typescript notes giving details of the figurehead and its ship. Dated 1974. Naval History Library, Plymouth.

HMS *Ganges, Figureheads at HMS Ganges*. A file containing twelve named photographs dated 1949. Admiralty Library Ref Dh 24.

Nore Command, *Nore Command, Sheerness Sub-Command – Figureheads*. Undated but c1948. Admiralty Library Ref Dh 22.

National Archives (The), Kew (TNA)

> ADM 87. Surveyor of the Navy – In Letters.
> ADM 88. Surveyor of the Navy – Register of In Letters.
> ADM 91. Comptroller and Surveyor of the Navy, Repair & Building of Ships – General Letter Books.
> ADM 106. Navy Board – In Letters.

Plymouth Command, *A Record of the Figureheads in H M Naval Establishments under Plymouth Command*. Undated but c1936. An album containing forty-four figurehead photographs with typed descriptions and pencil annotations. Admiralty Library Ref Dh 20.

Secondary Sources

A W, 'Figure Heads in the West Indies', *The Mariner's Mirror* Vol 28 (1921).

Admiralty, *Catalogue of Paintings, Busts, Relics, Models, &c., belonging to the Admiralty – showing in which of the various Naval Establishments at Home and Abroad they are Deposited* (London, 1883).

_____, *Catalogue of Paintings, Busts, Relics, Models, &c., belonging to the Admiralty – showing in which of the various Naval Establishments at Home and Abroad they are Deposited* (London, 1906).

_____, *Catalogue of Pictures, Presentation Plate, Figureheads, Models, Relics and Trophies at the Admiralty; on board H.M. Ships; and in the Naval Establishments at Home and Abroad* (London, 1911).

Carr Laughton, L G, *Old Ship Figure-Heads & Sterns* (Conway Maritime Press, 1991).

Chatham, *Catalogue of Figureheads, Models, &c. in the Museum in H.M. Dockyard, Chatham* (Undated but c1901–4).

Colledge, J J, *British Sailing Warships* (Ian Allan, 1964).

_____, *Ships of the Royal Navy* (Greenhill Books, 1987).

Conway's All the World's Fighting Ships 1860-1905 (Conway Maritime Press, 1979).

Costa, Giancarlo, *Figureheads: Carving on ships from ancient times to twentieth century* (Nautical Publishing Co, 1981).

Dalton, Tony, *British Royal Yachts* (Halsgrove, 2002).

Dennerly, Peter, *Clover's Folly – The Figurehead Collection of His Majesty's New Zealand Naval Base Devonport, Auckland* (RNZN Museum, Auckland, 2003).

Dewan, Janet, *The Photographs of Linnaeus Tripe – A Catalogue Raisonné* (Art Gallery of Ontario, 2003).

Endacott, Andy, *Devonport Dockyard – The Great Fire of 1840* (Plymouth, 1998).

Hamilton, Georgia W, *Silent Pilots: Figureheads in Mystic Seaport Museum* (Mystic Seaport Museum 1984).

Hansen, Hans Jürgen, *Galionsfiguren* (Stalling 1979).

_____, und Clas Broder Hansen, *Galionsfiguren* (Urbes – undated German edition).

_____, and Clas Broder Hansen, *Ships' Figureheads* (Schiffer Publishing, 1990).

Harland, Kathleen, *The Royal Navy in Hong Kong 1841-1980* (The Royal Navy, 1980).

Hughes, E A, *The Royal Naval College Dartmouth* (London, 1950).

Jackson, Instructor Lt Cdr P H O, *HMS Ganges Catalogue of the Collection in Nelson Hall and the Museum* (HMS *Ganges*, undated).

Kriegstein, Arnold and Henry, *17th and 18th Century Ship Models from the Kriegstein Collection* (Pier Books/Dupont Communications, 2007).

Laird Clowes, G S, *Sailing Ships, their History and Development as Illustrated by the Collection of Ship-Models in the Science Museum* (Science Museum, 1932).

Lavery, Brian, and Simon Stephens, *Ship Models 1650 to the Present* (Zwemmer, 1995).

Leslie, Robert C, *Old Sea Wings, Ways and Words* (Chapman & Hall Ltd, 1890).

Lind, Lew, *Fair Winds to Australia* (Reed Books Pty, 1988).

Littlewood, K, and B Butler, *Of Ships and Seas: Maritime heritage and the founding of the National Maritime Museum, Greenwich* (London, 1998).

Lyon, David, *The Sailing Navy List 1688-1860* (Conway Maritime Press, 1993).

_____, and Rif Winfield, *The Sail & Steam Navy List 1815-1889* (Chatham Publishing, 2004).

Manning, Capt T D and Cdr C F Walker, *British Warship Names* (Putnam, 1959).

Marshall, Gordon de L, *Ships' Figure Heads in Australia* (Tangee Pty, 2003).

Navy Records Society, *The Anthony Roll* (Ashgate Publishing, 2000).

Norton, Peter, *Figureheads* (National Maritime Museum, 1972).

_____, *Ships' Figureheads* (David & Charles, 1976).

Owen, Douglas, 'Figureheads', *The Mariner's Mirror* Vol III (1913).

_____, 'The Devonport Figureheads', *The Mariner's Mirror* Vol IV (1914).

Pack, A J, *The origins of the Figurehead – A description of the Figureheads in the Victory Museum and the ships to which they belonged* (Portsmouth, undated).

Portsmouth, *Catalogue of Figure-Heads, Models, Pictures, Relics, Trophies, &c in the Museum &c HM Dockyard Portsmouth* (Gale & Polden, 1911).

Pulvertaft, David, *The Warship Figureheads of Portsmouth* (The History Press, 2009).

_____, 'Warship Figureheads from the Royal Dockyards: Towards a National Collection?', *The Mariner's Mirror* Vol 95 (2009).

Rice, Tony, *British Oceanographic Vessels 1800-1950* (The Ray Society, 1986).

Sainsbury, A B, and F L Phillips, *The Royal Navy Day by Day* (Sutton Publishing, 2005).

Scarth, Alan J, *The Ship Models Collection, Merseyside Maritime Museum* (National Museums & Galleries of Merseyside, 1995).

Stammers, M K, *Ships' Figureheads* (Shire Publications, 1983).

_____, *Figureheads and Ship Carving* (Chatham Publishing, 2005).

Stephens, Simon, *Ship Models: The Thomson Collection at the Art Gallery of Ontario* (Skylet Publishing, 2009).

Taylor, David, *Figureheads* (National Maritime Museum, 1992).

Thomas, P N, *British Figurehead & Ship Carvers* (Waine Research Publications, 1995).

United States Naval Academy Museum, *Catalogue of the Henry Huddleston Rogers Collection of Ship Models* (US Naval Institute, Annapolis, 1958).

Warlow, Lt Cdr B, *Shore Establishments of the Royal Navy* (Maritime Books, 1992).

Whitfield, H F, *Plymouth and Devonport: in Times of War and Peace* (E Chapple, 1900).

Rif Winfield, *British Warships in the Age of Sail 1603-1714* (Seaforth Publishing, 2009).

_____, *British Warships in the Age of Sail 1714-1792* (Seaforth Publishing, 2007).

_____, *British Warships in the Age of Sail 1793-1817* (Chatham Publishing, 2005).

CIGARETTE CARDS

John Player & Sons issued two numbered sets of cigarette cards featuring ships' figureheads, each set having twenty five cards. The first set was issued in 1912, each card being 2½in x 1¼in with a coloured portrait on the front and a brief description of the ship on the back.

1. HMS *Princess Royal* – refers mostly to the 1798 mutiny.
2. HMS *Queen Charlotte* – Admiral Howe's flagship, renamed HMS *Excellent*.
3. HMS *Colossus* – shows the 1848 figurehead but the text refers to the of 1803 ship.
4. HMS *Seahorse* – the text describes Nelson's service in her as a midshipman. The illustration shows a figurehead in the form of a seahorse thought to have been created by the artist simply to accompany the text, as ship plan evidence is very different.
5. HMS *Eurydice* – telling of her tragic loss in 1878 [wrongly numbered 28].
6. HMS *Bellerophon* – showing the surviving head at Portsmouth and listing her battles.
7. HMS *Royal Albert* – showing 'a finely modelled effigy of the late Prince Consort'.
8. HMS *St Vincent* – describes how Sir J Jervis supplied a bust of himself for the carving.
9. HMS *Duke of Wellington* – includes the change of name from *Windsor Castle*.
10. HMS *Sybille* – 'carved from a portrait of Lady Hamilton as a Sibyl'.
11. HMS *Leander* – showing the bust of the 1848 ship while the text relates the bravery shown by the earlier ship of her name when captured in 1798.
12. HMS *Edinburgh* – giving a brief history of her service.
13. HMS *Formidable* – describing the Roman bust with plumed helmet.
14. The *Terra Nova* – Captain Scott's ship for the British Antarctic Expedition [not RN].
15. The *Half Moon* – a Dutch lion figurehead [not RN].
16. HMS *Warrior* – telling how the figurehead was by the Portsmouth Dockyard gate.
17. HMS *Victory* – showing the royal arms with a Royal Marine supporter.
18. HMS *Shannon* – telling of the capture of the American frigate *Chesapeake* in 1813.
19. HMS *Duke of Marlborough* – showing the figurehead of the 1855 HMS *Marlborough*.
20. HMS *Ajax* – reporting that the figurehead was then part of the Devonport collection.
21. HMS *Gibraltar* – showing the 'key to the Mediterranean' in the trailboards but confusing the 1780 *Gibraltar* in the text with the 1860 ship.
22. HMS *Royal Sovereign* – telling of the delays and changes made during her build.
24. HMS *Calcutta* – mentioning her involvement in the 1857 Chinese War.
25. HMS *Black Prince* – sister-ship to HMS *Warrior*.

The second set was issued in 1931, each card being of the larger 3in x 2½in, more than half of which showed the figureheads that were to be found on ship models. Several of the cards describe merchant or foreign ships but those relevant to this study are:

1. The *Great Harry* – from the model in the Royal Naval Museum, Greenwich.
2. The *Sovereign of the Seas* – quotes King Edgar trampling on the Seven Kings.
3. HMS *Prince* – from a model in the Science Museum, South Kensington.
7. HMS *St George* 1701 – a group figurehead on a model in the Metropolitan Museum, New York.
8. HMS *Royal George* – from a model in the Royal Naval Museum, Greenwich.
9. HMS *Achilles* – from a model in the Science Museum, South Kensington.
10. HMS *Egmont* – from a model in the Science Museum, South Kensington.
11. HMS *Boyne* – from a model in the South Kensington Museum.
12. HMS *Queen Charlotte* – from the model in the Royal Naval Museum, Greenwich.
14. HMS *Nelson* – from the model in the Royal Naval Museum, Greenwich showing the bust of Lord Nelson with two female supporters.
15. HMS *Victory* – showing the royal arms supported on each side by a cherub.
16. HMS *Trincomalee* 1817 – but by then renamed *Foudroyant* and afloat at Falmouth.
18. HMS *Duke of Wellington* – shown on the bow before being broken up by Messrs Castle.
19. HMS *Marlborough* – shown on the bow but reported as being in HMS *Vernon*, Torpedo School at Portsmouth.
20. HMS *Warrior* – shown on the bow but reported as being in Portsmouth Dockyard.
21. HMS *Black Prince* – shown on the bow but reported as being preserved at Devonport Dockyard.
25 HMS *Thames* 1885 – showing the royal arms and bow decoration.

INDEX

The index is to ship names only. Page references to illustrations are in italics. The index does not include entries in the Figurehead Directory. The dates quoted are for the year of launch, capture or change of name. Naval shore establishments are identified by the county in which they lie.